Design for Policy

Design for
Social Responsibility Series

Series Editor: Rachel Cooper

Social responsibility, in various disguises, has been a recurring theme in design for many years. Since the 1960s several more or less commercial approaches have evolved. In the 1970s designers were encouraged to abandon 'design for profit' in favour of a more compassionate approach inspired by Papanek.

In the 1980s and 1990s profit and ethical issues were no longer considered mutually exclusive and more market-oriented concepts emerged, such as the 'green consumer' and ethical investment. The purchase of socially responsible, 'ethical' products and services has been stimulated by the dissemination of research into sustainability issues in consumer publications. Accessibility and inclusivity have also attracted a great deal of design interest and recently designers have turned to solving social and crime-related problems.

Organisations supporting and funding such projects have recently included the NHS (research into design for patient safety); the Home Office has (design against crime); Engineering and Physical Sciences Research Council (design decision-making for urban sustainability). Businesses are encouraged (and increasingly forced by legislation) to set their own socially responsible agendas that depend on design to be realised.

Design decisions all have environmental, social and ethical impacts, so there is a pressing need to provide guidelines for designers and design students within an overarching framework that takes a holistic approach to socially responsible design.

This edited series of guides is aimed at students of design, product development, architecture and marketing, and design and management professionals working in the sectors covered by each title. Each volume includes:

- The background and history of the topic, its significance in social and commercial contexts and trends in the field.

- Exemplar design case studies.

- Guidelines for the designer and advice on tools, techniques and resources available.

Design for Policy

Edited by Christian Bason

Routledge
Taylor & Francis Group

LONDON AND NEW YORK

First published 2014 by Gower Publishing

2 Park Square, Milton Park, Abingdon, Oxfordshire OX14 4RN
52 Vanderbilt Avenue, New York, NY 10017

Routledge is an imprint of the Taylor & Francis Group, an informa business

First issued in paperback 2020

British Library Cataloguing in Publication Data
A catalogue record for this book is available from the British Library.

Library of Congress Cataloging-in-Publication Data
Bason, Christian.
  Design for policy / by Christian Bason.
    pages cm. – (Design for social responsibility)
  Includes bibliographical references and index.
  ISBN 978-1-4724-1352-9 (hardback: alk. paper)
1. Policy sciences. 2. Design. I. Title.

  H97.B377 2014
  320.6—dc23

                                                                  2014021933

ISBN: 978-1-4724-1352-9 (hbk)
ISBN: 978-0-367-67004-7 (pbk)

For Lillian

CONTENTS

LIST OF FIGURES

LIST OF TABLES

RACHEL COOPER

PREFACE

I am thrilled to introduce *Design for Policy* as part of this series of books on design for social responsibility. Social responsibility is, or should be, core in policymaking. Indeed, our governments – local, national and international – form and create policies that are translated into regulatory and statutory frameworks that have a profound effect on our lives.

The use of design for and in policymaking has its roots explicitly in the development of service design, especially service design in social situations, but more implicitly design for policy has evolved from the notions of user-centred design, participatory design and co-design, in which everyone is engaged in planning products, services, experiences and social processes, and in the visual and textual expressions of these processes. However as with any design domain, Potter (1982) reminds us that everyone can be a designer, but some do it as a profession. While this is equally true for design and policymaking, this book reveals that an understanding of both domains is important for practice in this field.

This book is part of a series aimed at illustrating the value of design; for example, we have tackled the application of all the disciplines of design to aspects of contemporary life, such as transport and sport, services and sustainability, illustrating the multiplicity of ways in which design is applied to serve society. I am pleased to introduce this volume as the book that finally illustrates the policy context to which design can and is being applied. The examples here reveal the innovation brought about by the application of design to policymaking, whilst sharing the tools available to design for policy.

Christian Bason, whose practical experience of applying design during innovative policymaking is world leading, was generous in his agreement to edit the book and bring together global and diverse contributions to address the topic. In addition, he has eloquently summarized the state of the field and the reasons why design for policy is necessary in an increasingly complex and interdependent political, social, economic and environmental landscape. We now have a solid basis on which, as Bason suggests 'to position design on the policy stage'. This book opens the stage curtain and narrates the first act, from which I hope much more research, practice and evaluation of design for policy can take place.

Reference

Potter, N. (1980). *What is a designer, things, places, messages.* Reading: Hyphen Press.

ACKNOWLEDGEMENTS

This book would not have been possible without the active encouragement of Rachel Cooper. Some years ago we both contributed to the European Commission's Design Leadership Board, an expert group established to generate ideas for strengthening design across Europe. Following one of our sessions, Rachel inquired if I might be interested in editing a volume, part of a series of design for sustainability, emphasizing the role of design for policy. I was immediately sympathetic to the idea, in particular since our work on the design board had confirmed something I had noticed in my national context in Denmark: whereas design for services is an increasingly acknowledged and well-defined discipline, design for policy is still an emerging and loosely defined field. To explore the notion of design policy would thus not only be a task of charting an existing landscape, it would have to be a contribution to defining it. What could be a more exciting challenge?

When some months later I asked the best people I could imagine if they would join me for the job, everyone accepted. This book obviously could not have been created without their efforts, dedication and, dare I say, patience throughout the writing and editing process. Many took up the suggestion, made by Joachim Halse, of collegial peer-to-peer feedback and made good use of that opportunity. I am indebted to everyone whose authorship is presented on these introductory pages for their generosity in sharing their research, insights and experience.

I do, however, wish to mention a few people who have played extraordinary roles in making *Design for Policy* become a reality. I wish to thank Eduardo Staszowski and Scott Brown at Parsons the New School for Design for not only writing (with Benjamin Winter) a strong chapter on the power-political implications of design in public contexts, but also for providing the map of global public innovation places as well as suggestions for improvement to the book's concluding chapter. Sabine Junginger's clear perspectives on design for policy, which we have discussed on numerous occasions, have been a strong contextual influence within and beyond her excellent chapter. Andrea Schneider worked diligently to draw on research originally carried out for the London School of Economics in drafting our chapter on emerging trends in design for policy. MindLab's Jesper Christiansen has been an ongoing dialogue partner on the notion of innovation in government, and always a constructive critic. I wish to thank Kit Lykketoft for providing a thought-provoking chapter on legitimating design while also taking care of day-to-day business as my right hand at MindLab, thus making the book possible. Our excellent student assistant Signe Dalsgaard supported my editing flawlessly, and project managers Runa Sabroe and Niels Hansen, both at MindLab, shared very useful feedback from their practical experience, with an emphasis on the final summary chapter.

Several people have contributed more indirectly to the work as sources of inspiration and help. Nina Holm Vohnsen of Aarhus University, previously a doctoral student at MindLab, has been a key critical inspiration for addressing the perspectives of stakeholders throughout the policy process hierarchy. My own doctoral advisor,

Rob Austin at Copenhagen Business School, has been very helpful in guiding my research and clarifying the linkages and insights to *Design for Policy*.

Finally I wish to thank my editor at Gower, Jonathan Norman, for being such a committed and patient supporter throughout the process, and his colleague Kathy Bond Borie for diligent production editing. Any errors or omissions are, of course, mine alone.

ACKNOWLEDGEMENTS

ABOUT THE EDITOR

Christian Bason is Chief Executive of the Danish Design Centre (DDC), which works to strengthen the value of all forms of design in society. Before joining DDC, Christian headed MindLab, a cross-governmental innovation lab, and the public organization practice of Ramboll Management, a consultancy. Christian is also a university lecturer, and has presented to and advised governments around the world. He is a regular columnist and the author of four books on leadership, innovation and design, most recently *Leading Public Sector Innovation: Co-creating for a Better Society*. Christian holds an M.Sc. in political science from Aarhus University, executive education from Harvard Business School and the Wharton School, and is a doctoral fellow at Copenhagen Business School.

ABOUT THE
CONTRIBUTORS

Mariana Amatullo is the Vice President of Designmatters, the award-winning social impact department at Art Center College of Design, Pasadena, California. She co-founded Designmatters in 2001. As the head of the Department, she is responsible for the strategic leadership of a dynamic portfolio of global and national educational projects, research collaborations and publications at the intersection of art and design education and social innovation. Through her leadership, Art Center is the first design institution to be affiliated as a non-governmental organization with the United Nations and a number of multi-lateral bodies such as the Organization of American States and the World Health Organization. Amatullo lectures internationally on design and social innovation; she is an active essayist and serves on a variety of advisory and executive boards of organizations engaged in the arts, design education and social impact, including Cumulus (the International Association of Universities and Colleges of Art, Design and Media), ideo.org and the USC International Museum Institute. In 2012, Amatullo was the recipient of inaugural 2012 DELL Social Innovation Education award for outstanding leadership in teaching and supporting student social innovators and was named to Fast Company's Co.Design 50 Designers Shaping the Future and the Public Interest Design 100. She is a Non-Profit Fellow with a Doctor of Management, Weatherhead School of Management, Case Western Reserve University. She holds an MA in Art History and Museum Studies from the University of Southern California and a Licence en Lettres Degree from the Sorbonne University, Paris. A native of Argentina, Amatullo was brought up through the diplomatic corps and grew up around the world.

Banny Banerjee is Associate Professor in the Design Division of the Mechanical Engineering Department at Stanford and teaches Design and Innovation at the Stanford d.school and the Stanford Design Program. His area of expertise is the use of Design Thinking for strategic initiatives and large scale transformation. His focus is the development of trans-disciplinary innovation processes directed towards complex challenges at the nexus of disciplines. He is also the founder of the Stanford ChangeLabs, formed to address issues of sustainability, next generation innovation processes and the dynamics of large scale transformation. He is collaborating with Stanford faculty from behavioural sciences, social economics, systems analysis, management science, engineering and art to generate new platforms for design thinking.

Tom Bentley was Deputy Chief of Staff and senior policy adviser from 2007 to 2013 to Julia Gillard, Prime Minister of Australia 2010–2013 and Deputy Prime Minister 2007–2010. His responsibilities included school reform, innovation and industry policy and the Government's white paper on Australia in the Asian Century. From 1999 to 2006 he was Director of Demos, an independent think tank based in London.

His publications include *Learning beyond the classroom: education for a changing world* (Routledge 1998); *The Creative Age: knowledge and skills for a new economy* (Demos 1999); *The Adaptive State* (Demos 2003) and *Letting go: complexity, individualism and the left* (Renewal 2002).

John Body founded ThinkPlace in 2005, leaving a senior role in the Australian Taxation Office where he had pioneered the application of design to Australia's taxation system. John now leads ThinkPlace as the Founding Partner. The company applies co-design across the full breadth of government challenges in Australia, New Zealand and the region. These challenges cover the design of policy, strategy, services and organizations. John moved beyond the field of corporate strategy into design, seeing the value of design because it can turn strategy into tangible transformations for people collectively and individually. John has a Masters in Chaos and Complexity Theory, an invaluable knowledge base when working with the challenges posed by most government services and systems. John is driven to deliver public value. Design thinking provides a means to combine many other disciplines to effect that positive change.

Christopher T. Boyko is a Senior Research Associate in ImaginationLancaster, a design-based research lab at Lancaster University. He is currently examining the relationship between well-being, the built environment and low-carbon on a five-year, £6 million UK Research Council project called Liveable Cities. This research builds on his previous work about urban density and the decision-making process for the Urban Futures project, and about mapping the sustainable urban design decision-making process for the VivaCity2020 project. In between these projects, Christopher co-wrote a UK Government report about the impacts of the physical environment on mental well-being. He also led a research project with colleagues at Lancaster University, studying key changes in the 'interaction order' of public spaces. His general research interests include sustainability, urban design, public space, environmental psychology and well-being. Christopher is an associate member of the Higher Education Academy and a member of the Environmental Design Research Association.

Scott Brown is a PhD student in anthropology at the New School for Social Research. His research is focused on issues of urban space, emerging modes of design practice and shifting forms of contemporary governance. He is currently working alongside the DESIS Lab at Parsons the New School for Design investigating questions of collaborative practice and social innovation in New York City.

Laura Bunt is Head of Policy for a national UK charity working on issues around social justice and citizenship. She was formerly Lead Policy Advisor at Nesta, the UK's innovation foundation. Her work explores the drivers and opportunities for innovation to improve how we deliver public services and address social challenges; in particular how new technologies and processes can deepen citizen participation in public services and decision-making. Prior to joining Nesta, Laura was at the Royal Society of Arts (RSA) working alongside the senior management team to engage the RSA's extensive Fellowship as a network of social action, helping the Fellows to connect to each other both on- and offline and to take more of an active role in the organization's work. She started her career at the UK think tank Demos working on issues relating to both social policy and the creative industries. Laura holds a degree in Classics from Oxford University, is an active member of her local government community and a proud resident of East London.

Jesper Christiansen is Research Manager at MindLab and a doctoral fellow at the University of Aarhus. Jesper studies and works with the complex change processes in the intersections between policy and practice. He has a special interest and expertise within citizen-centred systemic innovation, policy innovation and innovation capacity. His recent work activities include functioning as a university lecturer at Aarhus University, researcher at the British think tank Nesta and project manager at the Australian design agency ThinkPlace. Jesper is responsible for MindLabs research program and also functions as project manager and policy advisor. This involves continuously providing constructive links between research, knowledge and MindLabs practical experiments – including facilitating cross-governmental networks of learning and collaboration with leading scientific institutions, experts and research organizations. Jesper is currently completing a PhD thesis about the cognitive and systemic implications of public innovation.

Rachel Cooper is Distinguished Professor of Design Management and Policy at the University of Lancaster, and Director of ImaginationLancaster (a centre for research into products, places and systems for the future). Her research covers design thinking, design management, design policy, new product development, design for well-being, design in the built environment, design against crime, and socially responsible design. Rachel has undertaken research on design since 1995 and has written extensively in the field. She is commissioning editor for this series on Design for Social Responsibility. She was a member of the European Design Innovation Leadership board, and is founding editor of *The Design Journal*.

Sarah Forrester is an Executive Designer at ThinkPlace and has extensive experience in ethnographic and design research. ThinkPlace is the leading design firm in Australia and applies design to transform complex systems. Sarah began her career in visual arts, progressing to graphic design and she now applies the skills and methods developed through these disciplines to design research and service design. Sarah has played a significant role in a number of design research and service design projects for the Australian Government with particular focus on the welfare sector. Sarah has a particular interest and passion for using co-design to empower and to help create better outcomes for the most vulnerable members of the community.

Joachim Halse is Assistant Professor at the Royal Danish Academy of Fine Arts, School of Design. With a combined background in anthropology and interaction design Joachim has researched and taught participatory processes of knowing and making in close collaboration with partners in the public and private sector since 2003. Joachim has worked across a range of sectors and organizations, including public unemployment services, flexible hospital treatment rooms, smartphone usage, mobile work and ERP systems and waste handling and recycling. In 2008 Joachim earned a PhD from the IT University of Copenhagen with a thesis entitled 'Design Anthropology: Borderland Experiments with Participation, Performance and Situated Intervention'. He has written and presented widely on design interventions, democratization and ethnographic fieldwork in design research.

François Jégou created and leads the Brussels-based sustainable innovation lab Strategic Design Scenarios with 20 years of experience in strategic design, participative scenario building and new product-services system definition. François is active in various fields and research projects, from investigating social innovation for sustainable living in China, India, Brazil and Africa with UNEP to European research projects focussing on urban sustainable food, exploring the future of innovation or building a deliberative platform on nano tech. François is co-ordinator of the DESIS Europe, the European branch of the Design for Social Innovation and Sustainability network and Design Manager of the LUPI user lab for the Cité du Design in St Étienne, France. He teaches strategic design at La Cambre design school, Brussels and is visiting professor at Politecnico, Milan and Ensci, Les Ateliers Paris. His last publication, *Sustainable Street 2030,* is an ebook asking what everyday life might be like in a sustainable society. How would we eat food, move, work and take care of each other?

Sabine Junginger is Associate Professor at the Kolding School of Design in Denmark and a Fellow at the Hertie School of Governance in Berlin. Sabine received a Masters in Design (Communication Planning and Information Design) and a PhD in Design (Organizational Change Through Human-centred Product Development) from Carnegie Mellon University. From 2007 to 2012, she was a founding member of ImaginationLancaster at Lancaster University in the UK. Her research focuses on design in the organization and how designing as an activity relates to the activities of changing, organizing and managing. She is particularly interested in the design of public services where the design approaches chosen by public managers, policymakers and frontline workers have organizational, social and individual consequences.

Kit Lykketoft is Deputy Director of MindLab. Prior to her employment at MindLab Kit worked several years in the Ministry of Employment with both organizational and policy development. At MindLab, Kit is jointly responsible for the strategic- and competence-related development of MindLab. She has substantial experience in implementing user-involvement projects. Kit is a frequent speaker in Denmark and abroad about the work of MindLab, and advises on how to set up labs and units within government administration and renew the public sector. She is a skilled lecturer and organizer of training courses and seminars. Kit holds a MA from University of Copenhagen and an Executive M.Sc. from HEC/Oxford.

Ezio Manzini has been working for more than two decades in the field of design for sustainability, with a special focus on social innovation. On this topic he started DESIS: an international network promoting worldwide design schools as agents of social change towards sustainability. Throughout his professional life Ezio has been Professor of Design at the Politecnico di Milano. Simultaneously, he has collaborated with several international universities. Currently, he is Honorary Guest Professor at the Tongji University, in Shanghai, at the Jiangnan University, in Wuxi, and in 2014 at the University of the Arts in London. Recent awards he has received are the Sir Misha Black Medal in the UK in 2012, the Honorary Doctorate at the Aalto University in Finland in 2013, and Jiangsu Friendship Medal in China in 2013.

Simona Maschi's main focus is on envisioning future scenarios and experiences for people's everyday lives. In particular, she designs new concepts of product and services enabled by innovative technologies for both the public and the private sector. She is interested in new solutions that support companies' environmental and social responsibility. Her last works have explored different topics, such as private and public transportation, health and well-being, sustainable housing and smart cities. Simona is an active organizer of industry-focused workshops, seminars and training around the world and she really enjoys working in cross-disciplinary and cross-cultural teams of people. Simona holds a PhD in Design Methods from the Polytechnic University of Milan, Italy (2002). Her expertise includes Service Design, Interaction Design and Scenario Design.

Andrea Schneider is a career civil servant with a Master's degree in political science and systems change. As an internal change agent in local and federal US agencies, she has worked on a range of initiatives to develop public policy to support new practice models. Andrea has deep experience designing innovative programmes within justice, education, health, criminal justice, law enforcement and philanthropy. She was an expert witness to the US Congress on high-risk youth, served as an expert panellist to evaluate a US Department of Health and Human Services (HHS) $44M federal capacity-building system, led a $3M HHS federal demonstration grant to co-design community action prototypes and was appointed as a Fellow in the United States Department of Justice (USDOJ). Amongst other reports she co-authored the book *Community Policing in Action, A Practitioner's Eye View of Organizational Change* (US Department of Justice, 2003). Andrea lives in Palo Alto, California.

Andrea Siodmok is a mentor, champion and advocate for design-led innovation working with organizations large and small – from global corporations to charities and NGOs. Formerly Chief Design Officer at the Design Council and more recently Head of the Policy Lab at the UK Government's Cabinet Office, Andrea set up a number of design-led innovation labs to help turn today's policy challenges into new opportunities that make a real difference to people's lives. As an expert in user-centred design, she helps executive leaders and senior decision-makers to create the conditions for innovation to thrive. She has run workshops and given over 100 keynotes on design and innovation across five continents, as well as held various advisory roles advising government, academics and European policymakers on public sector innovation. She holds a first-class honours in design and a PhD in Virtual Reality and is a visiting fellow at the University of Northumbria.

Eduardo Staszowski holds a PhD in Design from the Politecnico di Milano in Italy. His current research at the New School focuses on the intersection of design, social innovation and public services. Parsons DESIS (Design for Social Innovation and Sustainability) Lab works at the intersection of strategic and service design, management and social theory, applying interdisciplinary expertise in problem setting and problem-solving to sustainable practices and social innovation. The lab develops externally funded research projects with local partners and promotes workshops, studios, toolkits, exhibitions and publications that facilitate social change through design-based sustainable community initiatives.

Marco Steinberg is founder of Snowcone & Haystack, a Helsinki-based strategic design practice focused on helping governments and leaders innovate. Marco is former Director of Strategic Design at the Finnish Innovation Fund, where he launched a portfolio of initiatives to address the acute need for strategic improvement in the public sector. Marco believes that there are solutions to the complex challenges that governments, societies and environments face. There is a need to shift from trying to improve the efficiency of what was to redesigning what could be. His passion is in helping leaders find the pathway to these strategic improvements. Marco is currently the Chairman of the Board of the Museum of Finnish Architecture and serves as advisor to many organizations. His previous experience includes: professor at the Harvard Design School (1999–2009); advising governments on small and medium-sized enterprise (SME) and design-funding strategies; and running his own design and architectural practice.

Nina Terrey is a Partner at ThinkPlace and is a leading expert in design applied to complex public sector challenges. ThinkPlace is the leading design firm in Australia specializing in the transformation of complex services using design methods and approaches to systemically create public value. Nina is author of a number of papers and frequently speaks at international design and management conferences in such topic areas as management and design, design strategy and culture, and changing organizations to become more design led, especially in the public sector. Nina holds a PhD in Management, and is an adjunct Associate Professor of ANZSOG Institute of Governance. Nina's research titled 'Managing By Design' traces the application of design thinking in a complex public sector context – The Australian Taxation Office. Nina's current passion and interest is in progressing design into the policy front end, looking for possibilities to experiment and scale the co-design into the decision-making of the policymaker.

Romain Thévenet is a designer. Initially interested in ecodesign and service design, he graduated from Ensci (Paris) with an MA in industrial design in 2008. In his end-of-studies project, he explored different ways design tools could contribute to build alternative local development policies. Since then he has been particularly interested in how innovation methods from the industrial sector can be used within the public sector, to change the ways public policies are designed and implemented. He took part in the creation and development of la 27e Région, a public innovation lab working with French regional administrations. Since 2009, he has coordinated the various design teams operating in its programs. Most recently, he has been working as a freelance designer, running projects both with la 27e Région and other organizations and remaining in the realm of public service issues.

Stéphane Vincent is the co-founder of la 27e Région, a French innovation lab dedicated to the public sector created in 2008. With a background in management and innovation, his career began in media companies. His first experience within the public sector was in 1995, when he was in charge of innovation policies in a regional government. Seven years later, he became an associate in a consultant agency for clients such as government ministries and public and local authorities. He developed the concept of la 27e Région, a non-profit 'do-tank', as a way to explore radically new ways to design and build public policies, inspired by service design, ethnology, social innovation and digital culture. He is a regular speaker in national and international events, and as a writer he publishes or contributes to many books and reports such as *Design des politiques publiques, la Documentation française*, April 2010. He received the Europe Design Management Award 2011, the Victoires des Acteurs Publics 2011 and was a German Marshall Fellow in 2005.

Jennie Winhall is a Senior Strategist and a founding member of Participle. Previously Jennie was Senior Design Strategist for RED at the UK Design Council. As part of an interdisciplinary team of designers, social scientists and economists, she developed a methodology for designing with end users and front-line workers to create new public services and delivery models. Prior to Participle she was project lead for Service Design agency live|work, who create user-centred, sustainable services for clients such as Experian, Norwich Union and the NHS Institute for Innovation and Improvement. Jennie's background is in product design and psychology and her work has won awards from the D&AD, the RSA, Germany's Red Dot and the Australian Design Association. Jennie has worked for design groups in the UK, India, Australia and France.

Benjamin Winter is a designer, researcher and teacher, working in service design and social innovation. He has an MFA in Transdisciplinary Design from Parsons The New School for Design, where he currently serves as adjunct faculty in The School of Design Strategies. Ben is also a fellow at the Public Policy Lab, an active member of Parsons DESIS Lab and a contributor to their Public & Collaborative project.

THIS BOOK: AN OVERVIEW

The contributions to this book are organized in three sections.

Section 1 addresses the current and emerging public policy context for design.

Tom Bentley outlines some of the core questions and challenges that are raised for policymakers in an increasingly interconnected and globalized world. As a highly experienced policymaker at the highest levels of government, and as one of the chief architects of the Australian government's strategy 'Australia in the Asian century', Bentley has been intimately involved with shaping policies in what he characterizes as a turbulent and contested environment.

Christian Bason and **Andrea Schneider** write on selected global trends towards embedding and institutionalizing design in government. Where is design practice headed, and what forms does it take in the public sector? This global tour takes a closer look at France, Denmark and the United States and highlights selected cases from these countries, while also touching on the state of play in the UK, Finland, the Netherlands, Australia and Italy. Additionally the chapter considers and maps the rise of design labs as organizational anchors for design within or close to public organizations.

Jesper Christiansen and Laura Bunt move from policy context to policy environments, arguing that there is an urgent need for re-thinking the practice of public policy in order to allow for social complexity, uncertainty and unpredictability in designing of public outcomes. They point to the need for establishing a new culture of decision-making based on reconceptualizing the development processes, policy tools, value of evidence and the public authority role itself, thus challenging the existing paradigm of public management.

Sabine Junginger highlights how the design discourse has to rise from policy implementation to policymaking to encompass and understand policy design as such from a design perspective. As a consequence, we must challenge the emphasis on policymaking as decision-making based on seemingly rational and objective models. Instead, there is a need to reimagine policymaking as designing through inquiry, experimentation and learning.

Banny Banerjee discusses the concept of 'super-wicked problems' which are characterized by massive scale, urgency and complex interactions between many subsystems that are themselves wicked problems. Banerjee expands our design vocabulary with a fifth dimension of design, which is suited to help drive large-scale system transformation.

Marco Steinberg's contribution completes Section 1 by emphasizing the role of stewardship in public sector design processes. How does one lead the process of uncovering the architecture of problems, and what are the leadership practices needed to steward design-led policy projects?

Section 2 examines a select number of cases of how design can help drive policies and implementation at all levels of government, including state, regional and local levels. The cases have been chosen to illustrate the diversity of the application of design for policy, and the intimate relationships between (top-down) policymaking and (on-the-ground) service provision.

Ezio Manzini writes on designing for community policy, emphasizing how a new kind of social services (*collaborative services*), involving active and collaborative citizens, generate value for them and, at the same time, for the whole of society. He examines the case of community gardens, where citizens commit themselves to set up and take care of neighbourhood resources. Manzini points out how collaborative and experimental spaces can facilitate positive loops between bottom-up change and public agency innovation, simultaneously.

Sarah Forrester and John Body show how design approaches succeed in linking policy intent with on-the-ground professional practices in the field of vulnerable families in Canberra, Australia. They highlight key components of a design-led process to reconfigure not only interactions with families, but also to reconfigure the overall governance systems.

Christopher Boyko and Rachel Cooper discuss the experience of design at city level, using the case of the UK-based research project *VivaCity2020*. Mapping a process for sustainable urban design decision-making, the authors discuss the different stages and contributions of design.

Kit Lykketoft explores how design might become a legitimate practice within a national, ministerial policy environment. By studying the case of MindLab, a cross-governmental design and innovation unit, she discusses the concept of legitimacy and the types of practices that strengthen and weaken it.

Mariana Amatullo shares lessons about design as a driver of cross-agency collaboration and better results for both end-users and system users, drawing mainly on a case driven by the Danish Business Authority.

Eduardo Staszowski, **Scott Brown** and **Benjamin Winter** take departure in the New York City-based 'Designing Services for Housing' project as a case study for identifying the various challenges designers face in working in collaboration with public partners to effect social change. Amongst other key issues they acknowledge that designers, by engaging with public problems, take on a political position, and that the management of (political) risk thus becomes part of their role.

François Jégou, Romain Thévenet and Stéphane Vincent use the term 'friendly hacking' to discuss the dilemmas that arise when design-led projects challenge the robustness of public policy instruments and services, identifying weaknesses and pointing to needed improvements. Using two case examples from design-led projects in French regions, they pinpoint seven key lessons for designers who wish to engage with government and make an impact.

Section 3 shifts perspective to design tools: The approaches, methods and practices that embody design as a tool for policymaking. The section focuses on the themes of intent, insights, ideation and implementation.

John Body and Nina Terrey consider design tools for *intent*: How can design improve the way that policy is delivered into communities in practice, to deliver the intended results? They show how one must invest in strategic conversations that can help galvanize a common understanding of the policy intent amongst all stakeholders across multiple levels of governance.

Andrea Siodmok shares a range of tools and cases that demonstrate the power of design to provide *insight*: design research methods for policymaking which range from cultural probes to ethnographic research and to citizen journey mapping.

Joachim Halse discusses how design can facilitate *ideation* via visualization and modelling. Through the concept of 'evocative sketching', Halse demonstrates how design can make seemingly complex and abstract policy concepts experientially available in order to drive the generation of new ideas.

Simona Maschi and Jennie Winhall finally share design tools for *implementation*: They discuss and demonstrate how design can help manifest policies in the world via interactive services, graphic expressions, interfaces and products.

Christian Bason concludes the volume with a consideration of the patterns emerging from across the different contributions: In what way is design being applied for policymaking? What are the dilemmas involved? What is a realistic promise of design for policy? Could the systematic integration of design approaches in the practice of policymaking warrant the term 're-invention', or is design rather positioned as an add-on, a more marginal contribution to the centuries-old practice of making policy? What are the main lessons for public managers and policymakers? And as for the academic community, what are the contours of the future research agenda for design in the context of public policy?

CHRISTIAN BASON

Introduction: The Design for Policy Nexus

> Governments can be brutal and stupid. But the best have helped their citizens to live stronger, safer, richer, freer lives.
>
> Geoff Mulgan (2009: 1)

We take for granted that governments on a daily basis take decisions that influence our lives and the societies in which we live. We also tend to expect that governments generally seek to improve the current state of affairs. Governments are, ultimately, the owners of public problems, and policies are ostensibly the strategies they pursue to address them. However, being far from simple and rational processes, policies are 'windows onto political processes in which actors, agents, concepts and technologies interact in different sites, creating or consolidating new rationalities of governance and regimes of knowledge or power' (Shore and Wright 2011: 1).

In an award-winning doctoral dissertation, Nina Holm Vohnsen looks through such a window. She describes how a young policymaker in the Danish Ministry of Employment sits one evening in her Copenhagen office and looks out the window from her office to another ministerial building across the street: 'We are 200 people sitting here, making paper ... We just sit here and write about what ought to be done, without *doing* ... I wonder what they are writing over there' (Vohnsen 2011: 18).

Similarly, I had the opportunity to look onto a different policy window as I conducted leadership training in design and innovation for directors in European Union institutions in Brussels. While our session was going on, European farmers were on strike and had effectively blocked most of the nearby streets with tractors and other farming machinery. As we discussed the challenge of innovation in the public sector, a director in charge of the Union's agricultural policy said with no apparent irony: 'How can they do this, when we do so much for them?'

In both these cases –from the perspective of a national ministry and an international institution respectively – policymakers lament the fact that perhaps they do not make the difference to people and society they could. How often do policies succeed in becoming the actual carriers of the change intended by policymakers? How does the planning and deliberation of the policy process translate into tangible outcomes for citizens? How can policies effectively promote certain behaviours, relationships and capacities? How can policy thinking and policy 'doing' be combined? As we observe the young policymaker and listen to her frustration, and as we listen to the surprise of the EU Director, we recognize that these are some of the most enduring questions facing policymakers and, indeed, contemporary society.

From Policy *Description* to Policy *Prescription*

There is no shortage of analyses of how such 'windows' on public decision-making unfold. Since Graham Allison's 1971 study on alternative decision-making models during the Cuban missile crisis, political scientists and decision researchers have developed increasingly finely tuned models for understanding decision-making processes in policy environments. On a case-study basis, we know how to interpret what happens between the point at which a public organization is called upon to address a societal challenge, and the point when it formally decides which policy levers it will use to tackle it. We can also understand the processes which are implicitly or explicitly put in place to help stakeholders navigate and ultimately reach decisions. And we can analyze the process through a variety of conceptual lenses (Allison 1971; Smith 1993).

However, despite our increasingly powerful analytical tools, the question remains whether the ability of policymakers to shape and drive policy in ways which lead to the intended outcomes has truly improved in recent decades. Arguably, policy-making in the twenty-first century has become increasingly difficult, as the contexts in which policies are formed and must work have become more complex, or at least complex in different ways than in the past, to the point where 'the journey to success in public sector undertakings is perilous, strewn with traps and snares that bedevil the efforts of best and the brightest' (Eggers and O'Leary 2009). The rise of a global networked economy driven by new technology, new patterns of global trade, finance and mobility, new media, new lifestyle and health patterns, combined with a literally more turbulent climate, poses daunting challenges.

The point of departure for this book is the belief that the practices and tools of today's policymakers have not kept sufficiently abreast of these developments.

What we do not know much about is whether there is a fundamentally better way of carrying out policy? Might we create policy processes which more deliberately oscillate between understanding the nature of the problem and understanding the potential effectiveness of public action? Might we become more skilled at inviting into the policy process, at an early stage, the complexities not only of the wider policy-making system itself, but of the world 'out there' in the form of insights about context and human behaviour? Could we become better at applying the tools and methods most appropriate for exploring particular problem spaces? Might we thereby create policies that stand a better chance of achieving their political objectives? How could policy be more effective both from a top-down and from a bottom-up perspective? Might we in the future become as skilled as *pre*scribing the 'good' policy process, as we currently are at *de*scribing it?

In short, could we reinvent the art and craft of policymaking for the twenty-first century?

When Policy Meets Design

There certainly is no lack of interest in improving the effectiveness of policymaking. Because of the trends described above, governments around the world are under unprecedented pressure to identify new, better and more cost-effective ways of producing public services and better societal outcomes. Increasingly, public servants, alongside academia, think tanks and consultancies, are undertaking an exploration of alternative 'tools of government' (Bourgon 2008; Mulgan 2009) which may hold more promise than the current repertoire available to policymakers.

These new tools span from a range of new financial instruments (social impact investing, crowdfunding) to new approaches to regulation (behavioural economics, 'nudging') and to new organizational forms (mutuals, collaboratives, social enterprises, place-based approaches, co-production), to name just a few (Policy Horizons Canada 2012). However, perhaps the most exciting development, both from a practical and an academic standpoint, is the exploration of different ways of creating innovation within the policy process itself (Bunt and Christiansen 2012).

Here, design enters the picture.

Over the last decade, design as an approach to policy and service innovation in the public sector – especially but not exclusively in the Anglo-saxon and Nordic countries – has increasingly been explored (Bason 2010; Boyer et al. 2011; Cooper et al. 2011; European Commission 2012; Bason 2013). Design can be defined as the human endeavour of converting actual into preferred situations (Simon 1996). This broad definition views design as the process of creating 'new integrations of signs, things, actions and environments that address the concrete needs and values of human beings in diverse circumstances' (Buchanan 1990: 20). Rather than viewing design merely as an addition to the repertoire of policy tools, this definition indicates that design offers a different way for policymaking to be done. However even though design is now explicitly entering the public policy and service space, literature that convincingly marries design, public organization and societal context, and explores their relationship, is extremely sparse. The ambition of this book is to help bridge that gap.

Design for Policy is intended as a resource for government departments, public service organizations and institutions, universities, think tanks and consultancies that are increasingly engaging with design as a tool for public sector reform and innovation. The book thus aims to contribute to actual policymaking as well as to the learning environments where our future public leaders and policy professionals are developed. This objective is reflected by the contributors, who span from high level government strategists, design thinkers and experts, to academics with backgrounds in design as well as public management and related disciplines.

The book is part of a wider series, edited by Rachel Cooper, examining design for sustainability. As a contribution to the series, the intent of this book is to point to new avenues for applying design-led processes of policy development and innovation at all levels of the public sector.

In this introductory chapter, I first discuss the concept 'design' in a public sector context, and pinpoint some of the questions we need to ask about the intersection of design and policy: Where are they heading respectively, what are their linkages and how can design and policy inform each other? What are the key questions we need to ask, and what are the emerging agendas for practice and for research? I then briefly give an overview of the contributions to this volume.

The Emergent Nature of Design in the Public Sector

According to Buchanan (1990), design affects contemporary life in at least four areas: symbolic and visual *communication*, the design of material objects (*construction*), design of activities and organized services (*strategic planning*) and, finally, the design of complex systems or environments for living, working, playing and learning (*systemic integration*). The way in which these forms of design play out in today's society is undergoing a number of transformations, two of which are of particular importance for this book.

First, design is shifting to the concept of 'co': to *co*-llaboration, *co*-creation and *co*-design as a central feature, emphasizing the explicit involvement of users, partners, suppliers and other stakeholders in the design process, in essence discarding the notion of the heroic single designer (Boland and Collopy 2004; Shove et al. 2007; Sanders and Stappers 2008; Michlewski 2008; Bason 2010; Meroni and Sangiorgi 2011). Design as a discipline is thus undergoing a significant transformation, which perhaps places it more squarely at the heart of an organization's ability to create new valuable solutions. Variations such as participatory design and service design, which focuses on (re)designing service processes from an end-user perspective, are in rapid growth (Bate and Robert 2007; Shove et al. 2007; Brown 2009; Cooper and Junginger 2011).

Second, design is increasingly embracing the social. Although not a new perspective to designers per se, Ezio Manzini (2011: 1) emphasizes that design as such has followed the evolution of economic thinking, as twenty-first-century design also reflects '*the loss of the illusion of control, or the discovery of complexity*' [original emphasis]. This has led to a wider change in design culture which has arguably been under way since the late 1960s, and which could be characterized as design for 'social good'. This shift is in part captured by the movement of social entrepreneurship and social innovation (Mulgan et al. 2006; Ellis 2010), and in part by the growing interest in public sector innovation (Mulgan and Albury 2003; Eggers and O'Leary 2009; Bason 2010; Boyer et al. 2011; Bason 2012; European Commission 2012).

Much of the conversation, both amongst practitioners and in the academic community, concerning design for social good has focused largely on the concrete articulation of design as services. A growing body of literature (Parker and Heapy 2006; Meroni and Sangiorgi 2011; Polaine et al. 2012) addresses design for services, including the series of which this book is a part. Design for policy has been far less elucidated. Part of the reason is perhaps that service design is a relatively malleable discipline, which lends itself to application in any sector – be it private, public or non-governmental. Policy, it can be argued, is almost uniquely a public sector enterprise.

The Promise of Design for Policy

Before turning to an overview of the contributions to this book, let's take a brief look at the promises and challenges of design for policy.

First, design offers a different approach to the task of understanding public problems. Design provides an array of highly concrete research tools, ranging from ethnographic, qualitative, user-centred research, to probing and experimentation via rapid prototyping, to visualizing vast quantities of data in new and powerful ways. Drawing on elements of systems thinking, design research can help policymakers better understand the root causes of problems and their underlying interdependencies – the 'architecture of problems' (Boyer et al. 2011; Mulgan 2014).

Second, the emergent and more collaborative aspects of design suggests that policy options could be increasingly co-designed through an interplay between policymakers at different levels of the governance system, interest and lobby groups, external experts and, not least, end-users such as citizens or business representatives themselves. Graphic facilitation and the use of tangibles and visuals for service and use scenarios can provide the means for cross-cutting dialogue, mutual understanding and collective ownership of ideas and solutions. Design, as a creative discipline, is ripe with ways and means of stimulating individual and group creativity, and can thus facilitate a wide divergence of views and ideas, enabling selection, then synthesizing them.

Third, design offers the devices – concepts, identities, graphics, products, service templates, system maps – that can help give form and shape to policy in practice: Design is perhaps at its best when it creates the tangible artefacts that we as humans can engage with physically and emotionally. The ability to create deliberate user experiences and to make services and products desirable and attractive is at the heart of design practice.

Across these three dimensions of defining problem space, developing ideas and concepts for policy and of articulating that policy in tangible ways, design should be well positioned to make a significant contribution. In a time when we search for ways to better manage and even benefit from the rising complexity and turbulence of our societies, design seems to promise smarter and more engaging ways of tackling problems.

However, one can also point to a wide range of challenges.

There appears to be an inherent clash between the logic of administrative organization and the sensibilities of designers. Far from being unproblematic in the private sector, the relationship between public decision-makers in government departments and agencies on the one hand, and designers on the other hand, can be fraught with misunderstandings, mutual distrust and apprehension. As Geoff Mulgan, Chief Executive of the UK's National Endowment for Science, Technology and the Arts (Nesta) has observed during encounters between British decision-makers in government and designers (2014: 6):

> Policy-makers have grudgingly accepted that they might have quite a bit to learn from the designers; but the designers appeared baffled when it was suggested that they might have something to learn from the policy-makers, or from the many other organizations and fields with claims to insight into service design: social entrepreneurs, professions, consultancies, IT, policy makers, etc. There are plenty of exceptions to this rule: but overblown claims that design methods are uniquely placed to tackle complex, holistic problems has not always helped to inspire a culture of collaboration and mutual learning.

Behind this chasm between the design community on the one hand, and policymakers on the other, lies perhaps not just unrealistic claims from designers, but a difference in the values – implicit or explicit – that characterize the two. Table i.1 illustrates some of the characteristics of these two 'worlds':

Table i.1   Design in the balance

Government	Design
Analysis	Synthesis
Rational	Emotional
Logical	Intuitive
Deductive	Inductive
Solutions	Paradigms, platforms
'Thinking it through'	Rapid prototyping (think through doing)
Single disciplines (e.g. law, economics)	Multiple disciplines, T-shape
Elegance	Impact, value, diffusion

Source: Inspired by Banerjee (2009), Brown (2009), Martin (2009)

This divergence raises the question of whether designers can ever become a respected part of the public sector, and recognized as partners with policymakers?

One could argue that the political, ideological and sometimes abstract nature of public policies make them unfit for design practices which are concerned with that which is attractive, functional and meaningful to people in practice. While the ability to give shape to abstract concepts and ideas is a core design skill, can designers come to terms with the sheer scale, interdependence and complexity of public problems? Can they contribute to the domains of law and governance? What is in practice the relationship between design for policy and design for services, and does 'policy design' in practice turn into 'service design'?

Finally there is the question of power. On the one hand, designers are not unaware that there is power in the ability to make and shape things and environments which can impact thousands or millions of people's lives. On the other hand, there is a different kind of power at play within and around public sector institutions, which are often nested in highly complex task environments, characterized by a multitude of stakeholders, interests and conflicts. Are designers able to navigate the intricacies and, indeed, conspiracies of public policymaking, and under which conditions and on what occasions can they play a legitimate role?

References

Allison, G. (1971). *Essence of Decision: Explaining the Cuban Missile Crisis*. Boston: Little, Brown & Company.

Banerjee, B. (2009). Presentation to Copenhagen Co-creation Conference; https://www.youtube.com/watch?v=OLqEQWmESe0.

Bason, C. (2010). *Leading Public Sector Innovation: Co-creating for a Better Society*. Bristol: Policy Press.

Bason, C. (2012). Public managers as designers – Can Design-led Approaches Lead to New Models for Public Service Provision? *Danish Journal of Management & Business*, Vol. 77(4), December 2012.

Bason, C. (2013). Design-led Innovation in Government. *Stanford Social Innovation Review*, spring 2013, http://www.ssireview.org/chapters/entry/design_led_innovation_in_government.

Bate, P. and Robert, G. (2007). *Bringing User Experience to Healthcare Improvement: The Concepts, Methods and Practices of Experience-based Design*. Abingdon: Radcliffe Publishing.

Boland, R.J. and Collopy, F. (2004). *Managing as Designing*. Stanford, CA: Stanford University Press.

Bourgon, J. (2008). The Future of Public Service: A Search for a New Balance. Keynote Address to the 2008 IPAA National Conference, Sydney, NSW, June 2008.

Boyer, B., Cook, J.W. and Steinberg, M. (2011). *In Studio: Recipes for Systemic Change*. Helsinki: Sitra.

Brown, T. (2009). *Change by Design: How Design Thinking Transforms Organizations and Inspires Innovation*. New York: HarperCollins.

Buchanan, R. (1990). Wicked Problems in Design Thinking, essay based on paper presented at Colloque Recherches sur le Design: Incitations, Implications, Interactions, at l'Université de Technologie de Compiègne, Compiègne, France.

Christiansen, Jesper and Bunt, L. (2012). *Innovations in Policy: Allowing for creativity, Social Complexity, and Uncertainty in Public Governance*. London: Nesta and Copenhagen: MindLab.

Cooper, R. and Junginger, S. (2011). General Introduction: Design Management – a reflection, in Rachel Cooper, Sabine Junginger and Thomas Lockwood, *The Handbook of Design Management*. Oxford: Berg Publishers.

Eggers, W. & O'Leary, J. (2009). If we Can Put a Man on the Moon ... Getting Big Things Done in Government. Boston: Harvard Business Press.

Ellis, Tania (2010). *The New Pioneers: Sustainable Business Success Through Social Innovation and Social Entrepreneurship*. Chichester: Wiley.

European Commission (2012). Design for Growth and Prosperity: Recommendations of the European Design Leadership Board, http://ec.europa.eu/enterprise/policies/innovation/files/design/design-for-growth-and-prosperity-report_en.pdf.

Manzini, E. (2011). Introduction in Anna Meroni and Daniela Sangiorgi, *Design for Services*. Farnham, UK: Gower.

Martin, R. (2009). *The Design of Business: Why Design Thinking is the Next Competitive Advantage*. Cambridge: Harvard Business Press.

Meroni, A. and Sangiorgi, D. (2011). *Design for Services*. Farnham, UK: Gower.

Michlewski, K. (2008). Uncovering Design Attitude: inside the Culture of Designers. *Organization Studies* 29 (2): 229–48.

Mulgan, G. et. al. (2006). *Social Silicon Valleys*. London: Young Foundation.

Mulgan, G. (2009). *The Art of Public Strategy*. Oxford: Oxford University Press.

Mulgan, G. (2014). Design in Public and Social Innovation – What Works, And What Could Work Better, http://www.nesta.org.uk/sites/default/files/design_in_public_and_social_innovation.pdf.

Parker, S. and Heapy, J. (2006). *The Journey to the Interface: How Public Service Design can Connect Users to Reform*. London: Demos.

Polaine, A., Løvlie, L. and Reason, B. (2013). *Service Design: From Insight to Implementation*. New York: Rosenfeld Media.

Policy Horizons Canada (2012). *Driving Policy on a Shifting Terrain: Understanding the Changing Policy Environment Amidst 21st-Century Complexity*.

Sanders, E. and Stappers, P.J. (2008). Co-creation and the New Landscapes of Design. *CoDesign: International Journal of CoCreation in Design and the Arts*, 1745–3755, 4(1): 5–18.

Shore, C. and Wright, S. (2011). Introduction in S. Wright, C. Shore and D. Pèro (eds.), *Policy Worlds: Anthropology and the Analysis of Contemporary Power*. New York: Berghahn.

Shove, E. et. al. (2007). *The Design of Everyday Life*. Oxford: Berg.

Simon, H.A. (1996). *The Sciences of the Artificial*. Cambridge: MIT Press.

Smith, M.J. (1993). *Pressure Power & Policy: State Autonomy and Policy Networks in Britain and the United States*. Hempstead: Harvester Wheatsheaf.

Verganti, R. (2009). *Design-driven Innovation: Changing the Rules of Competition by Radically Innovating What Things Mean*. Boston: Harvard Business Press.

Vohnsen, N.H. (2011). *Absurdity and the Sensible Decision: Implementation of Danish Labour Market Policy*. Doctoral dissertation. Aarhus: Aarhus University.

Section 1

Design in Context

TOM BENTLEY

Design in Policy: Challenges and Sources of Hope for Policymakers

The Global Financial Crisis (GFC) shortened the political life span of many governments and elected leaders around the world. This spike in turnover is not surprising. A shock triggering widespread recession, soaring unemployment and the collapse or takeover of many familiar institutions is likely to exhaust the reserves of political leadership and eclipse the credibility of those in office. For some new candidates running at the time, like Barack Obama and David Cameron, the ability to offer 'new hope' and a fresh approach to governing was an electoral asset. Being untainted by incumbency probably helps when shock and fear are coursing through electorates. But the size and complexity of the problems generated by the crisis mean that a lot more than hope and energy are required to govern successfully. Those fresh new faces are now grappling with intractable challenges.

Post-crisis Policymaking

Since 2008, a common goal for policymakers around the world, even in wildly varying circumstances, has become 'sustainable growth' (G20 n.d.). It is a common denominator across the G20, the group of economies and governments whose shared interests were confirmed during the initial responses to the crisis. But the blandness of the phrase still masks diverse circumstances and deep contradictions in the situations confronting policymakers in different nations and regions.

One thing they have in common, though, is that after the crisis, policymakers typically find themselves working with less time, trust and money to achieve their goals. They work in a more complex and demanding environment, where short term pressures and long term changes come together to create problems that can seem insoluble and situations that appear ungovernable. For many people, the collapse of Lehman brothers was an event that came out of nowhere, causing the seizing up of global financial markets, triggering a wrenching recession in many countries around the world and a shuddering, ongoing crisis of unemployment and public finances.

But the events may be explained as a manifestation of longer term forces which had been gathering for years, an expression of policy failures or distortions that had not been corrected in the trajectory of global markets and the design of key institutions, leading to large scale breakdown in a newly interconnected global economy. The crisis prompted action which went far beyond the standard responses and routines of policy. This was essential in order to unblock global credit, kick-start economic growth and seek to replace or repair institutions which had been massively damaged by their failures.

The immediate responses were focused on economic stimulus, on stabilizing and protecting key financial institutions and on intervening to prevent the further collapse of organizations like General Motors that were considered 'too big to fail'.

Of course, the crisis is not over. Many countries are still working to overcome the emergency and restore anything like acceptable levels of employment and public debt. In Greece, the whole society is still fighting to stave off basic collapse. In the US, the unemployment rate only fell below 7 per cent in late 2013. In the same year, those officially labelled as unemployed account for almost a quarter of all people aged under 25 across the European Union while the investment and demand that might generate new jobs for them continued to decline (Dorling 2013). Other countries which enjoyed more success in avoiding recession, such as Australia, Korea and China, still face the challenge of achieving 'sustainable growth', navigating the new environment and addressing their own specific structural or institutional weaknesses, as policymakers and citizens alike worry about the fragility exposed by global recession and the risks posed by collapses elsewhere.

The Public Policy Challenge

Despite the great diversity among countries, policymakers face a common challenge – to achieve simultaneously three basic outcomes: growth in jobs and incomes; basic social and public goods like health, education and environmental protection and security and stability for citizens through justice, policing, defence and sound public administration. The ability of governments to meet this triple imperative – providing for economic sustenance, social need and public security – has clearly been challenged by the GFC and its consequences.

The most obvious manifestation of the challenge is economic recession, destroying jobs and capital and reducing income and revenue. This economic decline in turn creates ongoing fiscal pressure arising from lower revenues, higher need and the costs of intervening to prevent immediate economic meltdown. As government budgets are pushed further into deficit, their ability to fund services and investment is diminished and public debt accumulates. In extreme cases, these twin pressures and the public's reaction to them also threaten the ability of governments to maintain stability and security. The shock exposes policymakers to greater pressure and scrutiny, and tests the established models and narratives on offer to solve public problems and meet public need. It is no accident that two rival explanations quickly emerged for the crisis; the first attacking too much deregulation of financial markets and explosion of greed, and the second seeking to blame unsustainable public spending and the over-reach of the state for creating an accumulation of public debt and deficit which placed too great a strain on the workings of the market economy.

Subsequently, two competing narratives are playing out in the politics of many nations. In the first, economic growth and stability are to be achieved through retrenchment and austerity, cutting back public spending and services until governments and nations can 'live within their means' and free markets can 'recover' from the damage caused by excessive public intervention. In the second, governments seek to build on economic stimulus, prioritize employment over debt and invest proactively in new sources of growth. These two choices do not exclusively capture the full range of approaches taken to governing for growth. But they recognizably influence the strategies and the politics of many nations today.

In reality, the policy prescriptions of both the centre-left and the centre-right have been found wanting by the crisis, not just in their failure to predict or prepare for it, but also in their ability to offer compelling, workable answers to the questions it has thrown onto the public stage. The quest for 'sustainable growth' partly reflects a hunger for longer term stability and vision, which is in greater demand from citizens precisely because the crisis has reminded them of how easily things can fall apart. The binary choice between austerity and stimulus does not, however, provide an adequate model for either economic growth or for successful governance. Political leaders find themselves seeking explanations and 'narratives' for the times we live in, to make sense of a complex reality and to chart a path through it.

In order to provide this coherence, however, policymakers need to generate new answers. The questions they face are about the sources of future growth and their sustainability, and the ways in which governments can create public goods, together with citizens and organizations in the private and social sectors, in situations where the rigid roles and demarcations between national and sectoral institutions have been broken down, and traditional social structures and hierarchies also eroded. The most familiar forms of governance and reform strategy, from privatization and deregulation through the target-driven new public management, social democratic tripartite consensus and authoritarian national development have all been found wanting. In response, a new focus on 'strategic', 'collaborative and 'networked' governance has begun to emerge (Parker and Parker 2006).

The Shock of the New: Acceleration and Innovation

Another effect of the crisis was to accelerate the transition from older to newer sources of power and influence. In 2006, none of the world's top 10 banks by market value were Chinese. In 2009, four were (Legrain 2010). China's economic resilience saw its strategic influence and credibility grow. The widespread criticism and predictions that China's institutions of capitalism and governance were built on sand have been muted, at least for now. China's government is visibly seeking to moderate its own growth path and to accelerate institutional reform, for the sake of greater sustainability.

The GFC accelerated the destruction of old business models, as companies and industries reliant on incumbency were left behind and economic hardship tested the resilience and productivity of firms forced to compete harder for more limited resources. This more intense competition further drives the growth of firms and networks in 'emerging' economies. In 2003, only 31 of the world's 500 largest companies by revenues were from emerging economies. By 2009 there were 91: China had 39, Korea 14, Russia 8, India 7, Brazil and Taiwan 6 each, Mexico 4, Singapore 2 and Malaysia, Saudi Arabia, Thailand, Turkey and Venezuela 1 each.

Companies and governments, particularly in Europe and North America, have become even more painfully conscious of the need for strategic investments and alliances in these parts of the world, and for economic strategies which prioritize innovation. But while the centre of economic and strategic gravity may continue to shift, the consequence for policymakers is not a reduction in a role or influence, but rather a proliferation of connections and pressures. This was the great lesson of the crisis, as problems created in specific US financial markets cascaded across the globe.

The growth of interdependence through connection, transparency and exchange applies to almost every aspect of life.

Pressures on Policymakers

The result of greater interdependence is an environment of great challenge and complexity to public policymakers. They are short of time, money and trust, but face immediate and pressing demands. Many of the established models, rules and institutions through which economic growth and public and social goods have been 'delivered' over the previous generation are unable to achieve growth, meet need or offer stability in the ways that people still expect. In an atmosphere of crisis the resources available to policymakers with which to generate alternative strategies have been limited.

Indeed, the drivers of innovation themselves contribute to the sense of crisis and illegitimacy confronting public decision-makers. The new technologies, social movements and markets are disruptive, challenging established institutional power and enabling coordination and collaboration that cuts across existing hierarchies and organizational structures.

Policymakers and organizational leaders need new ways to explain what is happening and mobilize communities to adapt. But the ongoing impacts of these changes make it harder for those holding institutional roles to communicate clear purpose and benefits to far-flung citizens. Digital technologies, for example, allow far greater specification of wants and needs in the fields of health, aged care, education, environmental protection or personal security. At the same time, they blur the boundaries between the different players responsible for their production. Social media networks are undermining the established hierarchies of political and public communication and the business models of traditional media, even while they accelerate the fragmentation of traditional social identities and public allegiances.

Policymakers around the world therefore find themselves with an array of interconnected problems and challenges in front of them, and a growing cacophony of demand to offer clear solutions. They must find ways to achieve the goods for which they are responsible, but in situations where their ability to control directly the actions which create such goods is limited. Yet the demands and expectations placed on governments have, if anything, multiplied in recent years. Government is just as much involved in different markets and sectors of society as it has ever been, grappling with long-standing functions from public transport and education to crime and cyber-security. The result is a pattern widely repeated around the world: a perception of political dysfunction and dissatisfaction, focused on the inability of political decision-makers to achieve satisfactory progress or articulate a common long-term purpose which can achieve the legitimacy of widespread public recognition and support.

Governments are not less powerful than in the past: The actions taken by national governments to address the GFC, stimulate the economy, nationalize banks and corporations, re-regulate markets and restructure the finances of other nations, not to mention participate in military interventions and invasions in recent decades, demonstrate the central role, vast resources and huge powers of nation states. But they share the stage with many other actors and increasingly operate through interconnected networks of communication and action which do not recognize the boundaries of geographical territory or functional authority through which governments are traditionally organized. It is not the case that governments have fewer opportunities to act or fewer options through which to act. Rather, the problem is that they work in an *environment* that has become more complex, less forgiving and more constrained, with others jostling for power and authority. This situation has created three particular challenges to the models of public policymaking that have dominated the last century.

The first is the assumption of a linear policy cycle, in which a rational process of decision-making is undertaken by those with formal authority to do so, starting with clear objectives and then selecting methods of intervention and allocating resources on the basis of options shaped by the available evidence. In this model, implementation then follows on from policy decisions as an equally rational, step by step administrative process, culminating with evaluation, which in turn informs future policy deliberations. This model, which is deeply embedded in the cultures of legislatures and bureaucracies around the world, is one of the main reasons why policy processes are primarily focused on the production of documents, rather than the production of outcomes.

The second challenge is the assumption that policy and implementation are carried out through functional, vertically separated organizations, or 'siloes' typified by national government departments holding policy authority over implementing agencies. Of course governments embody a wide diversity of structures, in part designed through the writing of democratic constitutions, and this diversity should not be oversimplified. However, the standard assumptions and forms of agency have enormous influence over how policy is produced and the capability of governments to implement their objectives.

The third challenge, as a consequence of the first two, is the assumption that policy and implementation are separate activities, conducted by different people and organizations with different kinds of specialist knowledge and capability.

These three assumptions maintain an extraordinarily powerful hold over the organization of public effort and the imagination of policymakers. They provide the structure through which the activities of government can actually occur. And they help to hold a balance between integration and fragmentation, action and paralysis, which enables government to function at all, given the relentless pressures they are under. However, the contemporary challenges of governing demand alternative ways of thinking and organizing, because the trends I have outlined present a direct, growing challenge to all three assumptions.

The Role of Institutions

Policymakers are therefore under enormous pressure to produce better outcomes, searching for more effective combinations of activities and organization, while continuously demonstrating progress to the wider world and learning to adjust, in real time, to events and innovations occurring beyond their control.

One key to understanding this challenge is through the lens of *institutions*. Public policymakers are not taking decisions and allocating resources through abstract processes disembodied from the societies they govern, but working through many and varied institutions to try to achieve outcomes that people value. Institutions are important because they act as both means and ends for public policy – they are the means of carriage for translating resources and goals into outcomes, but they also act as embodied forms of values that citizens recognize actors *in* society, and bulwarks against the unfettered use of state or market power. Democratic parliaments, for example, literally represent a particular way of taking the decisions needed to make laws. Democratic constitutions deliberately separate powers between different branches of government, prescribe a level of institutional diversity and spell out fundamental rights and duties which are then protected and enforced by specific institutions.

Institutions help to determine how well policymakers can interpret what is happening around them, and how well they can translate their policies into action. But institutions also have a double life in the policy process, because as embodied agents in the societies they serve, they define what is possible in practice and act as *barriers* to the achievement of policymaking intentions, either because they actively resist those intentions, or because of limitations in their capacity to carry them out. Institutional diversity is a pre-requisite for innovation, action and learning in complex societies. But the very fact of institutional diversity means that the process of translating policy goals into practical outcomes requires coordination, negotiation, learning and conscious effort. For example, during the GFC, 'Quantitative Easing' (QE) emerged as an important tool in the struggle to generate GDP growth in a number of economies, especially the US. It is a policy innovation undertaken by specific institutions – reserve banks, who have the power and capability to do so, and have resorted to QE – *precisely because* other market institutions and monetary policy tools have failed. Indeed, in many countries, existing governance institutions have become stuck in cycles of coping and persistent failure, 'muddling through' their terms of office and struggling to develop any coherence or momentum in tackling the biggest challenges faced by their citizens.

Such failures highlight the fact that, while governments are 'owners' of public problems, their organization does not reflect the shape and structure of those problems. In this context, the separation in organizational design between 'policy' and 'implementation' is an impediment to successfully or strategically influencing the evolution of systems which operate beyond their direct control. Policymaking, in this view, is primarily about adapting to changes taking place in the much wider systems of society, economy and environment and seeking ways deliberately to influence and shape them so that they produce desirable outcomes. Crisis forces action, and the constraints formed by the shortage of time, trust or money may provide the spur for innovation.

This emergent set of challenges and constraints creates a fresh opportunity for perspectives and methods grounded in design to intersect with, and perhaps reshape, the conduct of public policy.

Institutions are fundamental to this process, bringing scale, structure and patience to possibilities that would otherwise flicker at the margins of economic and social life. But equally, a fact of institutional life is that they are instinctively opposed to forms of innovation and experimentation that might threaten their power, routines and resources Because of this 'double life' of institutions, the 'design in policy' challenge also has twin edges. On one side, design-based methods, tools and insights can be applied to public policy processes, encouraging a broader perspective and a richer mix of options from which policymakers and implementers can draw. But on the other, unless these principles are concretely embodied and embedded as ongoing capabilities of policy systems, the dominant institutional norms of those wider systems will quickly reassert themselves.

In other words, without the active participation of public institutions it is hard to imagine being able to structure and bring valuable innovations to scale. But if this is a necessary part of governance, then proactively opening the space and developing the capabilities to do so, across widespread systems like health, water, education, transport, energy and so on, is as vital a function as democratic and financial accountability. As a consequence, we should think about what policymakers can do in terms of their ability to create, shape and link institutions, and focus more intensively on developing the tools and methods needed to fashion institutions to achieve public purposes in new ways.

Australia: the Best of Times, the Worst of Times

These pressures and tensions have played themselves out in Australia in recent years, despite its stand-out success in responding to the GFC. Australia began 2008 with no public debt, a budget in surplus and economic growth spurred by a decade-long surge of export income from mining. Australia continues to benefit from the extraordinary demand for materials and energy resources in Asia.

Nonetheless, the crisis dramatically reduced Australia's investment, aggregate demand and tax revenues and created widespread expectation of a recession. A combination of economic stimulus by the national government, continued demand from Asia and resilient financial and economic institutions (for example, Australian banks are well capitalized and well regulated) saw Australia withstand the global shock and grow both employment and GDP in 2009 (Barrett 2011).

In 2013, Australia's economy was 14 per cent larger and had created almost a million more jobs since the crisis, in contrast to the 28 million added to unemployment registers worldwide during the same period. But the challenge of 'maintaining normality' (given that Australia also recently achieved its 22nd consecutive year of economic growth) also had a high cost, which took some time to appear. The reappearance of budget deficits and public debt, combined with real-time coverage of the global economic emergency, shook public confidence and prompted an increase in the savings rate and a reining in of private consumption.

This fiscal prudence was actually a good thing for the economy, given the rapid growth in private consumption and debt in the decade before 2008. But a heightened sense of anxiety and uncertainty was palpable, fuelled by those with a political interest in creating a sense of crisis, helping to create the paradox that, in Australia, where the unemployment rate in July 2013 was 5.7 per cent, economic confidence among the public was lower than in Spain. But a further effect of the crisis, as elsewhere, was to lengthen the 'to-do' list for government, simultaneously adding new and complex commitments while taking away many of the financial resources needed to achieve other reforms. In the process of trying to move on from the GFC, implement stimulus programs and continue to negotiate and deliver major commitments, including a carbon price, a national broadband network, a restructure of health and hospitals and taxation reform, Prime Minister Kevin Rudd lost his footing and the support of his parliamentary colleagues and was replaced by his deputy, Julia Gillard.

Many reasons can be given for the change, such as the Australian Labor Party's culture and history of leadership coups, the behaviour of Rudd towards his colleagues and senior public servants as prime minister, the lack of trust among the most senior members of the government and the pressure caused by constant media speculation. What has been given relatively little attention, however, is the way in which the GFC contributed to the overload and paralysis of government even in a country which responded successfully, avoided recession and maintained a growth record that is globally admired.

With the benefit of hindsight, individual mistakes that might have been avoided can always be found. But it is striking that, even in a country that got it right, the experience, expectations and perceptions of government did not align with each other. In an atmosphere of paralysis and distrust, politicians are cast as weak, reactive and dependent for self-preservation on special interests.

Consequently, the perception at least of a vicious cycle is created, in which politics remains bogged in a mire of competing interests and claims, with governments and their leaders suffering from a lack of legitimacy *and* a lack of capacity to get things done, and the two problems feeding each other. In this sense, Australia fell victim to the growing perception that politics had become dysfunctional and paralyzed, incapable of achieving the clear solutions and long term plans that people need in order to chart a course out of crisis and into the future. In Australia's case, the irony is extreme, given the success with which it steered through the crisis and the effectiveness of Julia Gillard's subsequent reform agenda from 2010 to 2013.

Australia in the Asian Century

In this context, the Gillard Government set out to develop a longer term strategy which genuinely addressed substantive reform challenges and sought ways to achieve progress for Australia in a post-crisis landscape. On re-forming Government in September 2010, Gillard began systematically to complete the unfinished reform tasks, achieving the structural separation of the national telco, completing a national health funding agreement and legislating a carbon price. She also began work to construct a strategic framework around which the government could mobilize not just itself, but the rest of Australian society towards a coherent longer-term purpose. In September 2011 she announced the development of a government White Paper on Australia in the Asian Century.

The rise of Asia represents simultaneously a competitive threat and an enormous new source of opportunity for economies in other parts of the world. Adapting successfully to the shift in the world's centre of gravity, the transfer of economic and strategic power from the Atlantic West to the Pacific East, is a global preoccupation (Demos 1995; Barber et al. 2012).

For Australia, these seismic changes are even more acute. A federation of Westminster democracies, the nation is formally allied with the United States and China is its biggest trading partner, while Indonesia, the world's most populous Muslim nation and a vibrant young democracy, is its near neighbour. Despite the dominance of its Anglo-Celtic culture, Australia is an ethnically and culturally diverse nation. And despite their ongoing marginalization, indigenous Australians proudly represent the world's oldest living culture.

Australia's recent prosperity reflects the strength of its trading relationships with Asian partners, but its long-term prospects are vulnerable to the same risks and shocks faced by the region, and its remarkable endowment of natural resources will not be enough to secure sustainable growth. Australia needs further innovation and specialization to ensure that its economy successfully adds value in the vast global markets for goods and services now taking shape across Asia.

The 'Asian Century' itself demonstrates and illustrates many other aspects of the broad changes in the policymaking environment: the emergence of transnational production chains, the growing flows of people, goods and money through liquid networks, the shift of hard power towards new strategic centres and the growing importance of soft power, culture and people-to-people links in shaping the evolution and performance of different communities.

What Prime Minister Gillard announced was a comprehensive exercise to map the changes, consider their impact and lay out a long term strategy through which Australia could seize the opportunities they are creating. Such a project challenges the capacity of government, precisely because governments are organized to separate activities and problems into component parts, and operate most typically through fragmented routines which enable operational stability and day to day coordination, but militate against ambitious, cross-cutting and innovative patterns of action.

A full government review overseen by the head of government also gave the project an opportunity to transcend the factionalism of competing agencies, world views and ministers, by seeking to combine them into a whole that was more than the sum of its parts. Achieving that, however, was not a guaranteed outcome.

As a policy exercise it therefore sought to reflect the new principles or qualities of the environment: it sought to be open, long term, cross-cutting and deliberative. It took into account not just the economic and security dimensions of Australia's place in the region, but also the social, educational and cultural factors, and focused on how Australia's exchange of people and culture within the region it lives is fundamental to its future. The governance of the project combined traditional policy processes with some innovation: A committee of senior cabinet ministers oversaw the progress of the White Paper and included expert advisers from business and academia. A task force was formed in the Department of Prime Minister and Cabinet, made up of public servants from several agencies including the Treasury and Department of Foreign Affairs, to run as an integrated team.

The public consultation process included electronic forums and discussion networks hosted by a non-government think tank: the Lowy Institute for International Policy. And the engagement process included public servants travelling to and engaging with key countries in the region, as well as diplomatic representatives of those countries in Australia. The process was welcomed in most quarters and, after a slow start, prompted submissions and participation from many different organizations and interests.

A Shift in Strategic Perspective

The result was a document, and a strategy, which articulates the shift in perspective that many nations are attempting to make (Australian Government 2013). That strategy seeks to maximize the benefits of openness, while actively building and strengthening capabilities that will be a source of advantage in an interconnected, rapidly changing environment. Perhaps most significant, it is a strategy which seeks to build on those comparative advantages by cultivating stronger *relationships*. The White Paper set out long term goals for 2025, along with specific responsibilities for achieving them, and largely avoided making more incremental or programmatic commitments.

The goals included:

- The Australian economy being more open and integrated with Asia;

- Australian businesses being recognized for their excellence and ability to operate successfully in Asian markets;

- Australia's innovation system performing in the global top 10 and its school system reaching the world's top five;

- Deeper and broader people to people links;

- Having the necessary capabilities to promote Australia's interests and maintain its influence.

For each goal there were specific pathways and actions, including increasing the teaching of Asian languages and studies in Australian schools, creating a Centre for Asia Capability at the University of Melbourne, publishing individual country strategies for priority nations, creating new 'AsiaBound' scholarships for study overseas and focusing a network of 200 senior public servants on the skills and knowledge they need to prioritize to become 'Asia-capable'.

In some respects, the strategy reasserted orthodoxies which have been the pillars of Australian policy for decades, such as the commitment to open markets and low or no tariffs. Such re-commitment is appropriate where the settings remain correct, especially when it is contextualized by a more holistic explanation of why they matter. The process prompted a struggle between two views of the world, both of which are well represented within the federal bureaucracy and among networks of experts – between economic liberalizers committed to the evolution of markets, and national security guardians committed to projecting Australian interests and influence through the strategic use of hard and soft power. The logical extension of either view is to put more emphasis on either market integration, for example, through free trade agreements, or on strategic engagement, for example through military exercises and diplomatic representation, in order to maximize Australia's place in the new regional order. It is also logical that any established institution, when asked what is needed to prepare for the future, will put forward more of what it already does. This step is part of the ritualized conduct of government and the internal contest of ideas and influence. The question, however, is whether such a process can *also* generate new insights and articulate new priorities that also gain acceptance and support, and prompt innovations which might lead existing institutions to change their practices.

The broad shift that occurred through the means of the White Paper was the greater priority placed on innovation for Australia's economic future, and the important roles of human capital, culture and relationships in achieving innovation. This emphasis helped provide an explanation of how Australia can go beyond a narrow dependence on the mineral and commodity-producing sectors that have fuelled its recent growth and how it can develop the more specialized capabilities that will be competitive in global markets and justify higher costs. Australia's goal must be to build a diversified economy which can trade successfully in regional markets and build distinctive capabilities for adding value to materials, products and services. In turn, these capabilities should fuel the development of longer term collaborative relationships.

An emphasis on innovation and strategic collaboration alongside robust market competition can be found in many policy discussions around the world. It prompts a focus on the clustering of knowledge and connections in particular places, building on their existing comparative advantages (and on specific institutional foundations) and evolving their identities and cultures in the process. For Australia, a nation that has been a stand-out economic success by pioneering an approach to economic reform a generation ago, it is an essential development. Cushioned by its minerals income,

Australia has risked falling into a backward-looking, self-referential discussion of its future, on both sides of politics.

The White Paper provided a framework for working through a different storyline, visibly supported by the evidence and economic data and synthesizing some of the key intellectual and territorial disputes within the government. More importantly, it created a framework within which an open, content-rich *public* discussion of these issues could occur. In a political atmosphere still dominated by shrieking, character attacks and an artificial atmosphere of emergency, this was a welcome development.

When it was released in October 2012, *Australia in the Asian Century* received widespread welcome and support across business and civil society, in the media and among public decision-makers, including other governments. One commentator in the *Financial Times* described it as the best strategy of its kind in the world. The main exception to this constructive response came from the parliamentary opposition (now the Australian Government), who sought to marginalize the strategy by accusing the document of 'spinning', for solely political purposes, existing policies that they opposed, such as carbon pricing and the national broadband network. However, the widespread endorsement of the strategy and engagement with its implementation meant that the opposition did not dwell for long on attacking the White Paper. Indeed, many of their individual policy commitments reflected the direction and goals it set, despite their inability to offer public support for it.

Lessons and Opportunities for Policymakers

Australia in the Asian Century succeeded in creating a positive framework for planning a nation's future, looking forward more than a decade and underpinned by a coherent explanation of change. It was a conscious attempt to design a pathway for a whole society into the future, and to create a platform from which different sectors and institutions could work together towards shared goals. In many respects, it is a conventional policy document, generated using traditional policy disciplines. But it also went beyond the status quo of Australian policymaking, both in content and in process. It prompted acknowledgement, among many different institutions, that they must acquire new capabilities in order to adapt more successfully for the future, and that in many cases these capabilities are best developed through open collaboration.

Interestingly, this discussion of capabilities included a recognition that 'design skills' are an growing part of Australia's capacity for economic value-adding, as Australian excellence in fields like architecture, infrastructure planning, security and crisis management, software and social media, regulatory and market design becomes more recognized and embedded in the wider region. In this case, 'design skills' are a proxy for a cluster of capabilities through which we can visualize, integrate and learn through a broader range of methods, in order to solve complex problems and improve the functioning of interconnected systems. This, of course, is at the heart of the policymaking challenge explored in this book.

Growing and applying these capabilities is a long term challenge. The Asian Century project made some progress in identifying them more clearly and in pursuing an approach to policymaking and governance which can use them more effectively. It is an approach in which the capabilities of governing institutions co-evolve with the open movements of market exchange, people and information across our interconnected planet. The disciplines of policymaking must increasingly influence interdependent systems without abandoning specific responsibilities for particular sets of outcomes. In doing so, policymakers will have to forge alliances with broader coalitions of actors, generating a wider range of organizational platforms and sources of knowledge, than they ever have before.

References

Australian Government (2013). *Australia in the Asian Century*, http://pandora.nla.gov.au/pan/133850/20130914-0122/asiancentury.dpmc.gov.au/index.html.

Barber, M., Donnelly, K. and Rizvi, S. (2012). *Oceans of Innovation: The Atlantic, the Pacific, Global Leadership and the Future of Education*. IPPR, London, http://www.ippr.org.uk.

Barrett, C. (2011). *Australia and the Great Recession*. Princeton, NJ: Woodrow Wilson School of Public Policy.

Demos (1995). *The Age of Asia: Learning from the Sunrise Societies*. London, http://www.demos.co.uk.

Dorling, D. (2013). *Generation Jobless, New Statesman*, http://www.newstatesman.com/2013/08/generation-jobless.

G20. http://www.g20.org/documents/.

Legrain, P. (2010). *Aftershock: Reshaping the World Economy After the Crisis*. London: Little Brown.

Parker and Parker. (2006). Collaborative Government, Demos Collection.

CHRISTIAN BASON AND ANDREA SCHNEIDER[1]

Public Design in Global Perspective: Empirical Trends

Design as an approach to shaping public policies and services appears to be emerging rapidly from multiple points across both industrialized and emerging economies. International institutions, national government organizations, local government, foundations, philanthropies, voluntary and community organizations as well as educational institutions at all levels are taking up design approaches in various forms. The organizational anchoring (public, private or third sector) varies, as does the terminology: Service design, strategic design, macro design, public design, design thinking, human centred design, social innovation, social entrepreneurship are among the labels commonly used (Bason 2013). This development implies that it is virtually impossible to provide a coherent overview of the state of play – and that the state at any given point in time is subject to change quickly.

This chapter nonetheless seeks to present a range of concrete examples of how design is practiced within public service organizations, and attempts to briefly synthesize a number of the emerging trends. As part of the Context section of this book, the purpose of the chapter is to provide an empirically based overview of the growth of design practice within or close to government.

Our approach has been to draw on multiple sources to identify design approaches applied in the context of public sector organizations. These include secondary sources such as available books, reports, case studies, websites and analyses, and primary sources such as selected in-person and telephone interviews to uncover particularly interesting organizations and cases. Our emphasis has mainly been to highlight cases where the term 'design' is explicitly used. Usually, the word implies the use of methods such as design (or ethnographic) research, graphics, visualization, models, prototypes, rapid iteration, ideation and concept development. Typically these methods would have been in the form of distinct projects, usually with the assistance of external design consultancies or internal design or innovation resources. Further, we have mainly focused on public sector (governmental) organizations. In some countries, such as the United States and Italy, much of the design of policies and services for societal outcomes is not necessarily, however, anchored in government. In areas such as support for employment, entrepreneurship, health, education and social services, efforts are often anchored within the voluntary and community sectors, and fully or partly funded by philanthropies.

---

1   With a special contribution by Eduardo Staszowski and Daniela Selloni, Parsons DESIS Lab at the New School University, New York.

The chapter is structured as follows: First, we provide examples of how design for public policies and services is being articulated nationally via strategies, programmes and initiatives. Second, we turn to local and regional government applications of design, and share some case examples of concrete design-led innovations. Third, we consider the use of design for digital and 'open' applications in government. The key examples across these domains are drawn from countries where there is a critical mass of design-inspired activities within the public sector and/or in the voluntary and community sector. We draw mainly, but not exclusively, on developments in the UK, France, Denmark and the United States, in order to give a sense of the developments across geography in advanced economies. Fourth, we provide a particular consideration and visualization of the rise of design labs, or Public Innovation Places. This contribution, and in particular the visualization of design labs globally, has been made by Eduardo Staszowski and Daniela Selloni of Parsons DESIS Lab. Finally, we identify and discuss some of the key emerging trends and questions that synthesize the empirical developments we have covered.

National Design Strategies for the Public Sector

A number of countries are increasingly integrating design for public policies and services as part of national strategies and initiatives. This integration signifies a shift in which public sector organizations are more fully recognized as users and procurers of design for more strategic purposes.

UNITED KINGDOM

In the UK, initiatives ranging from the RED scheme in the mid-2000s, the Public Services by Design programme and to the UK Design Commission have helped place design centrally in the minds of public servants and key public sector organizations nationally. Recently an official All-Parliamentary Design and Innovation Group of the UK Parliament published the Restarting Britain Series, investigating *Design Education and Growth* (2011), *Design and Public Services* (2013) and (in development), *Design and the Digital Revolution*. These reports provide public policy recommendations and a thoughtful review of the public design field in the UK. While not a design-led organization per se, the Behavioural Insights Team (BIT) at the Cabinet Office has paved the way for systematic use of behavioural economics and psychology in the design of public interventions in areas such as tax forms and employment services. Backed by rigorous use of randomized controlled trials, BIT has gained significant momentum as a model for applying knowledge about human behaviour to shaping policy outcomes. On the back of this experience, and probably with an eye to the wider international trends, the UK government chose in 2013 to strengthen more open policymaking by establishing a Policy Lab. The Lab is a small team taking its departure in design approaches; with the intent to anchor more explicitly design competencies at the heart of Whitehall

DENMARK

In Denmark, design for societal purposes has been on the policy agenda for some time, although it is only within the most recent five to seven years that it has begun to take off in a wider sense. Some of the key triggers of the developments have been a pilot scheme on service design run by the Danish Business Agency (DBA) which provided support for demonstration projects in welfare institutions such as kindergartens and employment services. Another instrument was the Programme for

User-driven Innovation, also sponsored by the DBA, which funded more than DKK 400 million (EUR 50 million) worth of design-inspired projects, with perhaps 20 to 30 per cent allowed for public organizations. Also the Danish government sponsors MindLab, a cross-governmental design unit which is sponsored by a number of ministries and a city government. Funding for design projects within public service organizations in Denmark has to date largely been public, either through the above-mentioned support programmes, via academic research support, or via participating organization's own funding sources. From garbage management in the municipality of Copenhagen to reducing tension between inmates and guards in the Prison and Probation Service, and to high-level policymaking across multiple departments within the state administration, design is applied more and more broadly in the Danish public sector. There is a growing service design industry, although no single design consultancy has yet singled out the public sector as its sole client; most are still working mainly for corporate clients, and many are still focusing on (digital or physical) product design. A commission established by the Danish government to produce a vision for Danish Design in 2020 suggested that design is used explicitly to help tackle some of society's 'grand challenges', in areas such as ageing, health and climate change (Danish Business Authority 2011).

UNITED STATES

Design is also capturing interest within federal and local government across the United States. While the US has not explored design explicitly as part of national policy, there is increasing momentum for using design, as technology and data driven approaches have demonstrated limitations. There is a growing sense that digital approaches may be effective for fixing roads, paying parking, finding schedules, getting tax services online, but probably not sufficient on their own for reducing poverty, immigration, climate change, gun violence, aging and so on. When President Obama issued the Open Government Directive (OGD) in 2009, requiring federal agencies to act on the three major principles of transparency, participation and collaboration, it was a notable and ambitious change agenda for the federal government. The central role of the White House Office of Science and Technology set the pace for a focus on data, accountability, technology and tackling challenges through innovative uses of data and related applications. Additionally all public websites were required to be more accessible and easy to understand by the public. In 2012 President Obama launched the Presidential Innovation Fellows to 'harness new ideas and technology to remake our government'. The OGD has so far produced more results with transparency and participation, less with collaboration within and between federal agencies, building capacity or redesigning public services. The Office of Personnel Management (OPM) and Consumer Financial Protection Bureau cases represent a new direction (see below). The corresponding open government data movement made public data available for others to use, creating a vibrant civic start-up marketplace. Government leaders in local cities invested heavily in digital solutions to improve operations and increase citizen participation. The digital culture and entrepreneurial nature of the open government movement has closely linked data, civic apps and the start-up culture to public innovation. While digital and data driven approaches have dominated both discussion and action, there are several significant cases of design practices in federal and local government.

The Lab @ OPM is a new part of the broader federal mandate to deliver on President Obama's promise of a more effective, innovative and efficient government. During the early stage of Lab development, OPM leadership set out to learn from iconic companies and institutions such as Google, Facebook, IDEO and the d.school at Stanford. Located in OPM's sub-basement, the space was designed and constructed to inspire intense collaboration and co-creation. It was built to support innovative thinking, through the selection of Human Centred Design (HCD), as its idea-generating and problem-solving method. The work of the Lab falls into four focus areas: creative co-working, building capacity, immersion projects and targeted design support. Examples of recent projects include: making the federal health benefits selection process more user friendly for federal employees, revamping a signature fellowship (Presidential Management Fellowship) as an end to end service experience, developing more creative messages to send to young women to fill the STEM pipeline within the federal government, supporting the development of an Innovation Center at the US Coast Guard and running usability tests of federal websites.

The United States thus presents a complex picture of public innovation and design at the national level. In recent years there has been a dramatic interest in the idea of public design, not necessarily an understanding of the meaning of design thinking in public systems and policy. To make it more complicated, the idea gets mixed in with civic technology processes, government efficiency models and expansive ideas about what constitutes public participation and engagement. In a risk adverse system and highly politicized context, design in policy and practice is a hard reach. Public innovation is often associated with data and technology, not new processes for designing public services, building more effective programs or increasing employee capacity. The federal case examples provided here are relatively new and nested in a complex government bureaucracy. Leaders step lightly, as they make their case to polarized policymakers, with different views of the role of government and greatly reduced federal resources.

CANADA

Design for policy is at early stages in the Canadian national context, but it is gaining momentum. At national level, there has been increasing activity in terms of exploring the potential of design for public policy and services, not least driven by efforts to shape the conversation by the federal government's foresight unit Horizons Canada as well as by MaRS Solutions Lab and the nation-wide network Social Innovation Generation (SiG) (Bellefonte 2012; MaRS 2012). At the time of writing, multiple federal departments were actively exploring the possibility of establishing innovation labs and –hubs for driving policy design. The notion of a 'policy designer', for instance has been articulated as illustrated in Figure 2.1.

AUSTRALIA

In Australia in 2011, the federal government adopted a comprehensive Innovation Action Plan for the public service, which includes several references to design. Most significantly the plan proposes the establishment of a Design Centre, to act as a hub and catalyst for innovation within and outside the Commonwealth government. However, design is by no means new to the Australian public service. As is also portrayed elsewhere in this volume, the Australian Taxation Office has worked systematically for more than a decade to embed design into its organizational fabric; with the help of consultancies such as ThinkPlace in Canberra and Second Road in Sydney, other public organizations are now beginning to follow suit. For instance, the (federal) Department of Human Services has established an internal co-design practice.

THE NETHERLANDS

In the Netherlands, design is still broadly viewed as quite foreign to government; the notion of design is still very much linked with the image of 'posters and toasters'.

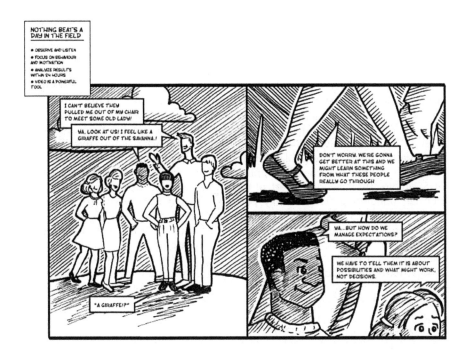

Figure 2.1   A day in the life of a policy designer
Source: Teresa Bellefontaine, David Cavett-Goodwin, Naomi Kühn, Jean-Philippe Veilleux, *A Day in the Life of a Policy Designer*. Policy Horizons Canada. Government of Canada, 2013.

Meanwhile, there has been a decade-long tradition of establishing physical innovation units, or 'Future Centres' within government departments. ranging from the Social Affairs ministry's innovation lab to the Tax Department's The Shipyard and 'LEF' of the Department of Public Works and Water Management. These units tend to apply a range of methods, some of which draw on aspects of design. Further, a major annual conference, held in Amsterdam, 'What Design Can Do' highlights how design in its many guises can contribute to shaping a better society.

FINLAND

In Finland, Helsinki Design Lab (HDL), was part of the national innovation fund Sitra, and worked from 2008 to 2013 to demonstrate how strategic design can help tackle complex societal challenges in fields such as sustainability, ageing and education. Through a series of ambitious design studios, HDL connected strategic designers with public servants and end users to build experience and share the value of design approaches for systematic problem-solving. Another related phenomenon in Finland is the merger of three major universities, including the school of art and design, into the new combined Aalto University. As part of its efforts to integrate the various professional disciplines around hands-on student learning activities, Aalto has established the Design Factory, a major facility that allows for design experiments, prototyping and incubation. The Design Factory hosts the annual Aalto Camp on Societal Innovation (ACSI), which gathers a large international group of experts to apply design methods to societal challenges.

In Italy, the explicit use of design within public sector organizations is currently not widespread, although there are signs of growing activity. For instance, design consultancies such as Experientia and Esterni carry out work for public organizations both at home and abroad (for instance, Experientia has worked with HDL on public challenges such as education, see above). Beyond government, in the not-for profit sector, an interesting example is the Fondazione Housing Sociale (FHS), an initiative designed along three axes: the promotion of ethical financing initiatives, particularly real estate funds dedicated to social housing, the testing of innovative, non-profit management models and a public-private partnership to develop these initiatives in a manner coordinated with and supplemental to existing public housing policies. At FHS, architectural design is part of a complex and varied process which, unlike a 'normal' building project, is only partially focused on the construction of the buildings themselves. The process extends to the management of the dwellings, the enhancement of community life and the services contributing to that enhancement. Design thinking is utilized throughout the life of these projects in how they develop the concepts and work with families, existing services and the various stakeholders. With long-term sustainability as a financial and community goal, these projects are designed with multiple stakeholders as end users. FHS is releasing a toolkit based on their work and discoveries.

GLOBAL ORGANIZATIONS AND SETTINGS

Finally, design seems to be making its way into a range of global organizations and settings. The European Union's Design Leadership Board launched a series of recommendations in 2012 which include specific proposals for fostering design-led innovation in the public sector. The European House of Design, an EU sponsored project, develops a design management toolbox for the public sector. Even more recently, the European Union, by way of a high-level expert group, has put forward a number of recommendations for strengthened public sector innovation which explicitly point to co-design as a key approach. In 2009 the United Nations employed design quite actively for the climate change campaign 'Nine Planets Wanted', including a major exhibition at the New York Headquarters. The UN also hosted a major seminar in 2010 in New York to explore the intersection of public policy, cultural studies and design and the potential to address the challenge of re-integrating ex-combatants in former war zones. (Building on this seminar and other experiences, think tank Policy Lab, based in Boston and Oslo, is venturing to apply design more broadly to UN projects.) UNICEF has for a number of years built a comprehensive platform for creating innovation labs as a tool for driving change processes. More recently, the UNDP and the World Bank have started looking to design as an approach to public sector reform through seminars in Europe and Asia. Finally, design for public and societal purposes is also promoted globally by organizations such as DESIS (DEsign for Social Innovation and Sustainability), and SIX, the Social Innovation eXchange.

Design for Regional and Local Government

Moving from the national to the regional and local level means that design practice becomes more widespread and understood with tangible, locally based outcomes.

UNITED KINGDOM

In the UK, the Creative Councils is a program between the innovation fund Nesta and the Local Government Association supporting local government innovators across England and Wales. The goal is to develop and implement radical innovations addressing a long-term, significant challenge in the participating local areas. Since launching in 2011, 17 Creative Councils have been formed to support innovative projects covering a wide range of ideas from how to support an aging population to finding new ways to create economic growth and support local youth. These projects focus on building local capacity in design and supporting the spread of innovation methods and projects across the country. With an idea similar to their Creative Councils, Nesta has become the implementation partner for the Bloomberg Philanthropies Mayor's Challenge in Europe, offering $12.16 million to city governments for bold and compelling ideas to address a major challenge. This new project replicates the Bloomberg Philanthropies Mayor's Challenge in the United States (http://mayorschallenge.bloomberg.org).

Another interesting case from the British context is how the London Borough Barking & Dagenham's Housing and Environment Services handled pressure from growing demand, the diverse nature of the local population and public sector budget cuts. The council wanted to understand how to use design to become more innovative, user-centric and to deliver services more efficiently. With the UK Design Council's help, they engaged the services of a design agency who trained staff to undertake ethnographic research and lead co-design workshops and service prototyping work. Through this intervention, initial savings were identified and reinvested into other service improvements, 70 ideas were generated for potential service improvements, residents felt more involved with getting their needs met and the staff have successfully adopted the new design methods and are now able to train their colleagues.

A final UK example shows how the Patchwork social services families project used a design approach to join up a disparate range of social workers involved with a single family, a common problem in government services around the world. Working with FutureGov, a creative agency that brings digital innovation to local government, the two councils developed the Patchwork App, which allows social workers, from multiple agencies to find out quickly and easily who else is working with their family. This app helped make complex systems communication easier for both the professionals and their clients (http://www.designcouncil.org.uk/our-work/Insight/Research/2013-restarting-britain-2/).

DENMARK

In Denmark, since 2007 Local Government Denmark's annual Innovation Awards, given to the most groundbreaking municipal innovation projects, have also seen a rise of design approaches, to the point where three of the winners were service design projects in food service ('meals on wheels', 2009) and services for adult mentally handicapped (2010, 2013), respectively. Camillagaarden in the city of Odense (the 2010 winner) is a workplace for adult mentally handicapped, many of whom have little or no spoken language, and who for many years were relatively passive 'users' of the institution's offerings of simple manual labour tasks. A few years ago, the institution had come to the point where it might lose its funding due to too few users. However, in a joint project with Local Government Denmark and the design firm 1508, the managers and staff at Camillagaarden were trained to apply design approaches such as cultural probes, photo diaries, prototypes, service analogies, testing and ideation methods to explore new ways of involving and engaging citizens. Within the duration of the project, the relationship between staff and the adult mentally handicapped users was transformed. The design methods allowed citizens to visually articulate their hopes, dreams and aspirations – and their concrete personal stories – about what a good experience at Camillagaarden was about, and how it could be made better. The staff built on these inputs to fundamentally redefine their professional role from experts to coaches and facilitators. 'We are still professionals, but in a very different way', is how they explain this transition. According to the managers, the citizens are now actively involved as the true innovators, coming up with new ideas every day, and driving the formation of various interest groups that pursue the activities they find the most fun and rewarding. User satisfaction and everyday engagement has skyrocketed and the number of users has gone up by nearly 300 per cent, to the point that the institution now has a waiting list.

FRANCE

In France, the organization La 27e Région, a non-profit foundation working to facilitate public sector innovation through design, is a prime exponent of design-led work at the local and regional level. For instance, in 2009 a multidisciplinary team composed of two service designers, a sociologist and an architect spent several weeks in a school in Revin, an economically devastated area in northern Ardennes (France). Created in the 1970s, this school was about to be totally rebuilt, with a project estimated at 40 million Euros mainly funded by the Regional Government of Champagne Ardenne. One of the projects consisted in organizing a balanced dialogue between the local community (pupils, teachers, parents) and the architect of the future building. In the course of one day, around 40 pupils and their teachers had the possibility to react, re-interrogate and criticize the new architectural project already selected, by drawing ideas and writing questions on large blueprints laid out on classroom tables. During the second day, the architect came to the school and presented the new buildings to the pupils, then visited an exhibition based on the blueprints re-written by pupils, teachers and the school staff. Both the architect and the regional government realized that they had to take the practices of people much more into account in the organization of interiors, such as classrooms and lobbies. Three months later, after changes to the architectural design, the result was a 1 million Euro savings in the cost of the building, which was reinvested in the quality of the interior design and furniture budget.

UNITED STATES

In the United States, a range of initiatives are bringing design to cities and local government. Public Policy Lab NYC is an independent 501(c)3 not-for-profit organization which, during the summer of 2013, formed a partnership with the New York City Department of Education's Innovation Zone (iZone) and the Office of Student Enrollment to explore improving the high-school admissions process. They recruited three fellows for design research, visual design and project strategy work over the course of several months. These fellows investigated and tested design-based innovation methods to help low-income and non-English-speaking families make more informed decisions when selecting a high school (http://publicpolicylab.org).

The Mayor's Offices of New Urban Mechanics in Boston, Massachusetts (2010), Philadelphia, Pennsylvania (2012) and Mexico City (2013) are good examples of embedding design-oriented approaches within City Hall policy environments. To speed the rate of municipal innovation, the mayors of Boston and Philadelphia established innovation incubators to build partnerships within and between city agencies and outside institutions and entrepreneurs. Each city focuses on three major issue areas: participatory urbanism, clicks and bricks, and education. Projects have included apps for smart phones, helping citizens report service problems, identifying potholes to improve roads and redesigning an entire city trash system. Code for America has been a civic technology partner is each of these cities (http://www.newurbanmechanics.org).

The San Francisco mayor's Office of Civic Innovation utilizes government as a platform for innovation. The office works closely with San Francisco residents, local creative and tech-minded communities and the technology companies located within the city. Their goal is to collectively use data and design solutions and apply them to long-standing civic challenges. They have three strategic focus areas: economic development, citizen engagement and government efficiency (San Francisco Office of Civic Innovation, innovatesf.com).

Finally, as also discussed later in this volume, the Parsons DESIS (Design for Social Innovation and Sustainability) Lab is a research laboratory housed at The New School in New York City. DESIS Lab works at the intersection of strategic and service design, management and social theory. It applies interdisciplinary expertise in problem setting and problem-solving to sustainable practices and social innovation. In 2011, DESIS Lab launched Public and Collaborative NYC, a program of activities to explore how public services in New York City can be improved by incorporating greater citizen collaboration in service and policy design. The lab created a learning space for civil servants to acquire critical and creative problem-solving skills through monthly lectures and project-based workshops. The lab has collaborated with New York City agencies such as the New York City Department of Housing Preservation & Development and the New York City Department of Education's Innovation Zone (iZone) to explore the potential for citizen-led service initiatives and to explore more collaborative, responsive and engaging educational experiences.

AUSTRALIA

Australia has also seen a growth in design practice regionally and locally. In the intersection between public, private and the NGO community, organizations such as Adelaide-based The Australian Centre for Social Innovation (TACSI) and Perth-based Social Innovation in Western Australia (SiiWA) are also looking to design as a key driver for tackling societal challenges. For instance, TACSI has successfully used design approaches to for 'radically redesign', South Australia's approach to hard-to-reach 'chaotic' families. By creating a family-driven mentor programme to connect 'sharing' families who have been through hard times but come out the other side and that have resources to offer, with 'seeking' families that are in a tough situation and need support, the Family by Family project has harvested remarkable results that had so far evaded the Adelaide public sector families administration: According to one assessment, for what it typically costs annually to place one child in foster care, the family by family approach could help 200 families thrive again.

CANADA

Finally it should be mentioned that Canada has seen the rapid spread of social innovation initiatives across the main provinces, in no small part driven by the cross-organizational initiative Social Innovation Generation (SIG). One outcome of this process has been the establishment, at Toronto-based MaRS, one of the SIG Partners, of the MaRS Solutions Lab. This innovation lab works closely with the Ontario government to address societal challenges especially at local and regional levels through a range of design approaches.

Design for Digital Public Services and Open Government

A growing range of examples are demonstrating how design can facilitate digital solutions for better public policy results as well as more transparent and open government.

UNITED KINGDOM

In the UK, Government Digital Services is a highly recognized example of a design-led approach to the development of a public service. Gov.uk, the new single platform government website, won the Design of the Year Award with a promise to revolutionize the government's digital presence. Thinking about building digital services, not websites, allowed the diverse design team to face a twofold challenge: to move all central government websites onto a single platform, thereby creating a unified look and feel, and a single point of entry for citizens wanting to interact with, or find things out from, central government departments; and to drastically simplify the experience of using the sites. Gov.uk has dramatically reduced costs and revolutionized how digital services are made available to the public.

DENMARK

Denmark is also leveraging design for digital solutions. In 2010, the Danish tax ministry collaborated with the innovation unit MindLab (see above) to better understand why young tax payers have great difficulty using online self-assessment systems. The current digital solutions were increasing error and bureaucracy, leading to frustration for the citizens and increasing public expenses. By conducting ethnographic research among a variety of young tax payers, MindLab's staff and their tax colleagues found that the young people were surprised that digital solutions are not better targeted towards them individually, and they got stuck online when the logic and language got too complex, and when appropriate actions required a large vocabulary of tax-related jargon that they rarely possessed. Building on such insight, the project team orchestrated a series of workshops to ideate solutions, develop concepts, create web mock ups and prototype new communication tools that could help make the digital service experience more effective. Today the Danish Ministry of Taxation is, amongst other things, redesigning its website (http://www.skat.dk), and using social media such as Twitter for citizen communication.

UNITED STATES

In the United States, digital applications of design have perhaps been the strongest trend. The Consumer Financial Protection Bureau (CFPB) has been one of the leading organizations applying design strategically in a policy environment. On July 17, 2009, President Obama established the Consumer Financial Protection Bureau (CFPB). The CFPB leadership had the task of creating a new bureau from scratch, with a public launch in July 2011. Agency leadership adopted an internet start-up model, which was highly data driven and consumer focused. With a mandate from President Obama, strong leadership by Elizabeth Warren and dual timelines, the CFPB turned to IDEO, a design company in Silicon Valley for help. IDEO's human-centred design approach matched up with the agency's need to deliver a logomark, brand guidelines, a consumer engagement strategy and a concrete action exemplified by the 'Paying for College' set of tools and information for students and parents. They set out to rebrand public service and create the capacity for a human-centred design approach in a federal bureau. The agency website is one clear demonstration of the results of this challenging endeavour.

Code for America (CFA) brands itself as a new kind of public service, to code for a better government in cities across the country. CFA Fellows are sent to selected cities to build apps, increase civic engagement and address a challenging local issue. The CFA Incubator supports the sustainability of these new applications into scalable business enterprises and retains talented civic technologists. The CFA model is expanding to international sites with adoption in Mexico City, Germany and Jamaica.

NYC Digital focuses on initiatives in five core areas: access to technology, education, open government, engagement and industry. It represents a whole spectrum of impressive activity in policy and practice. The NYC Digital Roadmap outlines the results of a myriad of activity from the iZone for Education to NYC BigApps Contest. Developed with a design firm, the newly designed NYC.gov website provides citizens with access to city information in one place.

The GovLab@NYU Wagner focuses on how to improve people's lives by changing how we govern, seeking new ways to solve public problems using advances in technology and science. GovLab operates as a network of networks and encompasses two major initiatives: GovLab Research and GovLab Academy. The director of the GovLab is formerly a deputy director of the White House Office of Science and Technology.

FRANCE

In France, the organization La 27e Région asked the question: Why do many politicians, their staffers and the civil servants they work with, not feel comfortable with the tools provided by their organization: intranets, laptop computers and around two to three mobile phones and communication devices? In late 2009, three politicians from the Regional Government of North-Pas de Calais accepted to take part in an experiment to explore 'from within' the way local politicians worked alone and with their staff. A team of service designers, graphic designers, one anthropologist and one political science researcher spent three months building a better understanding of the political 'black box', attending meetings, tracking politicians' journeys, visualizing social networks, co-producing insights and visions with the political and administrative community. One of the main insights was that confidence was a central value, and that digital tools should not only improve communication, but also improve the level and quality of confidence between politicians, staffers and civil servants. The team prototyped several projects which aim at building more confidence: a new kind of 'how to' meeting between staffers, dedicated to the exchange of tips and practical solutions (e.g. how to reach journalists? how to run agendas?), a toolkit for politicians freshly elected and a proposal for a brand new project-driven information architecture. The team also explored the possibility for the regional government to create its own 'innovation lab' that would promote design thinking and social innovation within the organization.

The Emergence of Design Labs: Public Sector Innovation Places

There is a growing perception that the state's ability to provide various forms of public service can be enhanced through public-private partnerships, the use of new technologies as well as various strategies for increased public participation. Such new approaches to provide better services for individuals and communities require breaking the established routines and traditional structures of government, and rethinking the opposition between government bureaucracies and community actors. As shown in this chapter, such new kinds of collaboration are emerging. These partnerships are characterized by horizontal practices such as co-governance, co-design or co-production where citizens, experts and governments work closely together to imagine, shape and provide better public services. Across the world efforts to promote radical innovations in the public sector are increasingly followed by the creation of different types of 'authorizing environments' that foster these experiments.

In this context, it seems that innovation units, design labs or public innovation places are on the rise. Some are positioned *within* government, while some work *with* government. A key trend is the emergence of design or innovation labs as new government resources (Bason 2010). From DesignGov in Canberra, to The Lab in Singapore's prime minister's division to the UK's Behavioural Insights Team and Policy Lab, Denmark's MindLab to the United States Lab @ OPM and the global DESIS Lab network, dedicated design resources and physical spaces for design activity play a growing role in a number of countries. Some are created with a significant focus on physical ('studio') space, while others rely mainly on their teams' skills and competencies. One might call them *Public Innovation Places*. By this we mean to suggest experimental sites, agencies or labs created to tackle innovative solutions to public/social problems, and dedicated to the creation of networks and partnerships – launching projects, events and platforms. Public Innovation Places can bring together a variety of actors, both public and private, with a diverse array of skill sets and expertise around a set of issues.

Within Public Innovation Places there are professionals from different backgrounds (design, economics, policy and social knowledge) who can operate in a more horizontal, non-hierarchical ways and provide a degree of freedom from many of the innovative constraints of agency-specific mandates, policy issues and procedural restrictions. While free to explore and produce new knowledge and practicable forms in a semi-autonomous fashion, these spaces can be supported by the larger institutional bodies whose services, interests and practices stand to gain from such collaborative work. How the results of collaboration are taken up might ultimately be up to the specific agency, organization or community which houses the space. A map has been created by Daniela Selloni[2] and Eduardo Staszowski[3] (with the expert advice of Christian Bason[4]) to illustrate the emergence of Government Innovation Labs across the world. Given the growing interest[5] and rapid expansion of Government Innovation Labs, this map was created to examine the existing structures and capabilities of labs by understanding the different organizational models, main activities and the degrees of government participation. See Figure 2.2 at right.

2 Service designer and visiting PhD Student, Politecnico di Milano.
3 Director, Parsons DESIS Lab.
4 Chief Executive of the Danish Design Centre.
5 The National Endowment for Science, Technology and the Arts (Nesta) in the UK is doing a research study in collaboration with Bloomberg Philanthropies to uncover the work done by innovation teams and units ('i-teams') happening in local and national governments around the world. In Canada, Dr. Frances Westley, the director of the Waterloo Institute for Social Innovation and Resilience (WISIR) at the University of Waterloo, is also leading a research on innovation labs. The Organisation for Economic Co-operation and Development (OECD) created in 2012 a task force (the Observatory of Public Sector Innovation) to collect innovative practices from across the public sector.

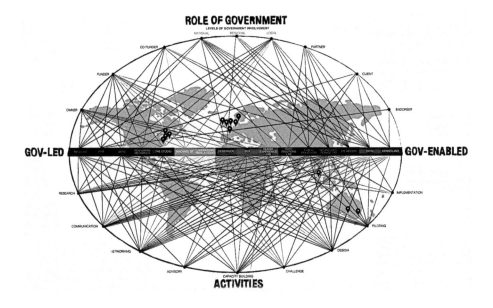

ROLE OF GOVERNMENT

LEVELS OF GOVERNMENT INVOLVEMENT

NATIONAL   REGIONAL   LOCAL

CO-FUNDER   PARTNER

FUNDER   CLIENT

OWNER   ENDORSER

GOV-LED   GOV-ENABLED

RESEARCH   IMPLEMENTATION

COMMUNICATION   PILOTING

NETWORKING   DESIGN

ADVISORY   CAPACITY BUILDING   CHALLENGE

ACTIVITIES

Figure 2.2   Government innovation lab constellation

Definitions and Approach

A Government Innovation Lab is a specific type of Public Innovation Place characterized by a direct connection with the public sector and created to tackle complex public/social problems that more traditional governmental structures fail to resolve, in particular, using design to experiment and propose innovative public services and policies and at the same time reform and change the way government operates.

Initially 17 labs were chosen to be represented in the map and selected on the basis of their relevance in the field (typology of partners, projects and so forth) and differences in organizational models. Desk research was carried out first to identify and then to categorize the different roles played by governments and the core activities/services provided by the labs. A survey with a prepared list of choices was sent to the labs in order to verify the classification model and the position occupied by the labs. Finally a map was designed to provide a visual synthesis of the data collected (see box on following page).

Labs can be differentiated by how they operate on national, regional or local levels. Most labs in the map appear to operate on local and/or national levels. Labs operating at the local or municipal level suggest an aspiration to work in proximity with citizens to improve public service delivery on a hyper-local fashion and could also imply that cities are emerging as gateways of government innovation. Labs operating on a national level suggest a trend in creating a new culture of innovation within large governmental bureaucracies. Labs operating on a regional or at multiple levels seem to be less common. This distinction proved to be useful for understanding the degree of *influence* and *scale* in which labs can operate.

HOW TO READ THE MAP

The map is divided into two main areas:

A. The upper part portrays the different roles government can play in the life of a lab, from weaker to stronger involvement. The roles identified in the study were organized in the map according to the following categories (from left to right):

- Government as **owner**: the lab appears in the government organizational chart, permanent (in the charter) or temporary;
- Government as **funder**: the lab receives public funds;
- Government as **co-funder**: the lab receives both public and private funds;
- Government as **partner**: the lab and government are associated in some action or project;
- Government as **client**: government pays and/or hires the lab for professional services;
- Government as **endorser**: government gives the lab approval or support by public statement.

Labs on the left side of the map are provided with stronger government support and participation. We call them 'gov-led' labs. Labs on the right side of the map still maintain a connection with government but with less support and a higher degree of independence. We call them 'gov-enabled' labs. Gov-led labs with stronger connections with government are often owned and funded by governments. Gov-enabled labs with weaker connections with government may engage governments purely as clients or endorsers of their activities. This categorization has proved to be useful for understanding the spectrum of possibilities in terms of *support* and *independence* ...

B. The lower part of the map portrays key activities performed by the labs, which can serve an array of functions, from performing research and writing reports to the design and implementation of real-world applications. The activities identified in the study were organized in the map according to the following categories (from left to right):

- **Research**: the lab develops studies, analyses and reports;
- **Communication**: the lab produces events and publications;
- **Networking**: the lab creates connections and links among different actors;
- **Advisory**: the lab gives expert advise to governmental agencies, citizens and community-based organizations;
- **Capacity building**: the lab develops skills and competences, improves capacities within agencies, individual citizens and community-based organizations;

- **Challenge**: the lab launches competitions and challenges to crowdsource ideas and projects;
- **Design**: the lab uses design to frame problems and to develop solutions, programs and services;
- **Piloting**: the lab develops tests and prototypes before wide implementation;
- **Implementation**: the lab is responsible for implementing and evaluation of new programs and services.

Activities such as communication and networking seem to be the most diffused, followed by capacity building and the launch of challenges. Few labs declared the direct participation in programs and services implementation after a piloting phase. These initial findings suggest that labs privilege activities that identify opportunities for change rather than having the mandate to interfere directly on them. When residing inside government their mandates appear to be limited to specific topics determined by their owners (ministries, specific agencies or departments) and when outside they are often hired as consultants for very specific jobs or depend on external grants to engage government in more experimental work.

The Role of Design in Labs

Most labs acknowledge and make use of design in fostering innovation. In their lexicon it is possible to find expressions such as design thinking, design management, user-centred design and so forth. Service design appears to be a crucial discipline for labs whose mandates are to improve the quality and accessibility of public services. Co-design and other participatory design methods appear as valuable tools for fostering citizen engagement and supporting shared models for decision-making.

Needless to say, this brief study of innovation labs in government is exploratory in nature and does not pretend to be comprehensive, but provides a starting point for understanding the phenomenon. As far as the geographical scope of the research is concerned (and given the volatility and speed of change in this field), it will be necessary to continue to monitor the appearance of new labs in other parts of the world and update the map.[6]

Key Challenges

This chapter has illustrated a tremendous variety in how design approaches are currently applied in public sector organizations. What are the patterns, and what are the challenges if public sector design is to contribute more effectively as a driver of innovation? Although the examples and analysis here are only partial, four themes seem to emerge.

---

6   The authors tried to reach out to all lab representatives portrayed in the map and wish to thank those who answered the survey. The data presented does not necessarily reflect the official positions of the labs and all errors and omissions are the authors' own.

Rapid Global Spread, but Mainly in Industrialized Countries?

First, public sector design seems to be spreading rapidly, at least among industrialized countries. It is in many respects a global phenomenon, and there are increasingly strong affiliations between organizations and communities not just across Europe, but also across continents. For instance, there is a potentially strong axis of public design between the Commonwealth countries, particularly the UK, Canada, Australia and possibly New Zealand, with a significant and mutual transfer of ideas and approaches. Additionally, the Nordic region, probably with Denmark and Finland as the current leaders, is rapidly embracing design within public organizations. One question arising from this pattern is how to link these trends to other regions, such as Latin America, Asia and Africa. Could they not benefit from being integrated with the growing community of public sector design? Organizations like DESIS and SIX seem well positioned to take up this challenge from the outside, while institutions such as the World Bank and the UN could build capacity on the inside of the public sector.

A Diversity of Design Methods – But Which Work Best?

Second, there is a very heterogeneous picture of the types of challenges that design approaches seek to address in a public sector setting: from high-level (macro) 'policy design' to the more tangible 'service design' of human-system interactions, and to 'participation design' to help drive citizen and community engagement. Part of the national trends in applying design may have to do with national tradition. In the United States, for instance, public sector innovation has largely been equated with technology; so when design is applied, it is in part to web-enabled 'crowdsourcing' solutions. Or design is used for enhancing public participation and open government, other key themes in American politics. Risk adversity counteracts the most basic process principles of design. Open versus closed systems is one way to think about the problem. Design thrives best in open ended systems where assumptions can be continually challenged on the way to finding solutions that work.

Public sector change is complex, time consuming and can easily be tossed aside with a change in political leadership and a lack of follow-through and even skill. The ability to startintroduce, let alone embed, design into public organizations is closely tied to everyday realities, including the political situation, public expectations, the economic climate and a complex set of values, leadership challenges, the will to make very difficult change and, not least, the human factor in all its dimensions. Have the challenges we are now facing finally grown large enough that we have to do something differently?

On the face of it, the most convincing current examples of the potential of design for public sector innovation seem to be in the service design category, where the ability of designers to visualize service interactions, engage end-users and redesign service processes and systems comes to the forefront. When the problems to address become more abstract, complex and cross-cutting, the more design approaches are challenged by the traditional governmental power-plays. This is where the strategic role of design is tested.

Concept Design or Value Creation?

A design is a plan for action. In that sense, it is perhaps not surprising that even well-designed plans are not always carried out effectively to create sustainable value. Thus, and third, some of the examples found in this global scan raise the question if design has sufficient impact. To what extent are new concepts actually implemented to create enhanced productivity, service experience, better outcomes or improved participation? The evidence, beyond anecdotes, is not always convincing; good metrics, especially concerning outcomes, are often absent. Perhaps part of the challenge is that the current trend in most countries is that design skills and methods are pulled in via outside consulting. The question that is raised by some of the identified cases is whether this leads to a lot of focus on concept design and early ideation processes, but not so much on driving actual, gritty organizational change and implementation.

Design may be viewed as an important driver of innovation, but it does not automatically lead to innovation; the 'innovation' label should be reserved for designs that ultimately generate value. The larger question therefore becomes how to get commitment from managers and staff to truly engage in a change process? One might point to co-design and co-creation approaches as the way forward; approaches which rely heavily on active engagement with people inside and outside the organization to ensure ownership and implementation focus all the way through the process. Nonetheless, while the process of ideating, developing concepts and orchestrating prototyping may be the domain of designers, long-term organizational change is not. Other people and other professions need to step in.

What Future for Innovation Labs and Design Places?
Finally, whether the existence of physical 'creativity' spaces is in itself any guarantee of wider organizational impact is probably questionable. However, it may be a significant development that design skills and resources are now being embedded consciously inside (or close to) the organizational fabric of public administrations.

The broader legitimacy of design for public policy and services could be enhanced through this top management backing; the transaction costs of using design methods are lowered dramatically when design becomes an easily accessible 'corporate' function. If such labs, or resources, can be utilized by existing leaders and innovation champions who understand the system that needs to be changed and are familiar with the politics of it, they might be powerful tools for change. Whether labs should be more focused on immediate problem-solving, or in the creation of new protocols and contracts that creates the conditions for systemic innovation to happen, remains an open question. The advantage of the current situation is that a range of different experiments are taking place around the world at the same time. Some will work well and some will not. The challenge could be to link them up sufficiently to take advantage of the best and move them forward together.

Finally, design for policy has to mean more than public policy; it needs to partner with internal organizational policies for those tasked with making sustainable change. Experience suggests, if it doesn't matter enough to be significant in day to day operations, outside of a brave few, it will never be taken on by champions and leaders. How do design-led public policies in countries such as Finland, the UK, Denmark, Singapore or Australia translate to practice, over time? How can they partner with the necessary resources, time, talent, people and money to integrate design into normal operations so that it becomes second nature, the new way of working?

Given that these common challenges and questions are now being raised globally, there is an opportunity to translate research into applied practice and anticipate challenges as different initiatives learn from each other.

Acknowledgements

This chapter has benefited especially from new insight into developments in design in the US context. Former OPM Director and current Ambassador, John Berry, Special Assistant to Director Berry, Matthew Collier, Deputy Associate Director, Sydney Smith-Heimbrock and Lab @ OPM Director, Abby Wilson were very helpful in sharing the development of the Lab from the early idea to its current implementation. Chelsea Mauldin, Executive Director of the Public Policy Lab NYC, continually demonstrated how to link design thinking to practical public policy; Nigel Jacobs, Director, Office of New Urban Mechanics, Boston shared his insight and experience in developing extensive community partnerships for city-wide innovation; Jay Nath, Chief Innovation Officer, InnovateSF, showed how civic technology works within city government and Los Gatos Police Chief, Scott Seaman lent deep insight into the importance of both internal and external policy to supporting organizational change over time. We also wish to thank Ezio Manzini for directing our attention to developments in Italy, and finally we are indebted to Eduardo Staszowski and Daniela Selloni for generously sharing their research, visualization and analysis of public innovation places.

References

Bason, Christian (2010). *Leading Public Sector Innovation: Co-creating for a Better Society*, Bristol: Policy Press.

Bason, Christian (2013). Design-led Innovation in Government. *Stanford Social Innovation Review*.

Bellefonte, Theresa (2012). Innovation Labs: Bridging Think Tanks and Do Tanks. Ottawa: Horizons Canada.

Bloomberg Mayors Challenge Europe, http://mayorschallenge.bloomberg.org.

Boyer, Bryan, Cook, Justin W. and Steinberg, Marco (2013). *Legible Practices: Six stories about the craft of stewardship*, Helsinki: Helsinki Design Lab.

Code for America, http://www.codeforamerica.org.

Danish Business Authority (2011). The Vision of the Danish Design 2020 Committee, http://erhvervsstyrelsen.dk/visiondanishdesignpubl/0/7.

GOV.UK, http://digital.cabinetoffice.gov.uk.

Helsinki Design Lab (2011). In studio: Recipes for systemic change, helsinkidesignlab.org/instudio.

MaRS (2012). Labs: Designing the Future, http://www.marsdd.com/mars-library/labs-designing-the-future/.

Nesta: Creative Councils, http://www.nesta.org.uk.

NYC Digital, http://www.nyc.gov.

Office of New Urban Mechanics, http://www.newurbanmechanics.org.

Presidential Management Fellowship, Office of Personnel Management, http://www.pmf.gov.

Public Policy Lab NYC, http://publicpolicylab.org.

San Francisco Office of Civic Innovation, http://www.innovatesf.com/.

The GovLab @ NYU, http://thegovlab.org.

The Lab @ OPM, Office of Personnel Management, Interview 2013.

The Open Government Directive/Initiative, http://www.WhiteHouse.gov 2009.

The Presidential Innovation Fellows, http://www.WhiteHouse.gov 2012–2013.

United Kingdom Design Commission (2013). Restarting Britain 2: Design and Public Services, http://www.policyconnect.org.uk.

JESPER CHRISTIANSEN AND LAURA BUNT

Innovating Public Policy: Allowing for Social Complexity and Uncertainty in the Design of Public Outcomes

Whatever has been planned, there are always unwanted consequences for a reason that has nothing to do with the quality of the research or with the precision of the plan, but with the very nature of action. It has never been the case that you first know and then act. You first act tentatively and then begin to know a bit more before attempting again (Latour 2007: 4).

Policy is a contested concept. In a traditional instrumentalist view, it often resembles what has been phrased as 'the authoritative distribution of resources with deliberate consequences for a society' (Easton 1981). In this understanding, policy is a practical concept applied in order to create predictable change and is characterized by an optimistic belief in social reality as programmable. Policy in its instrumental form aspires to show direct causalities between the projected plan, decisions made, actions carried out and particular processes, outputs and results. Here, the basic foundation for policy is the production of authoritative knowledge illustrating tangible paths or routes to implementation. It thus thrives on the 'high-modern' belief that it is within our reach to make the 'right' plan to govern the population effectively and correctly (Scott 1998). Consequently, an instrumentalist understanding of policy is applied by most policymakers and civil servants, which makes them explain failure in implementing the policy either as a policy in need of improvement or as people's inability to either understand or accept the rational intentions of the policy. This is also why so many evaluations of policy programs primarily often only prove or devaluate the theory or hypothesis behind them instead of questioning the underlying assumptions upon which the policy is based (Mosse 2007).

Yet many of the most pressing challenges faced by today's governments are those that confound traditional interpretations of policy as a rational problem-solving system of problem definition, administration and resolution. Problems of a global nature like environmental preservation, economic growth, demographic changes, democratic representation, education, homeland security or crime prevention are characterized by their complexity, and necessarily cut across different policy domains, professional sectors, organizations and political and administrative jurisdictions (Kettl 2002). At the same time, public service systems are struggling to manage responses to problems that are often bound up in the messy realities of people's daily lives and experiences. In areas such as healthcare, preventing long-term unemployment, helping older people to remain independent, reducing offending behaviour or family support programs, relational practices based on empathy and human-centred design are struggling in management and procedural systems that focus more on the agenda of the system than the citizens.

In designing policies and practices to respond to such complexity, public decision-making involves so much more than dealing with technicalities. These are issues for which it is difficult to articulate, or even identify, causal relationships (or mechanisms), and causes are multi-dimensional and interconnected, requiring more integrated intervention across different service silos, and therefore are unfit for compartmentalized systems. Social reality is constantly changing, creating a continuous movement of overwhelming complexity and multiple simultaneous rationalities to deal with (Vohnsen 2011). Such issues are consistently evolving and lack clear 'end' points, thus calling for more open-ended interventions. Therefore public interventions, no matter how well-planned and thought through, are likely to create unintended outcomes and unpredictable effects. In other words, while 'policies reflect the rationality and assumptions prevalent at the time of their creation, a key quality of policies is that once created they often migrate into new contexts and settings, and acquire a life of their own that has consequences that go beyond the original intentions' (Shore, Wright and Però 2011). So while much contemporary development work in the public sector still builds on a rigid planning paradigm where policies and programs are seen as something to drawn up separately from processes of implementation, the formidable character of public problems and the continuously changing complexity of social reality call for a subversion of instrumental logics of policy.

This complexity is where the concept of design becomes relevant. Design-led approaches to policymaking take a dynamic and integrated relationship between policy and practice as a premise in planning and development processes. Unlike understanding public policymaking as the rational development of stable models, design is predisposed to more iterative creation and stewardship, closing the gap between development of the model and its implementation. Rather than formulating a plan that sits distinct from practical application, it is in the testing and iteration that the plan truly comes to life. Policy, in this sense, can no longer be seen in its own right, but only makes sense when seen in relation to context, practical outlook and consequences and will inherently build questions of implementation and systemic implication into the processes of planning and development.

Design as a discipline is also comfortable with complexity and uncertainty, and is therefore commonly used as an innovation method – as a way of anticipating the future in a (still) unimaginable and intangible state which makes concrete processes, knowledge, means and results something that constantly have to be reinvented and validated. Though sometimes over-simplified, a core strength of a design approach is that it starts from understanding the 'architecture of the problem' to open a new space of possibility in touch with the practical realities of the people presumably influenced by or even involved in implementing policy; both focusing on the concrete causes and consequences involved as well as the interconnected systems and networks involved in dealing with it (Boyer, Cook and Steinberg 2011). The consistent emphasis on understanding and using the architecture of the problem as a driver in asking new questions and reframing challenges can introduce innovation into thought or action processes by creating a tension with common interpretation and point to different trajectories for addressing the problem; it is a way of adapting to changing circumstances and conditions rather than relying on static understandings of social phenomena.

In addition, processes of design are iterative in formation and implementation. This means that design is accustomed to being open ended, uncertain or in 'beta', using a set of bounded, disciplined techniques to test, learn and revise throughout the creative process. Prototyping, sketching, blueprints are the building blocks of design processes, using these 'objects' to reflect on and develop an approach. And the association with design as a creative practice is useful in this context as it provides the legitimacy for experimentation and imperfection that complex problems demand.

This chapter will focus on the challenges involved in introducing design into public policy and explore some broad principles for what should underpin a new culture of decision-making in public governance: a focus on outcomes, not on solutions; an enabling system for co-production; seeing experimentation as the grounds for conviction; recognizing a new type of authority and identifying and valuing useful evidence. These principles are not answers to the current challenges in themselves, but are meant to open up new avenues for exploring how public managers and policymakers can improve their ability to manage public planning and development processes in contexts of complexity and uncertainty. Designing for policy involves a role that has to be understood, explored and experimented with in creating and maintaining new public governance practices. Currently, these new processes of governance based on design approaches 'do not replace the old but interact with them, often uncomfortably' (Newman et al. 2004: 217). Viewing and applying design as policy introduces a different way of knowing (or not knowing), exploring and planning into public governance which create tensions with the existing approaches to public policy that value pre-established, instructive guidelines for development and implementation. In other words, even though public policymakers and practitioners are experiencing the limitations of existing administrative and governance approaches, what is left feels intangible and disempowering within current frameworks of administration and governance.

Principles for Enabling a New Culture of Decision-Making

Focus on Outcomes, Not Solutions

Ex: The Fredericia Model

In the municipality of Fredericia in Denmark, a new perspective on a problem brought about significantly better outcomes for elderly citizens at a lower cost. This shift was moving from silo-based service delivery based on perceptions of the needs of citizens to a more human centred approach, facilitating various collaborative efforts based on the desires of elderly citizens for their own future as well as building on their current physical and mental capability. Concretely, the initiative was about support socks – an issue that is not only costly, since it requires carers to come to the homes of elderly citizens to both put on socks in the morning and take them off at night, but it is also a service that creates a dependency and unwanted service relationship because the elderly citizen has to adapt her life to the schedule of the busy home carer. If the home carer comes at 7:15 in the morning, then that is the time when the elderly citizen has to get up and get dressed.

In the new service idea initiated by Fredericia, citizens that apply for help are offered the opportunity to participate in an intensive rehabilitation or training program in which the citizen is trained to take care of themselves in a six- to eight-week period.

This includes investing in what has been called 'service overload' sessions where social workers, physiotherapists, nurses, doctors and other relevant public staff engage in collaborative sessions with the citizen to understand his or her desires and interests in relation to their physical ability. From this, they then plan a rehabilitation process that will get revised and updated every week to make sure that the right combination of professional expertise is involved to improve the physical health and individual service experience of the citizen.

It is not only at the frontline where the outcome-focus has been established. Before this initiative was able to take shape, Fredericia reorganized their municipal practice on both a political and governance level – creating innovation and investment boardacross political boundaries as well as sectors and professional boundaries. Early results from this initiative include significant monthly budget savings, a better service experience for citizens as well as a better frontline staff experience – now they are actually contributing to improving the lives of citizens rather than just delivering a service to maintain the status quo.

In Fredericia, they had to address the challenge by focusing on outcomes. Here, you are not solving a well-defined problem; you are continuously addressing it by maintaining practices that are characterized by an empathic relationship to the real situation of the citizen. This not only poses a new logic in their way of working, budgeting and decision-making, but it also becomes a new way of thinking about scaling and implementing this type of approach elsewhere. The latter has become extremely relevant, since the 'Fredericia model', as it is now called, is currently the subject of national investment to scale the approach to municipalities across Denmark.

In traditional public governance, decisions tend to be related to the development of a specific policy, regulation, law or guide for action. Sometimes the goal can be the decision itself being made through political mandate or professional expertise. This rather static way of dealing with problems conceals a not so hidden premise which points to the solution as an 'endpoint' of development, improvement or innovation through the right application of effort, knowledge and strategy. Public solutions are often understood to be problems strictly defined by public institutions. Thus, efforts to 'solve' them are based on projects and programs developed according to criteria that are applicable with current systems and procedures. In this way, 'silver bullet' solutions become possible because social reality gets squeezed into projects where an intended plan in its theoretical shape can be put into effect through concentrated efforts within a stable system.

But as we have argued above, social reality does not pause for implementation just as public problems are not solvable in fixed terms. Whether they exist in order to secure civil rights, a well-functioning job market or a reliable tax regulation, public services operate within a wider system of organizations, influences and interventions that in various ways affect these problems. In this sense, the goal is not some kind of redemption in relation to the public problem, but to search out potential ways to address the public problem productively. There is a need to make the best possible use of public resources to create better outcomes for the population rather than merely ensure 'service delivery'.

In addressing issues that are complex or where causation is unknown, identifying and having an impact on outcomes is part of a continuous practice of addressing and working with the problem with those for whom the outcome is intended. In this sense, many public services are a matter of continuous facilitation rather than implementing 'solutions': their purpose, content, limits and outcomes have to be explored through creative and systematic iteration and adaptation. These practices develop over time and are reliant on numerous people, systems, organizations, institutions and stakeholders. The challenge in a public sector context is that these practices are never perfectly established as a solution to a problem, but need to 'live' continuously and dynamically within a community of people in order to create value.

If one accepts this premise, it offers new criteria for success and new perceptions of what the effects of public innovation can or should be. In recognizing that finished solutions to stable problems do not exist in public sector contexts and that 'best practices' are not scalable in a fixed way, the hard question thus becomes what *can* we transfer and scale? Diffusion and scaling are to a lesser degree about implementing 'best practice' and more about building the capacity to systematically facilitate local learning and experimentation processes to create intended outcomes. There is a need for investing, not in spreading solutions or 'best practice', but in 'localizing' useful ideas in various organizational contexts and authorizing environments.

In other words, we should focus on scaling certain approaches, principles or methods – the processes of understanding and developing service systems. This also has implications for measuring the impact of public intervention. Rather than assessing the efficacy of an approach as a 'fix all' solution, the primary goal of measurement and evaluation is to learn – to shape and adapt practice over time. Here, the challenge becomes how to institutionalize the adaptive capacity in public governance and ask how this approach affects performance measurement, evaluation and audit functions in government.

CREATE SYSTEMS THAT ENABLE CO-PRODUCTION

Ex: People Powered Health

In part due to the success of the National Health Service (NHS), the UK's population is growing and aging; we are living longer. The majority of NHS resources are now absorbed by managing chronic conditions we are able to live with long term, rather than responding to acute demand. Respiratory conditions, heart disease, poor mental health and diabetes are the sorts of long-term conditions that now account for half of all GP appointments, two-thirds of all outpatient appointments and 70 per cent of all inpatient bed days (Department of Health 2012). These conditions are often affected by social conditions – our behaviours, lifestyles and circumstances – and can be helped by effective self-management and the positive support of friends, peers, community and other social interactions.

Working with Innovation Unit, Nesta wanted to explore how the health system could be better designed to provide more social, co-produced support for people living with long-term conditions, finding ways to engage people in the design of their own care and drawing on community resources alongside NHS provision to improve health outcomes. Six localities stood out as teams with the ambition, permission and skills to achieve change at a system level, embedding 'co-produced' approaches to managing long-term conditions at the heart of the care pathway or organization rather than as a peripheral service. This included a primary care team in Newcastle wanting to employ 'social prescribing', where patients are referred to health trainers to support them towards achievable goals such as joining a local gym or social group as an alternative to a clinical care pathway; a practice in Calderdale experimenting with group consultations for patients with musculoskeletal pain, where patients are able to explore their conditions together and reflect on common experiences and a London borough designing a new commissioning model for all of the mental health services in the area, involving the community and providers much more actively in decision-making and service design to try and improve preventative services.[1]

The principles of more community based, peer supported and relationship focused support are fundamental to these new models, each demonstrating the value of a deeper partnership between professionals, service users and service providers born from greater understanding and empathy. Though in each case the emphasis was on people helping people to better manage a long-term condition, there were additional specific social and clinical outcomes in improving people's well-being, addressing social isolation and loneliness, improving diet and fitness and better signposting and take-up of services.

The NHS is a difficult environment in which to innovate, with rigid hierarchies, established professional cultures and significant resource constraints against consistent demand. For People Powered Health, the challenge was in how to integrate these new approaches within the mainstream system. One important aspect of this was how to account for the value of co-production. The program team supported each locality to develop a business case for the new model, to combine the qualitative feedback from service users and professionals involved with evidence to suggest the clinical and financial benefits of co-production (Nesta 2013).[2] This helped to establish further buy-in from professionals within the system and health policymakers, and has given the localities confidence in the value of continuing to embed co-production within their practice.

Particularly given the constraints on public finances, innovation is not only about creating better productivity, policy outcomes, service experiences and strengthening democracy (Bason 2011),[3] but is also deeply connected with an ability to draw productively and more broadly on society's resources. Many public and social innovation initiatives imply a blurring of boundaries between the public sector and other sectors, and require new means of collaboration – whether between the state and citizens, private businesses, social enterprises or civil society organizations (see Figure 3.1 below).

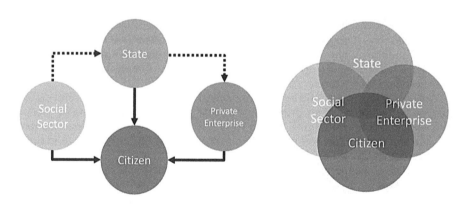

Figure 3.1   The changing relationships of government in delivering public outcomes

---

1   For more details on the People Powered Health program see Horne et al. (2013).
2   See Nesta (2013).
3   See Christian Bason (2011).

Current policy reforms affecting the public sector imply a move away from centralized control and regulation towards decentralized, localized, non-regulatory approaches and a stronger emphasis on the role for businesses, civil society and citizens in providing public services. This concept of 'co-production' – working together to produce public outcomes – tries to draw upon this outset. The ideal is that formal contractual relationships are replaced by more organic and informal social systems that make use of the resources of society in a much smarter and more efficient way. Co-production has had the awareness of governments for some time, but has shown to be very difficult for public organizations to facilitate and make a core part of their operations (Boyle and Harris 2009).

The challenge for governments and bureaucracies is that co-production implies a significant loss of control for institutions and organizations responsible for public governance. Co-production involves new types of relationships and dynamics between various actors of society, in particular a new relationship between citizens and the public state. The oppositional relationship between the public state and citizens – the state as 'deliverer' and the citizen as 'recipient' or 'consumer' of services – has been a feature of the culture of public decision-making for some time. This model builds on the public sector maintaining control through delivering what it knows to be best for the citizen or legitimate in relation to current budgets and criteria for civil rights. Changing the focus to the creation of outcomes rather than delivering services is thus problematic because it involves a loss of control, and introduces a new competitive landscape where the public sector is only one knowledgeable actor among many.

There is a new role here for public leaders and policymakers to be focusing more broadly on the resources of society and manage new types of relationships and interaction between the public state and citizens as well as between various different actors of society. The need for this role comes from a persistent focus on outcomes and the importance of understanding what outcomes matter from an individual or personal perspective rather than on the basis of what the system provides. For example, for a family coping with many different issues such as a consequence of unemployment, poverty or poor educational attainment, developing their own abilities to cope and remain resilient to sudden changes in circumstance may be the most valuable and effective outcome from their relationship with welfare services. Here, the ambition of government becomes not the delivery of services, but the achievement of outcomes that are informed by local insight, evidence and context and that comes about through new synergies between citizens, organizations, businesses and facilitated efforts of the public state.

This shift involves a change in the 'technique of government' from launching rigid programs implemented from the top and down to establishing and facilitating networks as the primary capacity to solve problems, productively share resources and learn (Sanderson 2009) – an approach also associated with 'networked governance' (Hartley 2005). What design approaches offer to co-production and networked governance are processes of exploration of and experimentation with new collaborative efforts and organizational setups in order to establish new local practice. It offers methodology that, rather than reduce or simplify reality, illuminate complex, interactive and interconnected realities with a sensibility towards the everyday lives and work activities as they are experienced in practice. Design thus aims to create concrete insight that can reveal how desired outcomes can be achieved in the particular local context.

EXPERIMENTATION AS THE GROUNDS FOR CONVICTION

Ex: Behavioural Insights to Inform Policymaking

How can governments use new behavioural insights to inform social policy and practice? As advances in behavioural science and psychology have shown, the way we act can be counter intuitive to the assumptions of traditional policy instruments. One example of this is a UK experiment to apply behavioural insights to reduce fraud, error and debt in tax collection. Based on hypotheses around what would motivate people to attend to deadlines, guidelines and criteria for tax administration – such as using more personalized language, highlighting social norms and local behaviour and rewarding desired behaviour – the Cabinet Office 'Behavioural Insights Team' worked together with relevant departments to design eight randomized control trials (RCTs) to test how these insights affect practice.

By making relatively minor changes to communication methods – using more personalized language in letters, including statistics of social norms such as others' response times, adapting the layout of forms – the teams were able to test how useful these insights were in preventing fraud, error and default in the public sector. The results were impressive: one trial investigating whether informing people how many others in their area had already paid their tax could boost payment rate advanced £160 million of tax debts to the Exchequer over the six week period of the trial. Overall, the trials showed effect sizes of up to 30 per cent in preventing fraud, error and debt through better understanding of human behaviour (Cabinet Office 2012).

The experimental approach allowed the team to adapt and learn from their insights, making small adjustments to practice and monitoring their effect. Randomization allowed the team to test whether the change in outcomes could be attributed to the change in intervention, as opposed to other contextual factors. Of course, experimentation as a basis for shaping policy for administering tax and payment systems is very different to using an experimental approach in education or children's services, for example. But the principle of knowledge creation through experimentation based on deep understanding and empathy of human behaviour could – within the right boundaries – inform action in uncertain contexts.

Governments always want to ensure that public intervention is as effective as it can be in positively changing public behaviour, and this is especially true in a time of constrained resources. Yet human behaviour is not rational and predictable. Our actions and responses are affected by our experience, our particular context, our social networks, social norms and personal beliefs (Wilson 2011).

The problem is that the dominant cognitive mindset from which civil servants are encouraged to act is linked to certain ideas of factual objectivity. This means that civil servants are compelled to put their knowledge to work in a way that, in the name of governance, has to assume that the public problem is and will remain addressable in a predictable way. If you want to redraw the map, or radically change public service systems, you cannot only use the existing known maps to inspire the process.

Thus, the idea of experimentation in relation to public governance and policy development has connotations of risk. This is to a large extent understandable given the important responsibility to ensure public accountability and civil rights through trustworthy bureaucratic procedures and structures. Therefore innovation, in that its outcome is unknown and unpredictable, is seen as risky in contrast to known, predictable outcomes (and familiar failures) of current practices whether or not they are successful. As a consequence, much innovation still tends to be carried out outside of the core operations of public organizations.

But what if we could turn this on its head, and see informed experimentation as the responsible foundation for decision-making in complex settings? That, given the current 'state of uncertainty', some of the legitimacy of public governance would come through policymaking as modelled on scientific experimentation and a process of discovery (Bakhshi, Freeman and Potts 2011). The experimental approach is necessary because innovation inherently destabilizes existing operational, organizational and administrative structures; experimentation necessarily challenges existing knowledge and experience in order to make new discoveries, asking people to contend with a high degree of uncertainty. This is at odds with the dominant culture of public governance that wants to minimize risk, waste and failure.

During periods of uncertainty, structured methods such as foresight and prototyping can be applied to anticipate and 'rehearse the future' in a more active and productive way (Halse et al. 2011). Using these methods to create a legitimate space for experimentation can be a way to contain and manage risk and expectation, and learn from (low cost) failure where the cause of a problem is unknown, or where practices still are evolving. This is different from running an initial pilot prior to launching a full program, which is often the way in which public policies are developed (and which has its own risks). When pilots hold profile, political capital and considerable investment, failure can have considerable costs. The expectation from experimentation is not necessarily success, but learning from practice.

The concept of 'beta' is relevant here. An established principle in technology development, beta versions are an early, prototype version of a platform, tool or web presence. They expect to be imperfect and exist as a 'working hypothesis' for future improvement. Beta is a powerful idea to apply to public policymaking. It changes expectations of performance and permanence of public services, given the signal of early stage development and ongoing learning. Beta not only welcomes feedback, but pro-actively encourages challenges and critique from the public, potential users, colleagues, partners, experts and other relevant actors. It goes beyond static consultation into ongoing engagement, iteration, co-production and collaboration, seeking contributions and suggestions for how practices could be improved. In this way, failures and complaints become opportunities for innovation and learning since imperfection becomes a legitimate and even expected part of the processes devoted to the experimental search for the possible. Polices are and must be 'perfectible'.

Adopting this does not mean that conducting experiments as a part of public governance in themselves are the goal or that experimentation should replace all other operational approaches. We wish to highlight their usability because, by the very nature of addressing public problems through policy and programs, public sectors are already 'experimenting' anyway. The question is if we wish to continue believing in our ability to foresee how our plans will unfold in practice or if we instead wish to accept the unpredictable consequences that go with any attempt to intervene in social reality?

RECOGNIZE AND EXERCISE A NEW TYPE OF AUTHORITY

Ex: Guiding Public-Private Innovation

During the last five years, political, administrative and operational levels of government in Denmark have developed an increasing awareness of 'Public-Private Innovation' (PPI) – dynamic and continuous collaboration between public and private sectors to innovate public services, lower the use of public resources and create opportunities for business growth. Despite multiple attempts in the form of various projects carried out in municipalities and regional organizations, the new welfare solutions have yet to create any significant value.

In 2011, the Danish Business Agency (DBA) and MindLab were given the task of developing a guidance tool for PPI which would provide support for municipalities and other public organizations wanting to work with PPI. However because this mode of collaboration was a significant move away from current development practices, there was no blueprint for guiding practice either at the ministerial level (policy) or on regional or local levels. This created a situation in which the different levels of the public sector became gridlocked. For this reason, the DBA and MindLab experimented with a new way of sharing responsibility. They involved public employees from both local and regional levels in a mutual process of learning and rehearsing future approaches of PPI. In this way, they sought to unlock the deadlock between the practitioners who previously had been awaiting 'authoritative guidelines' and thecivil servants who lacked the ability to give them guidance. The DBA thus took on a new role of facilitator of an ongoing learning process, actively engaging with its stakeholders and users, with the goal of creating a new community of practice.

In this way, a new type of authority for the DBA was involved that not only refrained from postulating that the complex processes were known in absolute certainty, but also altered the typically oppositional relationship between the ministerial agencies and local public organizations. Now responsibility was shared and continuously co-constructed by governmental, regional or municipal organizations through their active involvement in co-creating new knowledge and experience used to define, frame and guide PPI practices. Instead of putting their authoritative stamp on particular decisions or actions, the DCA had to participate in continuous processes of dialogue and knowledge sharing and actively explore what 'authoritativeness' could be and who should be involved in establishing the environment where it had to 'work'.

While public problems are increasingly understood in their complexity, accountability in public bureaucracies is still largely understood through traditional models of authority. The perception that it is possible to relieve the world completely of a particular problem is also reflected in an authoritarian role that involves the public sector as an 'all-knowing' entity and, as such, has the ability to objectively sanction or validate certain decisions based on authorized knowledge. Consequently, the professional culture of public leaders, civil servants, managers and frontline workers is one that values certainty, conviction and technical competency, rather than openness to uncertainty. Changing this authoritative role therefore implies the development of different skills, relationships and working cultures as much as it requires different practices. In other words, another kind of authoritative role – one that focuses less on sanctioning knowledge and information, and more on how to facilitate and enable the generation of knowledge and effective action. What is valuable to explore, then, is how government can warrant a more distributed approach in which the roles of the public sector are more focused on coordination, knowledge accreditation and stewardship than delivery or control?

This approach reflects a different way of taking responsibility and exploring how to act most appropriately as a public authority given uncertain circumstances. Where the prompts for public problems are unknown, authority comes not only from having access to superior resources or formal powers, but in understanding the context and conditions that affect problems. For example, a doctor prescribing treatment is endowed with formal authority, but in managing long-term conditions or in public health issues that require behaviour change, the experiential knowledge and particular actions of patients and the public are important methods to use to ensure an effective outcome. Consequently, the public state becomes a facilitator or a network leader that manages risk, uncertainty and social complexity by facilitating 'platforms' of collaboration and knowledge sharing.

In light of this collaborative approach, we suggest that a key feature of decision-making in complex public innovation processes is a different perception of what is 'authorized'. Intervention becomes about creating a new, productive 'authorizing environment' that is held up by various actors, different power relations and interconnected spaces of meaning and interpretation. The question is how we enable new approaches and practices in public service systems while simultaneously showing their actual public value and, at the same time, building the operational capacity and administrative capability to develop and govern them effectively (Bennington and Moore 2011). It is a paradoxical challenge of enabling certain actions and decisions (in relation to innovation) within systems that both their administrative and operational capacity is still unfit to authorize them.

We apply it here to open up a new type of role for public authority. One that, rather than controls or specifies activity and outputs, to a larger degree has to distribute various efforts and resources in order to effectively address problems in search of valuable outcomes – the authority of the State is used to lever the collective capacity for better public outcomes.[4] A role in which the public state recognizes itself as one knowledgeable actor among many and therefore deliberately seeks to draw broadly on the knowledge and efforts of various actors of society as a whole. In short, public governance that is concerned with outcomes necessarily requires co-production and collaboration and even creating new 'publics' and 'authorizing environments'.

This role by no means rules out that public authorities do have to step in at certain times and validate or sanction certain procedures to address the particular problem. It is rather that in public innovation there is not necessarily a direct causality between authoritative knowledge and public interventions since the reasons and conditions for making decisions have to be explored and learned rather than be known fully or in advance. In this context, there is a role for policymakers to ensure openness and veracity of information, ensuring impartiality and acknowledging dispute. Advances in digital analytical and communication tools have potential here in organizing information much more dynamically, with the state exercising its authority through facilitating shared decision-making. In the past decades, governments spent large amounts of resources on enabling market results. Now, the role of the public sector needs to involve enabling not only collaboration with private actors, but actively encouraging enabling and authorizing new types of environments for collaboration and co-production.

IDENTIFYING AND VALUING USEFUL EVIDENCE

Ex: Away with Red Tape

Young people between 18 and 30 years of age in Denmark are the demographic group least likely to be capable to do their taxes online. This surprising insight pushed the Danish Tax and Customs Administration (DTCA) to partner with MindLab to gain a better understanding of the experiences of citizens and their encounters with public sector bureaucracy. Under the headline 'Away with Red Tape', the broad agenda of the Danish government was to eliminate unnecessary rules and digitize and simplify complicated administrative procedures. While deregulation often focused on seemingly objective criteria, such as time consumption and the number of rules, this

---

4   We are grateful to Jocelyne Bourgon for this suggestion. See also Bourgon (2012).

project deliberately avoided predefining a rule or procedure as 'red tape'. Instead, the study examined the subjective experiences of citizens with public sector regulations, communication channels and service.

The initiatives that have emerged from the study stem from a design-driven process, which is characterized by systematic idea development and prioritization, the development of concepts and the description of specific prototypes in direct dialogue with citizens. These processes were all driven from an informational base coming from conducting interviews to be able to sketch out the service journey and experience in concrete and illustrative ways. This information led to various initiatives under the heading 'from digital access to digital self-reliance' meaning that usability must be understood as more than just a technical solution. In this way, the DTCA and MindLab created a new kind of knowledge foundation that set out a course of addressing problems in a more human-centred way, creating taxation procedures more in tune with the lives of citizens

An important part of this was the use of audio clips and radio montage, which were used to illustrate the experiences of the young citizens as vividly as possible. There were various audio representations of frustrated young citizens trying to do their taxes online. Some of these audio clips became consistent parts of internal meetings and workshops in the DTCA in their development work. These in-depth representations were intended to create a new understanding to engage decision-makers in novel ways by drawing them closer to the everyday experiences of citizens and applying a very different kind of 'knowledge' about the citizens compared to what they were used to. The audio clips became a new way of collectively relating to the shared challenge by continuously activating ongoing professional empathy for the experience of citizens. In this way, they contributed to creating a renewed sense of purpose and made new and useful decisions possible.

The shift to new types of processes and effects (innovation) and different types of roles, functions and activities (co-production) have significant implications for the way we think about the production and application of knowledge and information. Particularly, it seems to involve a fundamental discussion about what we consider as legitimate and not the least useful 'evidence' to work as a foundation for actions and decisions. To some extent, new forms of knowing (or not knowing) have become potential social assets to be explored in order to enable productive decisions in the process of changing (or innovating) welfare services.

This approach is particularly about finding ways to introduce less calculated or tangible insights more formally into decision-making processes. How can we, for example, make room for more outcome-focused initiatives when that typically involves highly relational and localized processes which make valuable evidence something that depends on contextual factors rather than standardized criteria? Or how can we support the application of qualitative insights about citizens in relation to their actual life experience that might be of a more unfinished and less tangible character, but will often prove to be the source of innovative ideas?

Building innovation capability in public governance simply requires other kinds of illustrating examples and representations to help decision-makers empathetically relate to the people and the problem at hand as well as see their purpose and possibilities in a new light. Creative methods building on ethnographic methodology, co-design approaches and social and interactive media provide opportunities to capture the experience and insights of citizens, to add legitimacy to interpretation and allow for processes of co-producing outcomes. This approach need not be at odds with more formal evaluation and evidence, as it provides a way to prompt the development of new hypotheses and questions for research and experimentation.

The challenges involved in legitimizing the practical and uncertain realities of public innovation projects also have to be taken into consideration. Often, public innovation project leaders spend more time on legitimizing and gaining support for the project itself within the organization. As a consequence of the practical, contextual or temporal reality of innovation projects, a substantial amount of resources goes into managing expectations about the process while much less is spent on imaginative experimentation and learning from practice.

What is particularly challenging for policymakers in this context is that (innovation) policy not only invents new forms of thought and foundations for decisions, but also involves the invention of novel procedures of documentation, computation and evaluation (Miller and Rose 2008). Given this multiplicity, you can certainly ask whether it is innovation projects that fail or whether they are failed by wider networks of support and validation (Mosse 2007). At least, one significant challenge for policymakers seems to be to figure out how to support and validate public innovation initiatives within the existing frames of public legitimacy. What should or could characterize the formalizing processes themselves in respect to evidence? Could different levels or expectations of evidence be applied and other types of systems and legitimizing processes be applied within governance practices? (Reis 2011).

Integrating Design in Practice

These principles imply new ways of thinking about the goals, means and authority of the public sector and government in responding to complex problems. How can these new ways become embedded within public administrative systems and governance structures? Bringing design into these settings requires a change in the way in which the public sector itself operates. This change involves much more than merely relying on new concepts and methods to integrate naturally into existing governance models and structures.

One approach that has seen increasing traction is for governments to set up distinct teams or units with a specific remit for innovation, often drawing on design methods. The UK's behavioural insights team or 'Nudge' unit mentioned above is an example of this, a team with a distinctive approach drawing on an understanding of psychology and behavioural economics and informed by experimentation to devise new approaches to policymaking and implementation. Another example is the recent establishment of an internal design lab by the Australian Government. Its purpose is to develop and test new approaches to complex policy challenges and create a different environment for collaboration and experimentation. The Centre for Excellence in Public Sector Design, or DesignGov, has positioned itself as a 'start-up within government', trying to introduce a new way of working across agencies to draw together different perspectives and prototyping new ways of addressing problems (DesignGov 2012). Consciously approached as an experiment, DesignGov provides an opportunity to test the usefulness of design approaches and principles in the context of complex policymaking. This approach is similar to the Danish public innovation unit, MindLab, which, as we have seen in the examples in this chapter, is working as cross-ministerial facilitator of human-centred design processes. Through this approach, MindLab is continuously experimenting with the integration of new kinds of knowledge in and spaces and processes for public development.

Yet the question remains whether such units or projects focusing specifically on public innovation can be successful in transferring the resilience and capacity for innovation broadly in operational competencies and mindsets. The risk for units of this type is non-integration: to create a separate practice outside of the core operations of the public sector. Public innovation does not necessarily thrive by only increasing deregulation or introducing innovation process models. It involves a change in the instruments of government and, along with this, changes in perspective and mentality that need to integrate effectively within mainstream decision-making cultures.

On the other hand, these units and design-led projects in general can legitimately create new 'authorizing environments'. As with the public-private innovation guide, where the public agency engaged as a facilitator in creating a new community of practice, innovation units and projects similarly have the potential of being sources of inspiration and legitimization, becoming central parts of social movements of introducing new approaches to public development. A crucial part of this exercise is to create powerful narratives to both inspire and operationalize the design approach. This was what 'The Fredericia model' succeeded with. In particular, they not only showed how the approach created better outcomes in relation to the service experience and the savings in public budgets, but they also illustrated the concrete implications that the new model would have for the political level as well as the administrative and organizational operations in the municipality.

Ensuring outcomes, facilitation and stewardship, openness to experimentation and comfort with uncertainty all require as much strength in vision in leadership as do more traditional approaches to developing and implementing public policy. Yet leadership in these contexts might look very different to authority achieved through conviction and certainty. It is perhaps, therefore, not just a consequence of dominant processes and practices that work against innovation in public governance, but the skills, leadership qualities and competencies that tend to be recognized as bringing authority and assurance to those in positions of responsibility. For example, the teams working with communities to identify outcomes in People-Powered Health or in Fredericia based their decisions on the aspirations and capabilities of service users. In both cases, it is evident that it requires leadership from assuming a different worldview and openness to an alternative set of values.

But even in the contexts of these developments, we are not suggesting that innovation and its accompanying practices should be the default approach to policymaking everywhere all of the time. Though the implications of these principles for public governance are profound and widespread, there may be some areas of public policy in which a more experimental, open-ended approach to developing policy is not (or not yet) appropriate, or socially acceptable. How much experimentation should we expect or hope for in areas of social policies? What sorts of problems lend themselves to a more experimental approach?

The question of where to start is largely an empirical one, as it is an empirical question whether variables cannot be meaningfully defined and measured. Where there is a relatively robust relationship between defined problem and effective intervention, a more traditional approach may apply. Where there is more uncertainty and complexity, these design-led principles might more usefully apply. These principles may therefore be relevant where:

- There is currently little on offer, either because of under-developed offerings or the emergence of new or newly identified need, such as in family support services;

- What is currently on offer is not working, either from a lack of take-up or lack of impact;

- There is little evidence of what works in terms of tackling a particular issue, such as in some areas of public health;

- The system needs to shift towards a more preventative approach, such as in reducing reoffending or in preventing the development of long-term health conditions;

- Commissioners are facing substantial cuts or changes to their commissioning context, requiring imagination and ingenuity in how to respond to local demand.

Where to begin integrating a design approach building on the new culture of decision-making described in this chapter thus involves some level of pragmatism. What is more important at this stage is to emphasize the need for reframing the practice of public policy through ideas, concepts and approaches of design. We see the emerging cultural shifts mentioned here as necessary in not only becoming more effective and constructive in creating better outcomes for citizens, but also as a way of increasing the legitimacy of public interventions in general. We see the productive integration of design capacity and capabilities in public policymaking and public governance as key in this respect.

Acknowledgements

We would like to thank many colleagues and friends for being such rich sources of insight and experience in these areas, in particular Christian Bason, Jocelyne Bourgon, Hasan Bakhshi, Halima Khan, Philip Colligan, Bryan Boyer, Dan Hill, Nina Holm Vohnsen, Marie Munk and Sabine Junginger as well as those who contributed to our expert seminars in Nesta in London and at MindLab in Copenhagen. All errors and omissions remain our own.

References

Bakhshi, H., Freeman, A. and Potts, J. (2011). *State of Uncertainty: Innovation Policy through experimentation*. London: NESTA.

Bason, C. (2010). *Leading Public Sector Innovation: Co-creating for a Better Society*. Bristol: Policy Press.

Bennington, J. and Moore, M., eds (2011). *Public Value: Theory and Practice*. London: Palgrave Macmillan.

Bourgon, J. (2012). *A New Synthesis of Public Administration*. Montreal: McGill-Queen's University Press.

Boyer, B., Cook, J. and Steinberg, M. (2011). *In Studio: Recipes for Systemic Change*. Helsinki: Sitra.

Boyle, D. and Harris, M. (2009). *The Challenge of Coproduction*. London: Nesta and New Economics Foundation.

Cabinet Office (2012). *Applying Behavioural Insights to Reduce Fraud, Error and Debt*. London: Cabinet Office.

Department of Health (2012). *Long-term Conditions Compendium of information* – third edition. London: Department of Health.

DesignGov, http://innovation.govspace.gov.au/2012/12/20/welcome-to-designgov-and-what-we-have-been-up-to-in-our-first-6-months/.

Easton, D. (1981). *The Political System: An Inquiry into the State of Political Science*, 2nd ed. New York: Alfred A. Knopf.

Halse, J. et al. (2011). *Rehearsing the future*. Copenhagen: The Danish Design School Press.

Hartley, J. (2005). Innovation in Governance and Public Services. *Public Money and Management* (January 25): 27–34.

Horne, M., Khan, H. and Corrigan, P. (2013). *People Powered Health: Health for People, with People and by People*. London: Nesta and Innovation Unit.

Kettl, D. (2002). *The Transformation of Governance: Public Administration for Twenty-First Century America*. Baltimore: Johns Hopkins University Press.

Latour, B. (2007). *How to think like a State*. Lecture transcript: http://robertoigarza. files.wordpress.com/2008/11/art-how-to-think-like-a-state-latour-2007.pdf.

Miller, P. and Rose, N. (2008). Governing Economic Life. In *Governing the Present*, edited by P. Miller and N. Rose. Bristol: Policy Press. 26–52.

Mosse, D. (2007). Is Good Policy Unimplementable? Reflections on the Ethnography of Aid Policy and Practice. In *The Anthropology of Organisations*, edited by A.C. Jimenez. Farnham, UK: Ashgate. 451–83.

Nesta, Innovation Unit and Private Public Ltd. (2013). *The Business Case for People Powered Health*. London: Nesta and Innovation Unit.

Newman, J. et al. (2004). Public Participation and Collaborative Governance (with Barnes, M., and Sullivan, H.) *Journal of Social Policy*, 33 (2), 217.

Reis, E. (2011). *The Lean Start-up: How Today's Entrepreneurs Use Continuous Innovation to Create Radically Successful Businesses*. New York: Crown Publishing.

Sanderson, I. (2009). Intelligent Policy Making for a Complex World: pragmatism, evidence and learning. *Political Studies*, 57 (4), December 2009, 699–719.

Scott, J. (1998). *Seeing Like a State. How Certain Schemes to Improve the Human Conditions Have Failed*. New Haven: Yale University.

Shore, C., Wright, S. and Però, D. (2011). Policy Worlds. *Anthropology and the Analysis of Contemporary Power*. New York: Berghahn Books.

Vohnsen, N.H. (2011). Absurdity and the Sensible Decision: Implementation of Danish Labour Market Policy. PhD thesis: Aarhus University.

Wilson, T. (2011). *Redirect: The Surprising New Science of Psychological Change*. New York: Penguin Group.

SABINE JUNGINGER

Towards Policymaking as Designing: Policymaking Beyond Problem-solving and Decision-making

Not the least because of stringent austerity requirements, governments around the globe have begun to look for new ways to develop and deliver policies, products and services that achieve the desired outcomes for their populations better, faster and cheaper.[1] In this effort, design is emerging as a central issue. Yet, the role of design skills, design knowledge and design capabilities in the public sector, that is in policymaking, policy implementation and in public management, remains largely unexamined. We need a better understanding of what designing constitutes in the public sector. We need to be able to scrutinize the current design approaches and design practices that public organizations pursue and engage in. We need to grasp the design concepts and the design processes that ultimately affect and shape the lives of millions of people. Where there is design, there is the potential for change. Thus re-framing policy as design or policymaking as designing opens new paths for us to generate, implement and instil changes to the public sector. These changes will be manifested in new products and services, but they will also ripple through the organizational fabric and re-shape organizational life for many public managers and civil servants. Lastly, they will affect how we think about policies and how we go about the design of policies.

The aim of this chapter is to position policy as a matter of design. I use the policy cycle described by Howlett and Ramesh in 2003 to study the current role and place of design in policy studies.[2] I find that design is portrayed as a problem-solving activity and policymaking as a problem-solving task. I show how this understanding frames and limits policy design because it enables almost exclusively responsive and reactive designing. I argue that the problem-solving approach leaves little room for human experiences or imaginary scenarios for desirable futures. To overcome these limitations, I suggest that we rethink – or re-frame – policymaking as designing.

---

1   The term 'product' remains a source of confusion. Generally speaking, a product is a consequence or outcome of a design activity. In this sense, a policy is a product as much as a service is. In this particular sentence here, a product describes the tangible design results – for example, a tax form or a web interface – that are necessary to create or deliver an organization's service. Public organizations may create these products themselves or hire design professionals to do so. However, everyday citizens associate these products with the organizations that 'deliver' them, even if they are part of a service.

2   My reason for singling out the Howlett and Ramesh policy cycle is that it beautifully captures the problem-solving approach and therefore lends itself to a discussion of this design approach to policymaking. I could also have looked more specifically into the design concepts that inform and shape policy implementation, for example by examining the role design is assigned in Hill and Hupe (2009).

In this role, designing becomes a means of inquiry and invention, of envisioning and of developing new possibilities for useful, usable and desirable policies. Policymaking as designing would equip policymakers and public managers with the full range of design tools and methods to develop and implement innovative policies. It can shift our focus from being problem-centred to being human-centred: from trying to solve a problem in isolation from the human experience to considering the actual human experience as a starting point. For this to happen, we need a new kind of design discourse in policy that looks into essential design practices, design concepts and design capabilities in these areas. But we also need to develop new educational approaches for policymakers, policy implementers and public managers. If the public sector is serious about its efforts to modernize administrations, become more citizen-centred and transform governance, design will have to become part of the curriculum of future policymakers, civil servants and other public managers. This chapter is an attempt to initiate such a discourse.

Policymaking as a Problem-solving Task

There are many different ways we can approach a new design discourse in policy studies. The term 'policy design' alone can depict many different kinds of design approaches to policy. For the purpose of this chapter, I have chosen to play with the design concepts at the heart of a policy cycle model which is still mandatory reading for many policy students and researchers: the Howlett and Ramesh (2003) policy cycle depicted in Figure 4.1. Admittedly, my selection is somewhat random as other popular works and models exist, notably those by Hill and Hupe (2009). Since the aim of this chapter is neither to provide an overview of policy design models, nor to provide a design critique of all of them, the Howlett and Ramesh model serves the purpose well. It simply presents an opportunity to reflect on the relevance of design to policymaking and to policy implementation. In short, it provides an opportunity to explore policymaking as designing (Figure 4.1).

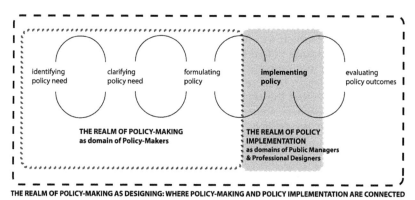

THE REALM OF POLICY-MAKING AS DESIGNING: WHERE POLICY-MAKING AND POLICY IMPLEMENTATION ARE CONNECTED

This diagram shows how the policy cycle by Howlett and Ramesh (2003) assumes a problem-based, linear, fragmented design approach. The original policy cycle is presented by the four loops in the center. This policy cycle assigns policy-makers the role of identifying, claryfying and formulating policy (realm of policy-making) before handing the formulated policy over to those responsible for policy implementation (realm of policy implementation). Policy-making as designing does not separate these two design activities (realm of policy-making as designing).

Figure 4.1   The policy design cycle (adapted from Howlett and Ramesh 2003)

The policy design cycle by Howlett and Ramesh suggests that policy design first and foremost serves to solve problems. As a consequence, it is only after a problem has appeared on policymakers' radar screen that the policy cycle can begin. Once a problem has been recognized as such (and we do not know how or why), the first task according to the policy cycle is to identify if 'this' problem warrants the need for a new policy. If the decision is affirmative and a new policy is considered necessary, policymakers have to *clarify* what kind of policy is needed. Now decisions have to be made about the *formulation* of the new policy. Once this task is completed and the policy has been formulated and put into words, policymakers, in this model, are done with their job. They have designed a policy that now awaits implementation. The responsibilities for any further action shifts from policymakers to policy-implementers whose task it is to develop the kinds of products and services through which the intent of the policy can be fulfilled and translated into reality. This handing off of tasks and responsibilities is indicative of a fragmented design approach that has come under increased scrutiny (cf: Adebowale 2009; Eppel et al. 2011). Yet, the policy cycle reduces policymaking to a problem-solving and decision-making task, which reinforces these fragmentations. In addition, policymakers who think of themselves as problem-solvers can find answers and responses only to those problems they become aware of. There is an implicit danger that policymakers tend to sense mainly those problems they can recognize as such – in other words, problems they are somewhat familiar with. But familiar problems can be symptoms, rather than causes for difficulties people experience.

Marco Steinberg, the former head of the Sitra Helsinki Design Lab (another public innovation lab) demonstrates the pitfalls of such thinking. He likes to tell the story of a city government that grew concerned about a significant drop of visitors to a local swimming pool complex. No visitors meant unsold tickets and less money for the swimming pool and the municipality: This was identified as a problem. To clarify if and what actions needed to be taken to solve this problem, the city council went to see the facility for themselves. They judged the poor state of the building as the cause. Back from their visit, the city council hired an architectural firm to make the facility attractive again. The architects, however, talked to local people and did some research around the area of the swimming pool. They learned that the drop in the attendance coincided with a change the city had made to its bus schedule. It was simply no longer possible for people relying on public transportation to reach the swimming pool during swim hours and this was a problem. But it was a problem that escaped the imagination and the experience of the city council, many of whom were used to taking their cars to get around town. Spending money on repairing the building would not have changed the attendance numbers unless the bus schedule would have been adjusted as well!

I like Steinberg's anecdote because it illustrates how well-intended efforts by national and local governments can fall short when the only tools they have available are based on solving problems they recognize and which they can see. Too often, we focus on the wrong problems in public matters because the problem-solving approach does not equip us with the means to explore issues from the experiences of everyday people and citizens. Instead of understanding the real cause for the situation, the city council isolated the facility as 'the' problem. This allows us to detect another weakness in the policy cycle by Howlett and Ramesh: it does not consider how people engage with each other and their environments. Instead, it depicts policymaking as making top-down decisions around a problem that can be isolated. In the anecdote, the city council executed the tasks assigned to policymaking in the policy cycle in Figure 4.1. The architects were assigned the role of the 'policy-implementers'. In this case, alert architects caught the flaw in this approach. Brought in by the council in the 'implementation phase', that is, to solve the problem the city council had identified (fixing the swimming pool interior), they were able to point out that the council had misconceived of the problem itself. The architects were able to re-place the problem of the swimming pool within its context. They successfully shifted the focus from an isolated problem to a problematic situation.

The anecdote reveals another flaw of the problem-solving approach that I have briefly mentioned above: its insistence on compartmentalizing and fragmenting design activities, of separating and prioritizing one kind of design, planning and formulating, over another kind of design, implementation and delivery. Returning to Figure 4.1, we find the overall policy design approach split into two isolated *design activities*: policymaking on the one hand, and policy implementation on the other. Steinberg's anecdote teaches us that this approach is often counter-productive. As innocent as the design of a bus schedule might be, changes to how buses run have direct implications for how people live, work and how they can access public services, leisure facilities or reach their work places. The example reminds us that the biggest and costliest mistakes tend to happen in the first and earliest stages of a design process, although the consequences and implications of these errors are often experienced and visible only in later design stages, often, when it is too late for changes owing to monetary, legal or technical commitments made earlier. This then means that we need to be more alert to when our design activities begin – and at what point our design understanding can inform and enhance the way we go about policymaking.

Problem-solving as a Partial View of Design

We can summarize that the problem-solving approach to policymaking is based on several assumptions that limit our design options from the start. First, it builds on the notion that policymaking is a responsive, reactive activity. Policies then are not the forward-looking, future-oriented frameworks they could be. Instead, they are rooted in the past, responding to present and past facts, fears or other forces. Policies in problem-solving are not so much tools to create future experiences but rather tools to regulate experiences of the past. We might say that 'the' problem shapes our policymaking and our lives because we only begin to shape policies that shape our lives in response to this problem. Second, the dependence on 'a' problem encourages policies to be developed in isolation from their larger contexts. Third, the problem-solving approach teaches policymakers to take action only when policymakers themselves are prepared to recognize a problem to be a problem. But it fails to consider and embrace people's everyday experiences and interactions. It also pays little regard to the realities of employees in those organizations that have to implement and administer policies. As the above anecdote demonstrates, what may seem to be a problem for policymakers may not be the problem experienced by people outside of policymaking. Furthermore, the problem-solving approach has a tendency to disconnect the different design activities that together constitute policy design by separating them into different design processes. The linear, top-down decision-making promoted in the policy cycle does little to remedy these fragmentations. If we take all these aspects together, we can conclude that policy design driven by problem-solving does not lend itself to envisioning and inventing futures. It does not encourage or enable us to develop innovative policies towards achieving more desirable futures.

In other words, the policy cycle based on problem-solving does not serve policymakers as well as some textbooks make it appear.

If this is the case, then why has problem-solving come to dominate policy design? One possible answer can be found in design studies. For a long time, the problem-solving ability of design has received more attention in design studies than its necessary companion, inquiry. Problem-solving has been discussed over time by many influential researchers, including Archer (1967), Simon (1969), Cross (1992) and Gorb and Schneider (1988; also Gorb 2011). For early design researchers, emphasizing the role of design in problem-solving was a way to relate design to the strategic and managerial realm of the organization. Establishing design as a problem-solving activity served to raise design awareness and to demonstrate commonalities between designing, managing and decision-making.

> The design act consists of a problem-solving activity which is goal-directed and is identical in kind with those problems familiar to management students and decision theorists. (Archer 1967)

As a result, policy researchers and practitioners have had few incentives to look to design as a driver to generate innovative policies. Only recently have scholars linked human experiences and human interactions that are mediated by products and services with organizational design approaches (Boland and Collopy 2004; Buchanan 2004; Junginger 2008). Design's ability to inquire into organizations and other systems from a human perspective has yet to be understood in terms of the value and relevance for public organizations and the public sector at large. The time is right to do so. In light of ever more complex and formidable problems that challenge us to enhance human living in sustainable ways, the responsive problem-solving approach no longer suffices. Policymaking in the problem-solving mode remains a reaction, a response that overlooks how policies can create possibilities for action towards improved or better futures. The move to policy as design is therefore an effort to correct this and to unfold the full range of design and designing into the policy cycle. We need to shift beyond policymaking as problem-solving towards policymaking as designing.

Policymaking as Designing

The generation of new, innovative and transformative policies depends on the ability of policymakers to inquire into situations before they turn into problems. How we frame problems influences the kinds of solutions we are seeking to address them. There are encouraging signs that we are headed this way: Martin Rein and Donald Schön have been articulate about the role of problem-setting in policy research and in policymaking (Rein and Schön, 1977, 1993, 1994), on framing and re-framing policy problems. Rather than accepting the problem-solving mode of policymaking, they propose to reflect on the problem as it appears, to state and re-state a problem. Questions and inquiry are essential in this effort.[3] Rein and Schön define a frame as 'a perspective from which an amorphous, ill-defined, problematic situation can be made sense of and acted on' (Rein and Schön 1993). Importantly, Rein and Schön

---

3   Schön's work in this area can be seen as an expansion on his work on the reflective practitioner (Schön 1983). *The Reflective Practitioner* has made an impact in management and organization studies and is now beginning to make inroads in public management.

talk about situations, not isolated problems. But a policy statement does not only make sense of an amorphous, ill-defined and problematic situation, it also frames the possibilities for any design that follows. This framing links the design of policies with the design of the products and services through which the policy comes alive and is implemented. It also means that the design of public services does not begin at the implementation stage. The design of public services starts already at the policymaking stage because policies effectively establish the criteria and the framework that make specific products and services possible. Policymaking and policy implementation therefore pose fundamental and connected design problems and are not disconnected design activities. Moreover, different design practices, design principles and design methods can lead to different kinds of policies.

The moment we link policy implementation and policymaking with the products and services that people actually experience, the human experience moves into the foreground. Human experiences can guide our questions and inquiries into ill-defined and problematic situations that we encounter in policy design. We might turn to human experience to guide '... the controlled or directed transformation of an indeterminate situation into one that is so determinate in its constituent distinctions and relations as to convert the elements of the original situation into a unified whole' (Dewey 1938).

This definition of inquiry by John Dewey provides a rationale and a roadmap for policymaking as designing, for connecting policymaking with policy implementation. Policymaking as designing adds two important elements to the current problem-solving mode: 1) the ability to inquire into *situations*; and 2) to explore what makes them problematic for people. In other words, policymaking as designing begins with an inquiry, not with a problem. The aim is to arrive at policies that are meaningful, useful and usable to people and society. The current problem-solving approach to policy design does not support this kind of inquiry. This has not gone unnoticed by researchers in public administration (Shields 1998) and in public policy (Forester 1993; Sanderson 2002). Likewise, the artificial separation of policymaking from policy implementation has been identified as an obstacle to policy implementation (Eppel et al. 2011) and as one of the causes that disconnect policymakers from frontline workers (Adebowale et al. 2009).

Policymaking and Human-centred Design

The role of human-centred design in policymaking is just beginning to receive attention. Human-centred design is about first principles of human existence, such as human rights and human dignity (Buchanan 2001). In human-centred design, symbols, things, interactions and systems (in the broadest sense) are in relationships with people but they also mediate and shape how people do and can relate to each other (Buchanan 1995). For this reason, design assumes an important role in our everyday lives, in our organizations and in our society. What, why and how we communicate, build or interact and what, why and how we organize these communications, things and interfaces into systems that work well for individual people and the collective are central concerns. Transposed onto the public sector, human-centred design offers a way to assess our design successes and failures along human dimensions: Are we achieving the kinds of human environments and human experiences we are striving for? Do our products help us fulfil our policy intents and organizational purposes?[4] And if not, how could they? Through designing, we can effect change: changes in services, changes in organizations, changes in the way we think about a problem.

For policymakers and public organizations alike, human-centred design is a mandate, not an option. The design concepts, design methods and design practices we employ in the design of policies and their implementations have consequences for millions of people. Despite this mandate, civil servants seldom receive design education that is relevant to their specific line of work. In fact, government organizations that strive to develop their design capabilities in human-centred design are left on their own to develop internal educational programs.[5] Rare is the policymaker or public manager who is given opportunities to reflect on their own design concepts, their own design practices and methods and to develop new design skills that embrace methods such as inquiry, user research, co-design and prototyping.

These methods and design skills can help us arrive at more citizen-centric policies and services while improving the efficiencies in the public sector in a time when policymakers and policy implementers have to engage and enable people like never before. They have to change their internal organization's design processes to arrive at products and services that reach the right people in the right places at the right time and in the format these people can access, use and understand. But they also have to find ways to change their organizational structures, mindsets and capabilities to do so. Human-centred design practices, design concepts and design methods can support these efforts. With its systemic, integrative approach, human-centred design allows us to overcome the weaknesses of the problem-solving approach. Kevin Lynch (1965) raises the hope that policies might achieve more humanizing outcomes if they were to start with imaginative explorations through which new, more suitable and sustainable policies can be discovered. How so becomes more obvious when we contrast the problem-solving approach with a human-centred design approach in Table 4.1.

Table 4.1   Approaches to problem-solving and human-centred design

Problem-solving Approach	Human-centred design Approach
Concerned with isolated problems.	Concerned with indeterminate situations.
One-directional, linear, top down, though with feedback loops.	Works simultaneously in several directions, neither top-down nor bottom-up but rather crisscrossing through an organizational system (Junginger 2009), thereby linking its elements.
Frames policymaking as a response mechanism: policymakers passively wait for a problem to appear and then respond, promoting reactive rather than pro-active policy design. Allows predominantly for discovery and selection of already existing alternatives.	Envisions futures and develops scenarios to bring them to live. Begins with inquiry, includes discovery, selection but also promotes invention.

---

4   'A' product in this context stands for the outcome of a human design effort. Therefore, organizations and policies, too, are treated and discussed as products.

5   Public innovation labs have emerged as major places for design education in the public sector. Examples include The Lab by the US Office of Personnel Management and the cross-ministerial research unit Mindlab in Denmark. The Australian Tax Office conducted a series of in-house seminars on human-centred design for its staff in the 1990s.

Fragments the design process. Treats policymaking as one design activity: the one that results in a first designed product, the policy, and policy implementation as another.	Integrates the different design efforts through participatory, collaborative and co-designing methods that inquire into all elements of a system (cf: Sanders and Stappers 2008; Bason 2010).
Presents policymaking as an abstract exercise built around decision-making but does not consider the experiences and realities of people concerned by the policy – citizens, external stakeholders, public employees.	Includes and involves people to learn about issues and opportunities for improvement of a particular situation. Civil servants, ordinary citizens, external stakeholders, public managers and others relevant to a particular situation, product or service often participate, collaborate and co-create towards a solution.
Values design only for its problem-solving ability and as an instrument for policy implementation.	Covers the whole range of designing, which includes inquiry, discovery and invention.
Takes policy design out of its context and suggests a policy problem can be treated in isolation.	Situates and integrates the design of policies and policymaking in organizational life but also in the human experience of everyday people.
Relies on abstract data drawn from the past.	Relies on actual and present human experiences.

Conditions for Reframing Policymaking as Designing

If we were to approach the development of a policy as a design challenge rather than a problem-solving task, we would have a chance to transform an ill-defined or in-determinate situation and all its constituent elements into a unified whole. We would be able to apply design not only to problem-solving tasks but also to generate and envision new and desirable futures and policies. And besides, because design as problem-solving remains useful and beneficial, we would become better at knowing in which situations problem-solving is a good approach and in which we might begin an inquiry to generate new possibilities and to invent new futures. This would aid policymakers in envisioning desirable futures and enable them to develop strategies to realize these visions – product for product, service for service. We could be analytical by examining what outcomes we can achieve through human-centred design approaches and which ones are out of reach. We would be able to reflect on our current design approaches and our current understanding of design. We could better deal with unintended outcomes, as the design approach incorporates testing and failing as integral parts of the process and thus embraces unintended consequences. We are just at the beginning of understanding the implications of policymaking as designing. However, we already know that the following factors facilitate a shift towards policymaking as designing:

1. Acknowledging that design does not just happen, nor do policies just come into being. It is people who take actions, make decisions and who do involved in these design processes.

2. Recognition by policymakers and others involved in the policy cycle that they are already making use of specific design concepts and are applying particular design methods and design practices, even if they are not aware of them. This is an area where design educators and design researchers have to develop materials, visualizations and provide examples.

3. Research into organizational design practices relevant to public organizations: This is a new area of research into the ways in which organizations engage with designing. How do public organizations engage with design? What possibilities do they have? What practices do we find?[6]

4. Encouraging and enabling people involved in policy design to engage with each other and to work in cross-ministerial, cross-agency teams: policymakers with policy implementers, policy implementers with citizens, citizens with policymakers, and vice versa. This is akin to a license to co-design, co-create and co-produce but requires new skills and new capabilities. Working in such a constellation and pursuing these activities means that designing can avoid the power games of being implemented top-down or bottom-up. Rather designing takes place across different departments, involves different levels of the organization and in this process realigns structures and processes. In visual terms, we can think of designing as weaving together the different organizational elements (Junginger 2009).

5. Empathizing with people whose lives will be touched in one way or another by a policy, be it as a private citizen or as a public employee. This requires tools and methods to experience what everyday citizens and ordinary employees struggle with. Design researchers and design educators have paid much attention to 'end-users', that is, the citizen in the public sector. However, we also need to find ways to empathize with civil servants, frontline workers and other members in the organization.

6. Overcoming the notion that designing is synonymous with problem-solving: to design is to envision desirable futures and to develop products and services through which this desirable future can become reality. This depends on our ability to inquire and raise questions not to close off paths by providing immediate answers.

7. To develop and advance design methods and design practices. Policymaking as designing promotes the idea that policymaking is iterative and informed by trial and errors.

In the public sector, these conditions often still need to be created. Currently, it is public innovation labs that seek to prepare the grounds for human-centred design approaches. Public innovation labs are research labs within national or municipal government agencies that are set up to change both the mindset and the practices of identifying problems and of developing solutions within their agencies. They are heavily influenced by design thinking, design methods and especially by the ideas around human-centred design. Public innovation labs may benefit from a new crop of civil servants who will enter into public offices over the coming years. This generation is equipped with new skills that include language and computer proficiencies and comfort with social media and the networked society. These public workers have little in common

---

6   I have developed an organizational engagement matrix in another paper. The matrix is based on three approaches public organizations can choose to pursue: designing for, designing with or designing by citizens.

with 'organization men' (Whyte 1978). Instead, these men and women will have grown up with a critical view of hierarchies and a great respect for people who act and make. They will have learned to be risk-takers early on in ways their predecessors could not even think of. The backgrounds of these new policymakers and public managers will be diverse and we may find in one government office, an anthropologist next to a lawyer, next to a designer, next to a political scientist and an economist. In addition, many of these new incoming civil servants will have previously worked in private businesses. They will be prepared for teamwork and have good communication skills. And they will insist on questioning and on inquiring into how we can enhance human living through appropriate and improved public services. This skill set also means that they will bring new design approaches with them – some knowingly, some unwittingly.

If we are indeed seeking to change the way we go about policymaking and policy implementation, it is our task and challenge as design educators and design researchers to support these new public managers and the new policymakers. We need to develop appropriate and suitable curricula for design education in the public sector. In 1960, Bruce Archer insisted that there is a place for design in management education. Not only is management a key area in the public sector, it is increasingly obvious that design education would also benefit public affairs. Design management has done much for business organizations but remains to be more widely used in public organizations. We still need to develop practical tools and methods for the public design manager and ask core questions like: How is design to be managed in a public organization? What is the role and task of a design manager in that realm?[7] We are in need of theoretical work that studies where designing takes place in the public sector, where it is being done when, by whom and for what purpose. We need to make essential design education accessible to students in policymaking and in public management. If human-centred design is a core requirement for people we leave in charge with designing the policies, products and services that affect the way we live as individuals and as a society, we should become better in preparing them for these roles. The aim of design education in the public sector would not be to turn civil servants into designers. The aim would be to raise the awareness of their own design activities and to familiarize them with design methods and concepts that are useful, usable and meaningful in their work.

Concluding Thoughts

This chapter demonstrates the importance of design research and design education in the public sector. I have shown how problem-solving drives policy design and why we should move from policymaking as problem-solving towards policymaking as designing. Reframing policymaking as designing sheds light on many already ongoing design activities and design practices in the public sector, that once revealed and in the open, can then be discussed and, if necessary, changed. Wood (1992, cited in Taylor 2011), for example, has pointed out that the design of policy texts, which serve a crucial role in the policymaking process, have a tendency to 'embody the authors' prejudices, biases and partialities' (Wood 1992, p. 24). In an environment too often driven by the ideas and concepts of 'objective' decision-making, Taylor felt the need to point out that 'the objectivity of a text stands in an inverse relationship to its perceived subjectivity' and the 'actual decision-maker can hide behind the text' (Taylor 2011).

---

7   This is also a call on researchers in design management to move into public design management.

In other words, such policy texts close off any questions, as they present themselves as objective facts. Policymaking as designing means to visualize and articulate current design practices, to reflect and question their current assumptions and our design approaches.

To achieve this comprehensive style, we need to study and reflect on the strengths and weaknesses of design approaches in the public sector. Although there is agreement that human-centred design is not an option but rather a mandate in the public sector, design education for policymakers, policy implementers and public managers is rare. Public innovation labs can fill this educational gap on a local level. Their presence and their actions are indicative of the awareness of human-centred design in the public sector and more specifically, in government. But we cannot possibly expect them to stem the necessary education and research on a macro level.

Not the least owing to the work of public innovation labs, we can now state with more certainty than ever that when a policy problem concerns social innovation or innovation of governance and the transformation of the public sector, responsive problem-solving approaches cannot reach these objectives. New approaches need to be generated, envisioned and pursued proactively to give shape to future policies and to desirable social outcomes. They pose new challenges for policymakers and policy implementers to get their hands and heads around but they also pose challenges for the rapidly growing field of design theory and design practice. Both fields can benefit from each other by developing these areas academically and practically in close collaboration.

Public innovation labs offer yet another clue that design does not just happen in design studios where design students experiment and prototype. Design is not just relevant to innovation in the private business. Instead, a consciousness and an awareness has arisen that designing is a core organizational activity, necessary to develop and to deliver products and services that make an organization relevant, useful, usable and at times desirable. Public organizations in particular are among the most prolific design places we can think of, generating products and services that often shape the lives of millions of people. From this perspective, the Howlett and Ramesh policy cycle clarifies why so many professional designers, especially service designers, are confused about their contribution to public design and to the design of policies. As part of the policy cycle, they are caught in promoting and supporting an overall fragmented design approach when they enter as problem-solvers at the policy implementation level. Their design activities in policy implementation are not to be confused with actual policy design (Woodham 2010).

In concluding this chapter, I feel a need to state that I am not calling on policymakers and public managers to abandon 'problem-solving design' in policymaking and in policy implementation. There is a rationale, a place and a role for design as a problem-solving activity. Many of the day-to-day problems in the public realm are served well with this design approach. What I am asking for is a critical reflection to understand when a human-centred design approach offers a path to improvement and innovation. And while politics will always interfere, the human experience remains central to politics and policy design (Chandehoke 2003):

> *Politics is a two-way activity ranging from what is experienced into how it is represented in the form of the expressed, and from what is expressed into an interpretation of what is experienced. But politics is also a plural activity inasmuch as it negotiates between different and contested forms of the expressive. Out of the web of contestation we derive a sense of what people want and need, desire and yearn for.*

Acknowledgements

This chapter has been a work in progress and I am particularly grateful to comments of earlier versions of this paper by Jesper Christiansen, Laura Bunt, Eva Sørensen and Arnand Hatchuel.

References

Adebowale, O. and Starkey, K. (2009). *Engagement and Aspiration–Reconnecting Policymaking with Frontline Professionals*. Sunningdale Institute Report for the UK Cabinet, March 2009.

Archer, L.B. (1960). A Place for Design in Management Education? *Design Journal* 220: 38–43.

Archer, L.B. (1967). Design Management. *Management Decision*, Vol. 1 (4): 47–51.

Bason, C. 2010. *Leading Public Sector Innovation: Co-creating for a Better Society*. Bristol, UK: Policy Press.

Buchanan, R. (1995). Rhetoric, Humanism and Design. In R. Buchanan and V. Margolin (eds), 1995, *Discovering Design: Explorations in Design Studies*. Chicago: University of Chicago Press. 23–66.

Buchanan, R. (2001). Human Dignity and Human Rights: Thoughts on the Principles of Human-centred Design. *Design Issues*, Summer 2001, Vol. 17(3): 35–9.

Buchanan, R. (2004). Interaction Pathways to Organizational Life. In R. Bolland and F. Collopy, *Managing as Designing*. Palo Alto, CA: Stanford University Press.

Chandhoke, N. (2003). Governance and the Pluralisation of the State: Implications for Democratic Citizenship. *Economic and Political Weekly*, Vol. 38, No. 28 (Jul. 12–18, 2003): 2957–68.

Cross, N. (1992). *Research and Design-Thinking*. Delft: Delft University Press.

Dewey, J. (1938). *Pattern of Inquiry, in Theory of Logic*. New York: Holt, Rinehart & Winston. 101–19.

Eppel, E., Turner, D. and Wolf, A. (2011). Future State 2–Working Paper 11/04. Institute of Policy Studies, School of Government Victoria University of Wellington, New Zealand, June 2011.

Fisher, T. (2009). Needed: Design in the Public Interest, http://chronicle.com, Section: *The Chronicle Review*, Vol. 55, Issue 34: B6.

Gorb, P. (2011). Foreword in R. Cooper, S. Junginger and T. Lockwood (eds), *The Handbook of Design Management*. Oxford: Berg Press.

Gorb, P. and Schneider, E. (1988). Design Talks, UK Design Council, January 1, 1988.

Forester, J. (1993). *Critical Theory, Public Policy, and Planning Practice: Toward a Critical Pragmatism*. New York: State University of New York Press.

Hill, M. and Hupe, P. (2009). *Implementing Public Policy* (2nd edn). London: Sage.

Howlett, M. and Ramesh, M. (2003). *Studying Public Policy* (2nd edn). Oxford: Oxford University Press.

Junginger, S. (2008). Product Development as a Vehicle for Organizational Change. *Design Issues*, 24(1): 26–35.

Junginger, S. (2009). Designing from the Outside In: The Key to Organizational Change? *Conference Proceedings of the 8th Conference of the European Academy of Design, Aberdeen, Scotland*.

Lynch, K. (1965). The City Sense and City Design. *Design Issues*, reprint 2000, reprinted from *Scientific American*, 213(3): 209–14.

Marlin, W. (1975). The Critic's Eye. *Design Quarterly*, No. 94/95, Second Federal Design Assembly: The Design Reality (1975): 21–2.

Rein, M. and Schön, D. (1977). Problem Setting in Policy Research. In C.H. Weiss (ed.), *Using Social Research in Public Policy Making*. Lexington, MA: Lexington Books. 235–51.

Rein, M. and Schön, D. (1993). Reframing Policy Discourse, in F. Fischer and J. Forester (eds), *The Argumentative Turn in Policy Analysis and Planning*. Durham, NC: Duke University Press, 1993. 145–66.

Rein, M. and Schön, D. (1994). *Reframing: Controversy and Design in Policy Practice*. New York: Basic Books.

Sahni, N.R., Wessel, M. and Christensen, C.M. (2013). Unleashing Breakthrough Innovations in Government. *Stanford Social Innovation Review*, Summer 2013, online: http://www.ssir.org.

Sanders, E and Stappers, P.J. (2008). Co-creation and the New Landscapes of Design. *Co-Design*, Vol. 4(1): 5–18.

Sanderson, I. (2002). Evaluation, Policy Learning and Evidence-Based Policy Making. *Public Administration*, 80: 1–22.

Schön, D. (1983). *The Reflective Practitioner. How Professionals Think in Action*. London: Temple Smith.

Schön, D. (1987). *Educating the Reflective Practitioner*. San Francisco: Jossey-Bass.

Shields, P. (1998). Pragmatism as Philosophy of Science: A tool for Public Administration. *Research in Public Administration*, Vol. 4: 195–225.

Simon, H.A. (1969). *The Sciences of the Artificial*. Cambridge, MA: MIT Press.

Taylor, J.R. (2011). Organization as an (imbricated) Configuring of Transactions. *Organization Studies*, 32(9): 1273–94.

Woodham, J. (2010). Formulating National Design Policies in the United States: Recycling the 'Emperor's New Clothes?' *Design Issues*, Vol. 26(2) Spring 2010: 27–46.

Whyte, William, H. (1958). *The Organization Man*. New York: Simon & Schuster.

BANNY BANERJEE

Innovating Large-scale Transformations

A Case for New Approaches to Scaled Transformations

We have arrived at a critical juncture in the history of civilization. Traditional objectives such as providing adequate services and means for a civic society to thrive and now being challenged to do so with more limited means. In addition to already challenging problems at every level, we have entered an era with grave questions regarding the very existence of the civilization as we know it. On one hand we have pressing issues such as the quality of healthcare, education and maintaining economic growth with ever-increasing difficulty as a result of greater demands being made with fewer resources. On the other hand, these immediate targets are couched within larger '*bedrock*' issues such as the future of social equity, food, water, energy, biodiversity and climate stability. The challenges represent a '*tragedy of the commons*'[1] playing out at a grand scale, with the larger challenges being the cumulative outcomes of our patterns of growth, including our vast population. It is imperative that these global challenges receive international commitment, but they compete with the more localized and immediate crises. There exists a profound conflict between long term and short term issues which behoves us to pose the question: *How do we simultaneously address urgent short term issues as well as the more longer term critical challenges?* Implicit in the question is another more fundamental question: *How to address challenges that are simultaneously massive, integrated, pressing, and highly complex that are a natural result of our history, and the interaction between our human and natural systems?*

The innovation and policy world not only has to gain institutional expertise at addressing *wicked problems*[2,3] but also must grow the capability to deal with *super-wicked* problems.[4] Super-wicked problems have most notably the additional attributes of massive scale, urgency and complex interactions between many subsystems that are themselves wicked problems. A 'Grand Challenge' such as ensuring global water security certainly transcends our current disciplinary limitations but the real difficulty lies in the possibility that the nature of these challenges are emblematic of deeply entrenched

1   G. Hardin, The Tragedy of the Commons. *Science* (AAAS) 162 (3859) (1968): 12438. DOI:10.1126/science.162.3859.1243 (1968-12-13).
2   C. West Churchman, Wicked Problems. *Management Science* 14:4 (1967). Guest Editorial by W.J. Rittel Horst and M. Melvin.
3   Webber, M. Dilemmas in a general theory of planning. *Policy Sciences* 4:2 (1973), 155–69. DOI: 10.1007/BF01405730.
4   Kelly Levin, Benjamin Cashore, Steven Bernstein and Graeme Auld, Overcoming the tragedy of super wicked problems: constraining our future selves to ameliorate global climate change. *Policy Science* Springer 45 (2012): 123–52.

flaws in our institutional structures, our underlying theories, definitions of success and our inability to act.

'Every system is perfectly designed to get the outcomes it gets' is a quote attributed to Dr. Paul Batalden, Professor Emeritus of Dartmouth Institute. If we look at some critical global targets, we see a massive gap between the kinds of targets that we would desire and the ones that our current systems seemed to be designed to produce.

One way to examine the integrity of our current systems is to list some critical targets against our chances of meeting them. Table 5.1 presents a global scorecard against 2030 projections, keeping in mind that by that time we will have added close to another billion people to the planet.

Table 5.1   Critical sustainability targets

Issue	Confidence level in meeting challenge
40% more freshwater needed	Low
45–50% more food needed	Low
39–45% more energy needed	Low
50% reduction in CO2 needed	Low
700M people under poverty line and a much larger number in extreme social and financial inequity	Low
Mass extinction: 3–4 orders of magnitude higher extinction rates compared to normal	Practically nil
Preventing climate change from drastically affecting populations and biomes dependent on its relative stability	Extremely low

There is much debate in the scientific community about the exact magnitude of the rates of decline and the projected shortfalls in resources. But what is clear from their orders of magnitude is that these targets and the inter-relatedness between them (such as the unfortunate relationship between higher energy demand and reduction in green house gas emissions) present a class of challenge that we have never had to face in such aggressive time frames. Our dominant disciplines and institutions are caught flat-footed in the face of such immense challenges. In addition, there has been a marked lack of political will and ability to act while precious years slip by and sharply declining conditions become that much worse.

While these issues listed are a sampling of the 'grand challenges', the triple attributes of scale, complexity and urgency can be found in any city, regional or national level issue. The inadequacy of our current thinking and toolsets to create systemic change are just as pronounced at the local levels as at global levels. For example, many cities would wish to reduce their crime rates, reduce their carbon footprints or create more employment but are stymied by decision gridlock, incremental policies, an absence of a systems view that is broad enough, and resistance to change at every level.

This class of challenge demands a much higher degree of innovation in order to leverage limited resources. For any intervention to have any degree of success, it is first necessary to make sure we understand that there are different regimes in innovation challenges and it is important to match innovation techniques to the type of challenge being addressed. The following are different types of innovation challenges organized in three different classes.

Class A: Implementation or Adaptation Type Problems

Type 1: Known and bounded problems with proven solutions. For example, developing an online interface for making an appointment with your doctor.

Type 2: Open-ended known problems with implementation of known solution archetypes. An example might be limiting traffic in downtowns through zoning and expensive limited time parking.

Type 3: Semi-familiar problems with solutions adapted and extended from existing solution sets, for example, meeting the water challenge in developing countries with distributed installation of hand-cranked bore wells, water purification education and water co-operatives.

Class B: Open-ended Medium-scale Design Challenges

Type 4: Pure technology or business or policy based interventions that are directed at specific needs, such as developing biofuel technology to offset petroleum or a consumer goods corporation aiming at market expansion or a public health policy intervention related to mandatory and subsidized health insurance.

Type 5: Closing system gaps through human-centred design and creative optimization. (Note: most systems are sub-optimal in their understanding of the human factor and deserve optimization on that front alone.) For example, reducing the long waits at the Department of Motor Vehicles (the agency that issues drivers licences) through online services, advanced scheduling, automated form filling and pre-emptive opt-out direct online billing. Another example is designing the process of transition between nurse shifts in a hospital in a manner that prevents communication gaps leading to preventable mis-medication and lapses in post-surgery care

Type 6: Using Human Centred Design to shape experiences and *pathways* through a system (service design tends to make use of this approach). An example might be designing the entire customer journey for a public transport initiative that takes into account, bad weather, cultural and language barriers for visitors, picking children up from day-care, buying groceries on the way home and also taking into account occasional personal journeys such as going to the airport with bags, meeting friends for a hike over the weekend or returning home from a night shift in a factory located in a crime-ridden neighbourhood.

Class C: Scaled Transformation Challenges

Type 7: Designing new system and scaling paradigms for unfamiliar and scaled problems, for example, reducing the energy footprint of an entire nation by a significant percentage through a combination of approaches.

Type 8: Transforming the behaviour, roles and the relationships of the constituent stakeholders within the ecosystem, including non-human elements such as resource flows and natural systems, for example, an intervention to the food security problem by simultaneous engagement by banks, government, agro industry, farmers, small business enterprise, telecom companies and non-profit companies.

Type 9: Transforming the behaviour, outcomes and trajectories of the larger ecosystem, for example, changing the way in which our institutions, civic societies, industry and government work so as to get entirely new trajectories regarding social, economic and environmental issues, while building a more resilient, more shock resistant future.

Class A requires innovation and design, but in bounded ways. *Class B* problems require a deeper understanding of the underlying human experiences and unmet needs, and also taking a systems point of view. *Class C* problems require ecosystem design, use all the methodologies from the other two classes, but are fundamentally predicated on an ecosystem behaviour point of view, following a more nuanced and 'ecosystem acupuncture' based innovation processes.

From a design taxonomy perspective, Richard Buchanan's[5] model depicts four orders of design activity:

1. Design of visual and symbolic expression;

2. Design of physical objects: tangible objects that meet functional or aesthetic demands;

3. Design of interactions and experiences;

4. Design of systems and pathways through a system.

A Fifth Order of Design

With each order, the tools and skills in the lower order are employed towards the higher order objective. These four models suffice for Class A and B. But Class C implies a fifth order, namely, *Design of Large-Scale Transformations*. It takes into account the larger implications, scale and speed of diffusion. The *'fifth order of design'* is conceptualized as an applied trans-disciplinary field that establishes a new epistemology and a set of processes. Given the multi-dimensional nature of scaled challenges, these new approaches and tools can only be arrived at through the strategic combination of different disciplines and agencies in order to create new paradigms necessary for scaled impact.

Discipline-centered Approaches versus Scaled Challenges

While the characterization of complex phenomena such as social systems or economic systems have been the ambit of disciplines for centuries, we are still left with a critical gap in our ability to create balanced, sustainable systems that give us satisfactory outcomes.

Our disciplines such as economics, law and engineering along with our government administration systems have organized themselves in silos in order to give themselves focus, but in doing so have acquired two important biases. The first bias has to do with the inevitable perceptual lens that comes with a disciplinary focus. The model

---

5   Richard Buchanan, Education and Professional Practice in Design. *Design Issues* 14:2 (1998): 63–6.

of 'lens' was originally proposed by Egon Brunswik and later developed by Kenneth Hammond[6] among others and is an important factor to understand varying perceptual fields and decision biases. For example, the department of taxation might be primarily concerned with taxes, and the department of health wears blinders about issues related to health. The singular focus, although understandable in order to conduct day-to-day business, creates a perceptual bias for most disciplines, wherein experts from a given discipline see the world in terms of factors that concern them and relatively oblivious to the others. Information systems experts see the world in terms of information flows, and a sociologist will see social phenomena. These disciplines work in silos with thick walls that impede communication across silos, and concern themselves mainly with questions that tend to be framed in narrower and narrower terms), thus creating a culture of hyper-specialization. Each discipline or agency looks at the world through their perceptual lens and operates within the rules of the silo. However, this profound lack of integrative thinking has a critical shortcoming when it comes to scaled challenges. Large-scale challenges are interlaced, with interdependencies *that have no respect for disciplinary silos*. This class of challenges belong to (Class C), and hence they need to be co-created by trans-disciplinary teams, working with holistic pluralistic perspectives and adopting philosophical frames of anti-reductionism, taking care to avoid overly deterministic and simplistic solutions (Figure 5.1).

Figure 5.1   A visual metaphor of a complex interrelated challenge viewed through the discrete perceptual lenses of different disciplines, all acting within silos

---

6   Kenneth R. Hammond, *Human Judgment and Social Policy: Irreducible uncertainly, inevitable error, unavoidable injustice* (New York: Oxford University Press, 2000).

Horizontal and Vertical Co-creation

Co-creation involves engaging members of different disciplines or agencies to create the solution together, rather than breaking the problem down and having them create piecemeal solutions. Co-creation is a universe unto itself and there are many nuanced aspects that drive successful co-creation. Horizontal co-creation refers to co-creation across disciplines or agencies on an equal footing regarding power or sphere of influence (Figure 5.2). A ministry of economic affairs creating solutions together with the ministry of education would constitute horizontal co-creation, as would be a case with a behavioural scientist working with an interaction designer. Vertical co-creation, however, involves members representing different power positions or different operational levels engaging in co-creation. In a public sector innovation initiative, an example of vertical co-creation might be policymakers co-creating with city officials, public servants who provide services and citizens.

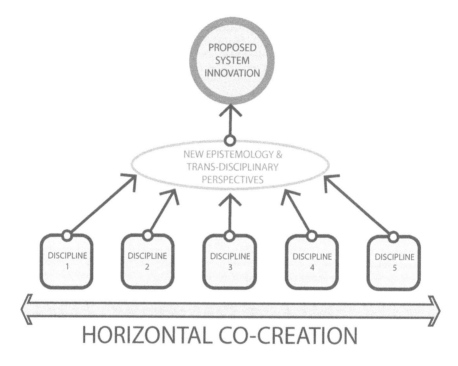

Figure 5.2   Co-creation across disciplinary boundaries allows for the creation of new perspectives that are informed by the diverse insights and make for more holistic, integrated solutions.

Horizontal co-creation is essential in harnessing the insights from a diversity of disciplines in designing holistic, cohesive interventions that outperform normative techniques while vertical co-creation ensures that top down strategy is matched with operational and contextual realities of the field and the conditions in which the initiative will be implemented. The combination of horizontal and vertical co-creation increases the odds of achieving integrative solutions that have broad impact and yet have potential failure modes identified before they're implemented at scale. Apart from the solutions being holistic and integrative, one of the key advantages to co-creation is the engagement of diverse parties and the various stakeholders buying into the initiative with an increased level of ownership and motivation (Figures 5.3 and 5.4).

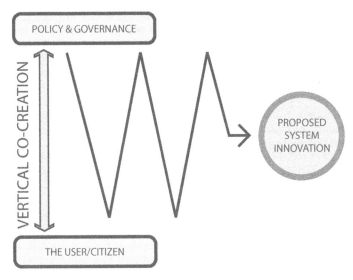

Figure 5.3   Vertical co-creation combining top-down and bottom-up thinking enables high-level strategic considerations to be fused with on-the-ground realities, making the users a part of generating the solution.

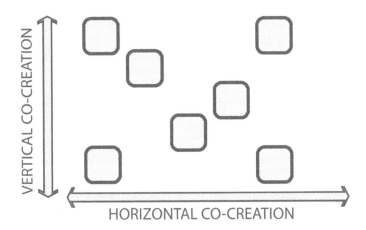

Figure 5.4   Vertical co-creation when combined with horizontal co-creation can yield deep transformations to integrated challenges, where solutions have to be designed with leveraged use of different perspectives and knowledge sets.

Dealing with the Integrated Challenge Canvas

Complexity requires that we rethink the way we approach problems. In the words of Herbert Simon,

> We have learned very well that many of the systems that we are trying to deal with in our contemporary science and engineering are very complex indeed. They are so complex that it is not obvious that the powerful tricks and procedures that served us for four centuries or more in the development of modern science and engineering will enable us to understand and deal with them.[7]

If all of us are mired in tunnel vision of our own agencies and disciplines, then how are we to escape it without losing the power of the hard-won expertise? The answer to this question lies in the notion of trans-disciplinary and trans-agency co-creation.

Trans-disciplinarity is quite different from inter-disciplinarity. A mark of inter-disciplinary or multi-disciplinary activity is that members stay within their respective disciplinary expertise and seek a consensus within intersection of their rubrics. In trans-disciplinary teams, however, the members certainly leverage their disciplinary insights, but transcend their disciplinary roles to engage in the co-creation of new solutions, processes and epistemologies. Successful trans-disciplinary co-creation is akin to a game of soccer, where there might be larger objectives such as scoring more goals than are scored against you, but the game consists of passing the ball back and forth and generating goal-scoring moves, without regard to who scores the goal. Trans-agency is conceptually quite similar, but leveraging the diversity of different agencies in order to co-create combinatorial interventions that are much more powerful than anything a single type of agency would be capable of. An example of this might be the private sector, the public sector and the education sector coming together to create a national innovation policy to solve critical social issues while simultaneously creating an engine for economic growth.

One of the key advantages of a trans-disciplinary system is the disciplinary parallax that is brought about by members from different disciplines looking at a more complex reality from different angles. Each discipline brings its own perceptual lenses, but the collection of perceptual lenses and the rich discourse that ensues gives the team the ability to perceive what lies beyond any single vision. Figure 5.5 depicts a metaphor of an understanding that can only be arrived at through the interpolation of different points of view.

The task lies in understanding the ecosystem behaviour from the diverse set of perspectives. It is important to create a more nuanced understanding through a discourse that simultaneously uncovers root causes, while building theories to explain causalities. This understanding of the behaviour of the ecosystem is the first step towards identifying leverage points and the creation of strategies that would change the behaviour of the ecosystem.

---

7   Herbert A. Simon, *The Sciences of the Artificial* (Cambridge: M.I.T. Press, 1968), 83.

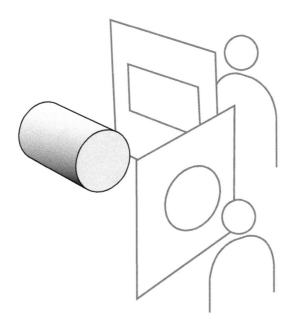

Figure 5.5   A metaphor for disciplinary parallax: the different perceptual lenses embody biases and allow for understanding different phenomena of ecosystem behaviour which, if interpolated, can then lead to a better understanding of the real ecosystem behaviour. The real behavior tends to lie beyond what an individual discipline is capable of perceiving.

Meeting Exponential Problems

Governance systems, policies and regulations have the potential of having broad impact. Similarly, civic societies, corporations and institutions also have the potential for bringing about new outcomes and large-scale impact. Each of these sectors, while containing great potential, is also coupled with inbuilt barriers that impede scaled transformations. The design of new policy, regulatory mechanisms and governance systems tends to be incremental, overly risk averse and slow. The actions of corporations tend not to be directed towards the interest of the commons, and civic societies rarely self-organize in ways to bring about rapid large-scale sustainable transformations. Consequently, the transformations that we have come to expect of our current institutions are slow, incremental and largely ineffectual in the face of continually increasing magnitudes of the challenge.

But if we look at some of the larger challenges such as climate change or population pressure, the future of food, water or energy, they have implicit growth rates that are exponential in nature. Apart from the exponential rates, even a small percentage difference in a large global phenomenon can me a much larger intrinsic number than a large percentage of a more localized problem. Systems, such as our planetary life support systems that have taken eons to build dynamic stability, become more and more fragile and vulnerable as they are subjected to over-exploitation.

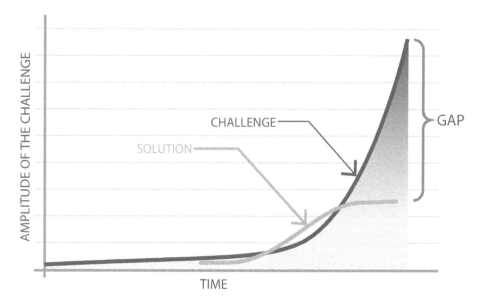

Figure 5.6   Many of our challenges have exponential growth rates due to positive feedback loops, but most solution sets tend to follow S-curves, where the rates flatten out over time. This creates a theoretical gap between problem and solution.

This implies that we must find approaches that can meet exponential problems with exponential solutions. Even an innovative solution, if linear in nature, would ultimately be outstripped by an exponential challenge (Figure 5.6).

A Behavioural Lens

The behaviour of an ecosystem is defined by attributes such as the behaviour of the various stakeholders, their motivations and mental models, the nature of the relationships including the feedback loops, the resource flows, the extrinsic or contextual conditions and the paradigms within which the system operates. Looking at a system through a behaviour lens allows us to perceive the causal pathways that lead to patterns of system behaviour, and eventually the outcomes and trajectories of the system. Similarly, looking at the stakeholder through a behavioural lens gives us a nuanced view of not just the forces that shape that behaviour, but also the motivations, cultural barriers, opportunities and leverage points that could change the behaviour.

This is particularly significant since behaviour is often where best-laid plans get compromised. Behaviour change is considered difficult to achieve, and yet this disbelief is contradicted by the rate at which populations adopt new technology, or the speed with which new social norms such as being active in digital networks are formed. Behaviour change can be far less expensive and rapid than infrastructural changes. A matter of great significance is that behaviour change allows us to meet challenges from *both the demand and supply side of the equation*. Many of our grand challenges can't just be met by supply side innovations, and hence behaviour change interventions hold great promise.

Ethnography techniques used in the Design Thinking process gives us deep insights about the human issues playing out including inefficiencies in the system, underlying motivations or unmet needs. Insights from behavioural sciences such as cognitive psychology, social psychology, behavioural economics and neuroeconomics gives us a lens that enables not only the parsing of behaviour in more sophisticated ways, but also in baking in the principles of behaviour change deep into the intervention.

Principles for Scaled Innovation

While any solution has the potential for scaling, it stands to reason that if the desire is to achieve scaled transformation, then the design process would need to aim for such scaled targets. The design process needs to follow a set of principles and heuristics in order to increase the odds of being genuinely transformative. Following is a list of principles that have emerged out of the work being carried out by ChangeLabs. These principles, organized in three loose categories help innovators navigate the ambiguous realm of complex challenges and crafting interventions designed to bring about deep and scaled impact.

1. MINDSET AND PERCEPTUAL LENS

(a) **Scale-mindedness:** Scaled outcomes and solutions can only result from *scale-mindedness*. It is a mindset and perceptual lens that focuses on opportunities for scaled impact. Scale mindedness guides the process towards scaled solutions.

(b) **Potency of leverage points:** Identify higher order leverage points such as the overarching paradigms, goals of the system, the nature of information flows, and gain rates on positive feedback loops.

(c) **Diffusability:** Build the ability for the strategy to diffuse into the innovation, rather than treating diffusion as a post-hoc feature, leveraging network effects, key influencers, mavens and the principles of diffusion.

(d) **Multi-objective goals:** Create multi-objective goals and solutions that take into account the integrated and indivisible nature of complex systems. Holistic solutions achieve holistic results. Piecemeal solutions tend to create unintended problems on some other front or fail to address deeper causal pathways. Multi-objective strategies leverage mutually reinforcing opportunities.

(e) **Agency systems and action repertoire:** Create ways of increasing agency in order to unleash the latent potential of communities, networks and social networks. Creating a visible set of options and actions for communities reduces the imagination gap, and serves to translate intention to action.

(f) **Build resilience:** Create multiple pathways for success; build in redundancy and the capacity for a system to withstand shock and turbulence.

(g) **Build capacity:** Create innovation and transformation capacity in communities and organizations. Design the system for continued innovation.

(h) **Simplicity:** Target simplicity on the far side of complexity. An ounce of good innovation buys ten in implementation savings.

(i)   **Plurality:** Maintain plurality of means and approaches with rapid iterative feedback loops between conceptual framings and testing of prototypes.

2. PROCESS TECHNIQUES

(a)   **Deep human insights:** Understand the underlying human dynamics, the motivational frames, unmet needs, predicaments and cultural norms.

(b)   **Focus on creating new paradigms:** Strive to create new paradigms and replicable models/archetypes that have the capacity to change the norms.

(c)   **Piggyback** on existing infrastructure, systems and behaviour that have already scaled, rather than betting on a small initiative that will have to undergo scaling before they cause widespread impact.

(d)   **Stakeholder relationships:** Modify the relationships between the key stakeholders as well as the resource flows in ways such that the new behaviours and outcomes align with system goals.

(e)   **Behaviour change methods:** Use behavioural interventions to change norms, mental models and patterns of behaviour in rapid time frames. Behavioural changes have the potential of spreading much more rapidly through a population than infrastructure.

(f)   **Demand side interventions:** Transform the demand side of the equation, not just the supply side – this reduces the magnitude of the supply side target and has the effect of getting there faster, while creating new hybrid models for transformation.

(g)   **Positive feedback loops:** Chase exponential problems with exponential solutions. Build in positive feedback loops so that the solution does not get outstripped by the rapidly growing nature of the problem.

(h)   **Multi-agency co-creation:** Surround the problem with engagements from different agencies in order to generate integrated solutions.

3. STRUCTURAL

(a)   **Platforms not just solutions:** Solutions that are designed for specific contexts might fail in a different context. Solutions designed more as universal platforms allow a variety of solutions to be developed that respond to contextual variations and different business models..

(b)   **Technology strategy:** Use technology strategies and platforms to outperform the natural time-constant of change in systems and institutions.

(c)   **Creative business models:** Most scaled challenges tend to work within the constraints of limited economic resources or political will. A creative business model treats the challenge as an opportunity to find elegant ways of creating economic activity to support and accelerate the desired transformation.

(d)   **Create economic complexity[8] and adjacencies for economic growth:** Growth takes place along adjacent paths and interstices, hence

8   César A. Hidalgo and Ricardo Hausmann, The building blocks of economic complexity. *Proc Natl Acad Sci USA* 106:26 (2009): 10570–5. Published online 22 June 2009. doi: 10.1073/pnas.0900943106.

designing for economic complexity, increases the chances of economic growth.

(e) **Measurement and feedback:** Design the right metrics, measurement systems, dashboards, decision systems, early indicators and definitions of outcomes. Drive outcomes towards measurable target outcomes and using measurements to guide the development rather than measuring an after the fact.

(f) **Find distributed solutions to distributed problems:** Often scaled challenges occur at the tertiary ends of a long network of distribution chains, thus increasing the cost of delivery. Distributed challenges require that we seek (and leverage) solutions, such as mobile phones, that are capable of crossing the 'distribution chasm'.

(g) **Multiple pathways and system acupuncture:** Find a collection of interventions that together have a disproportionate integrative effect.

(h) **Clarify higher level goals:** Build the success criteria into the culture of the new system so that the system can learn over time, but maintain higher level objectives that serves as continual compass for decision making.

These principles have guided the innovation in a diverse set of large-scale innovation projects at the ChangeLabs, and have resulted in a process and a set of versatile innovation tools.

ChangeLabs: A Platform for Scaled Transformations

The scientific era gave us departments of science and technology in government, granting agencies for science research, science-based educational programs, R&D labs in industry and an economy enabled by science and technology. We have a new era that ought to create a new set of agencies. The new era defined by massive global challenges suggests the question, *What is the nature of an entity or platform that will generate the thinking, processes, agencies and community to drive scaled transformations in rapid time scales delivering sustainable, manageable and equitable futures.*

ChangeLabs is one such platform designed to be a model that drives the development of a new field of Scaled Transformation, generating the practices that would be used for innovating such impact, and the global community that would shape this field.

ChangeLabs is not just structured as an institution, but a *function* that any organization or institution would naturally have, not unlike accounting or marketing – a function that would concern itself with creating desirable futures and building resilience against turbulent futures.

Currently ChangeLabs is a network with its hub at Stanford University, but we envision this as a network of networks joining similar agencies in the drive to generate powerful approaches to the most pressing challenges of our time. We see ChangeLabs as a *paradigm* to drive a different type of thinking, co-creation and the shaping of initiatives. We expect new processes, new frames for leaderships, organizations, impact, innovation, resource management and multi-objective intervention models to emerge out of such a platform, and we are already seeing early evidence of such models, theories and initiative creation.

A New Field for Scaled Interventions

ChangeLabs is not a just a think tank, but a *think-do tank*, with its focus on bringing impact that will move the needle in the direction of our most pressing challenges. We see this endeavour as the creation of a new field, albeit a *trans-disciplinary* one, crossing many existing silos. This new field that we are calling *Scaled Transformation* would create a capacity for trans-disciplinary co-creation towards challenges where scale, complexity and urgency are the defining attributes. A new field such as this would have to build a cohesive stack of structural layers, that any mature discipline is made up of. The stack of layers would include (a) a value system; (b) ontology; (c) epistemology; (d) an action repertoire; (e) a system of processes; (f) a platform for a cohesive praxis; (g) a method of propagation; (h) infrastructure and tools relevant to the field; and (i) a global community of researchers, thinkers and practitioners.

For this to be successful, there are three fundamental functions that need to be built in any ChangeLabs:

1. A function that continually generates new thinking, theories, models and processes for scaled transformation. (This is to be seen as the supply chain of thinking.)

2. The second function is the practice and incubation of large-scale interventions that the theories can be tested in; processes can be honed, and tried in a 'petri dish' for new theories while going about catalyzing scaled impact.

3. The mechanisms would propagate, accelerate, amplify and multiply the field and the community working towards the creation of this new field.

We have already embarked on the creation of ChangeLabs, and it is remarkable to note how quickly our perceptual lens has shifted from Design Thinking-based processes to a much more sophisticated, nuanced transdisciplinary process that is lending itself to much larger scale, complex challenges and spawning initiatives that are massive in scale.

Designing for Large-scale System Transformation

Agencies and leaders with large spheres of influence need to use processes that take an aggressive stance towards deep transformation of the system behaviour and key outcomes. The process needs to create a co-creative space that engages members and innovators from different disciplines and agencies from various vertical echelons, to look for scaled, multi-objective paradigms and to build in effective ways of implementing at scale. Such processes can be used in shaping, strategizing and implementing *any initiative*, whether or not they are directed towards the grand global challenges. Integrative, future based innovation needs to become commonplace in any context that touches matters of importance.

Each city and region faces systemic challenges that need addressing. Some of them are issues of inefficiency, poor design, and poor implementation or resource shortage. They might manifest themselves as high crime rates, poor education quality, obesity, corruption and tax evasion. The need to address global challenges while dealing with the immediate crises presents a very dynamic canvas on which to innovate.

This chapter does not attempt to go into detail about a scaled innovation process, but we are finding that once the scaled transformation gauntlet is picked up, a powerful set of processes naturally emerge, combining disciplines such as design thinking, behavioural sciences, diffusion theory, resilience theory and system analysis.

In brief, a process designed to bring about large-scale transformation would incorporate the following design activities conducted in iterative cycles with increasing levels of fidelity:

(a)   Creating the preconditions for trans-disciplinary co-creation and engaging of representatives from different sectors.

(b)   Gaining a nuanced understanding of the system behaviour and causal relationships, including the human dynamics, looking at the ecosystem as a multi-stakeholder, multi-dimensional space with causal relationships and flows. An understanding from a historical perspective also gives a deep understanding of the reasons behind the system dynamics.

(c)   A process of synthesis and framing to understand the key phenomena with a strategic view of finding leverage points and transformation modalities.

(d)   The generation of a set of integrated strategies at a high level comprised of strategic framing of the challenges, a theory of scaled transformation and a set of strategic propositions, which if implemented, would carry the theoretical power to change system behaviour and yield the desired outcomes.

(e)   Concept generation around the strategic goals so as to find innovative options that embody the choice of leverage points, theories of transformation and the combination of desired outcomes.

(f)   Co-creating the details of the concepts, turning them into tangible interventions, experiences, roadmaps and pilots.

(g)   Creating the metrics of success, the instrumentation for measurement of indicators of success and the feedback loops to ensure success.

(h)   Communicating the story, the vision, the plan and the roadmap to the additional stakeholders who need to engage within the frames of their own motivations.

(i)   An iterative co-creative path to implementation, with much prototyping, testing of prototyping and strategic re-framing of the intervention and engaging of new stakeholders.

(j)   Building in the scaling mechanism, harnessing the resources and shepherding the scaling, with a keen eye towards tuning it for contextual variations, and emergent phenomena.

Conclusion

Scaled transformation is not just a process; it is a mindset. The human mind perceives what it is looking for, and if we look for scaled, integrated solutions, we will develop the capacity to innovate such solutions. Apart from a responsibility of creating such a capacity in the face of urgent challenges that are seemingly intractable, it is also a tremendous opportunity to develop paradigms that enable new ways of collaborating with the future. If we find better alignment between our models of growth, our institutions structures and the type of scaled outcomes that we would like to see, we would not only have made strides towards addressing some of the confounding challenges, we will have created new platforms for simultaneously addressing social needs, environmental sustainability, economic progress and resilience.

In order for us to have the capacity for such transformations, we need to adopt new processes and create a broad network of platforms that will amplify, diffuse and advance such innovation approaches.

References

Buchanan, Richard (1998). Education and Professional Practice in Design. *Design Issues,* 14:2: 63–6.

Churchman, C. West (1967). Wicked Problems. *Management Science,* 14:4. Guest Editorial by W.J. Rittel Horst and M. Melvin.

Hammond, Kenneth R. (2000). *Human Judgment and Social Policy: Irreducible uncertainly, inevitable error, unavoidable injustice.* New York: Oxford University Press.

Hardin, G. The Tragedy of the Commons. *Science* (AAAS) 162 (3859): 1243–8. doi:10.1126/science.162.3859.1243 (1968-12-13).

Hidalgo, César A. and Hausmann, Ricardo (2009). The building blocks of economic complexity. *Proc Natl Acad Sci USA* 106: 26 (30 June): 10570–75. Published online 22 June 2009. doi:10.1073/pnas.0900943106.

Levin, Kelly, Cashore, Benjamin, Bernstein, Steven and Auld, Graeme (2012). Overcoming the tragedy of super wicked problems: constraining our future selves to ameliorate global climate change. *Policy Science* Spring 45: 123–52.

Simon, Herbert A. (1968). *The Sciences of the Artificial.* Cambridge: M.I.T. Press.

Webber, M. (1973). Dilemmas in a general theory of planning. *Policy Sciences* 4:2: 155–69. doi:10.1007/BF01405730.

MARCO STEINBERG

Strategic Design and the Art of Public Sector Innovation

The viability of nations and communities is being threatened by our inability to innovate on large-scale issues such as healthcare, education or food. The public sector is especially vulnerable as it owns a key role but is ill equipped to respond. A viable public sector is increasingly dependent on its ability to transform itself beyond its traditional administrative mode towards an innovative one. As an innovation and integrative practice, design can help contribute to building a new leadership model to help in this transformation. But to meet its promise, design needs to operate from within government at a strategic level, help provide studios or free zones for strategic improvements and connect new opportunities to impactful delivery through the art of stewardship. This paper examines the emerging practice of strategic design in the public sector on the basis of experiences garnered at Harvard University leading the Stroke Pathways Project during 2005–2008, and in building Sitra's (the Finnish Innovation Fund) Strategic Design capability between 2008 and 2013.

Design is a term associated with the art of shaping products and more recently with shaping services. In this context design and innovation have been closely interconnected, the former being a means to create new and more meaningful product or service innovations. The idea of strategic design is rooted in shaping decision-making and stewarding decisions towards impact.

May 12, 2004. Houston, Texas

My colleague Justin Cook and I are in an elevator at the Texas Medical Center with Dr. James Grotta, Chairman of the Department of Neurology, considered the preeminent stroke care innovator. We were there to observe first hand the realities of delivering stroke care in the field. A week of living stroke around the clock consisted of being on call at the emergency room; riding with ambulance providers; seeing doctors on rounds in the intensive care unit; talking to hospital administrators; meeting with families of patients; and so on. This was part of our fieldwork for the Stroke Pathways Project, an initiative focused on redesigning healthcare care delivery, from cradle to grave. How would you innovate the system from first principles up? This was not a project about process improvement, or improving the efficiency of the current system. Rather it was a project about redesigning our care systems to deliver strategic improvements. Could we radically lower care costs while radically improving outcomes (morbidity and mortality)?

'I am so happy you finally arrived!' Was Dr. Grotta's comment as we rode up in the elevator. 'Why is that ?' was my first reaction. Why would the globally acclaimed stroke expert be interested in the work of designers? 'For most of my life I've tried to build better care delivery systems in the US, only to realize that I have not been trained to do this work. I've been facing a design problem but I am not a designer, I am a doctor.'

The challenges our society face today are, for the most part, complex and interconnected and yet we don't have the institutions, science or practice to deliver the kinds of innovations at their intersection. While we saw a lot of innovation in stroke care, most of it was arguably about process improvement, preoccupied with creating efficiencies within the current structures. It's easier to work within the current logic than to rethink it: after all you have incentives, markets and knowledge domains that are in support of the existing, rather than the impending. As a result a lot of innovation work is actually focused on taking the existing structure or engine and making it a bit leaner, a little cheaper. But, as exemplified by our stroke work, the problem is also increasingly in a public sector engine that is fundamentally flawed as it is incentivized to administer existing processes, rather than rethink its underlying principles. The siloed nature of the sector, its central planning culture and the political aversion to real experimentation all work against modalities of innovation that strive to rethink solutions and systems. And the problem is not limited to sectors where there are established systems, but applies also to emerging ones too. While at Sitra, we led Low2No, a project to help build a sustainable carbon neutral development market in Finland. But to achieve real carbon neutrality one can't focus on energy efficiency, transportation or embodied energy alone. Rather one needs to have the capability to understand how a much broader set of drivers impact the carbon footprint of development. And to believe that this kind of systemic innovation will emerge from within markets is simplistic to say the least. It must emerge from a concerted effort to disrupt the current dynamics towards a new 'whole'. This must be built through purposeful intention – through design. While each ministry, institution or municipality is working on its own piece, Low2no clearly demonstrated that the public sector is fundamentally not structured to deliver strategic improvements on systemic challenges.

The only way to deliver strategic improvements is to re-examine and redesign the drivers that govern health, carbon or any of the principles underpinning most of today's complex issues (Figure 6.1). To do so you need to have the ability to challenge principles, core beliefs and vested interests, all in the pursuit of a more purposefully designed future.

Strategic design in our work at Sitra was about shaping decision-making to see the broader architecture of solutions. While there may be immense innovations in healthcare, it's questionable if healthcare as a whole has improved. In the US where there is arguably an increasing abundance of healthcare innovations, overall health has declined over the last 20 years compared to the leading countries. As such, it's easy to see that a lot of good parts don't make for a great whole. The 'architecture of the solution' is understating the positive sum blueprint of many coordinated efforts. Without it, many good ideas will invariably pull in competing directions, with no positive sum effect.

The challenge of innovating the whole is also evident within the service design practice that is emerging in the public sector. This recent emergence is a very positive development, but left alone it may not help us beyond the current logic of efficiency. If we relegate innovation to service delivery alone, we run the danger that we will improve the wrong solution, or at best create value through efficiency. As such we

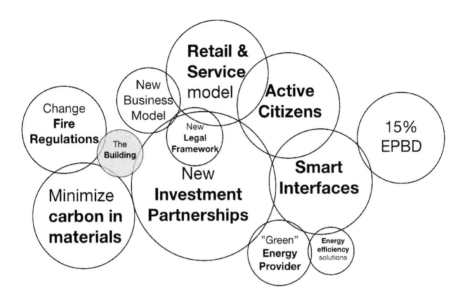

must also ask ourselves are these the services that we need? What really creates overall improvement and what is the architecture of that solution? To innovate on large themes we need to connect the service solutions to the strategic questions.

The work we did at Harvard under the Stroke Pathways project would lead to a radically different blueprint for stroke care. As a result we would also define an approach to innovate systems. This approach would later help us create the 'Studio model' through our HDL (Helsinki Design Lab) initiative at Sitra. The impetus for the studio model was the realization that the Stroke Pathways model, while effective in helping redesign the system, operated at a clock speed that was not commensurate with that of the political cycle. Four years may be a short timeframe in academia but it's an eternity if you want political traction on new ideas. The challenge we took on is to compress those four years into a one-week model. Doing that would position the model to work in support of the current system and its political cycle. But this compression had some tradeoffs, one of them being depth and refinement. A one-week design effort could only go so far, but we also realized that the culture we needed to operate within would be more receptive to a quick process of sketching rather than a prolonged one of absolute definition. Our experience in public sector strategic processes had evidenced that it was the latter that was missing and desperately needed; there were very little, if any quick, integrative, real-time strategy approaches focused on systemic challenges. As such we decided to prepare our model by investing significantly in the upfront 'brief' or problem definition; the team and its selection; and the stewardship of opportunities that emerged from the week towards impact. While we succeeded in compressing a four year process into one week, the week needs to be seen as a 6- to 12-month investment.

In 2010 we ran three studios to help create transformative innovations on three large-scale challenges effecting Finland's future competitiveness. The idea of a studio was to create a space that would allow for a strategic conversation about alternatives to the current path development.

At the core of delivering this kind of innovation are four basic principles:

1. The ability to work across multiple disciplines. The world is a very interconnected place and so are the challenges afflicting it. To identify the principles that govern value one must be able to see how different things affect each other. There are lots of aspects, ranging from interpersonal to disciplinary, that are required in building the necessary continuum between cultures and disciplines. Rarely do innovation challenges fit the boundaries of our existing institutional or knowledge silos.

2. The ability to visualize a new kind of complexity. Most of today's challenges defy words, numbers or traditional reports. The complexity at hand is caught between human behaviour, cultural traits, ideals, values, physical principles and perceived facts. The task is to find the right simplifiers for issues spanning many domains. Minard's famous map of Napoleon's march on Russia (Figure 6.2) is a great example how new modes of visualizations can bring together multiple data points into a coherent, synthetic, simple whole.

3. The ability to work with indeterminacy and relative precision. We are never going to get all the facts on any large-scale challenge that we encounter. The only way to go is to begin to understand the relative nature of things and find ways to work with limited knowledge. Many of the tasks we face require inventing, rather than adopting, solutions. As such our ability to have certainty beforehand may be limited. Also, many of our great challenges evolve at a quick pace, defying our desire to know everything before we act.

4. Capacity to connect the 'think', with the 'do', with the 'achieve'. One of the underlying challenges today is in creating a continuum from inception to implementation. There's a lot of thinking, a significant amount of doing, but it's the achieving that is elusive to all. So how do you build the continuum? This is particularly challenging on issues that have no real precedent or known solution. In the context of strategic design, it's the ability to steward interest, resources and values through the iteration between inception and implementation; between value and impact.

Innovation, by definition, is bringing something to life that does not yet exist. The call for strategic innovation that the studios were responding to was not so much a response to ignorance, but rather of existing logic and our inability to break out of it. As the old adage goes, today's problems won't be solved by the logic that produced them. Thus we consciously realized what a studio needed to do is to create a space free to create new logics, better aligned with today's social/economical/environmental needs. The stewardship model of strategic design in these studios helped us create this 'free zone', paving the way to the creation of alternative pathways for strategic improvements on three critical issues for Finland's well-being: aging, education, sustainability.

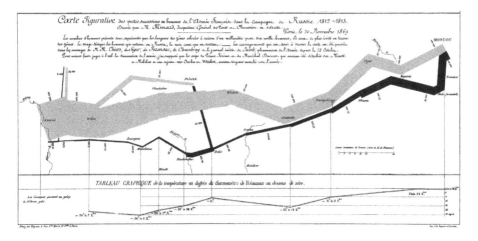

Figure 6.2   Minard's map of Napoleon's march on Russia

What Is a Studio?

A studio is a term borrowed from design education and practice that refers to a space, a team and a process. In our context a studio is a team of eight individuals representing diverse backgrounds who are brought together for a one-week, in-depth exploration of a strategic issue. The objective of a studio is to develop a roadmap to strategic improvements and identify a 'top 10' of implementable opportunities to help get us there. These need not be ideas about how one would redesign an ecosystem around an issue, but rather about identifying the things one can do right now to help us get closer to that end objective. For policymakers one of the biggest challenges of working in an innovation process is 'what do we do next?' A studio is positioned in such a way whereby it maintains its outside status and independence but can use all the resources and access available to the public sector.

The 2010 HDL studios were positioned to address significant questions at the heart of a viable Finland: aging, education and sustainability. They were developed independently of the system, to create a strategic conversation that seemed to be missing from the Finnish landscape. The studio had legitimacy by virtue of Sitra's innovation remit; our task was to use the positive experience of the studio with stakeholders to build legitimacy for further action within the system at large. We recognized that this body of work and capability building was at its infancy, so the immediate objective was to see if the studio could be an effective upfront innovation mechanism. The question of objective and legitimacy will always be critical and should be addressed within the unique circumstances and mechanisms of a given context.

What Are the Keys to a Successful Studio?

There are a lot of factors that determine the success of a studio, but there are four key principles that drive the overall outcome. We call them the four Ps: problem, people, place, process (Figure 6.3). Let's examine each one briefly.

PROBLEM

A studio is predicated on the idea that innovation starts by asking the right questions. As such framing the challenge is critical in setting an innovation agenda and trajectory. About three to six months before the studio week, we prepare a studio challenge brief. This is the problem and opportunity definition document (about 30–50 pages) that the studio team will receive. It's the client brief, so to speak, that includes the key datasets, ideas and insights that are known about the topic at hand. The opportunity space is a brief statement that challenges the studio team to see how this problem could be an opportunity. Both aspects of the brief are to be understood as points of departure, rather project specification, and a way for the studio team to quickly develop their own working hypothesis.

PEOPLE

Defining a challenge is critical, but useless if you don't have the right people to pursue it. We start with the belief that this kind of intense, immersive innovation is best achieved with eight people. We then balance the need to create a good working team dynamic with obtaining deep and representative expertise. We look for people who have deep, unique and complementary expertise. We then look for people who have good social skills (ability to work with others) and the ability to suspend disbelief. The latter is especially important with people who have a lot of knowledge about a particular issue in that they may understand things too well to want to entertain other realities. Finally we look to balance the studio in terms of demographics; age, geography and gender. Our first studios had six foreign members – because outsiders will touch all the taboos and bring other reference models that will broaden the team's range of ideas more quickly. Two of the six are local and one is a strategic designer with the task of leading the team. While the term 'designer' will quickly get you in trouble outside of the design community, experience told us that these kind of large-scale systemic challenges required a specific kind of leadership. It called for a form of leadership that could help integrate disparate inputs, build an architecture of the solution and be capable of operating where facts would be incomplete, datasets partial and where one would have to lead with propositions rather than analysis. Once you ask 'what kind of leadership do I need for this kind of innovation mission?' you quickly start sketching out the attributes that are most likely to be found in someone with a design background. But at the end of the day, whether it's the design lead or the team at large, the task of recruiting relies on meeting and talking extensively to potential candidates and striking the right balance between expertise, experience, mental disposition and social skills.

PLACE

Where the team works is also critical. We give them a home: a place they can work out of that has all the necessary physical, infrastructural and staff support necessary. The place is selected so it's conducive to the kind of integrated work the team will do, with ample working surfaces (both tables and walls to write on) but also a place that feels good to come to. The space is close to the vitality of the city, offering the team the opportunity to digress for a coffee, a conversation, to break the rhythm. It's located in a place where it's easy for guests to come to, and a place where it's easy to do a range of activities: whether it is studio work, a public presentation or a high level final review dinner. The spaces we've used have been rented out of house so that they are neutral (not ours) and so that the team can easily feel it is their home away from home. As a symbolic gesture we give the team a key to the space so they can use it anytime.

Their housing is within easy reach; coming to 'work' is a pleasure in a light-filled, flexible and beautiful working space.

PROCESS

Our HDL studios were structured in three parts. First there was the brief writing period where we took on an investigative journalistic approach to help define how the current system sees the nature of the challenge and what it thinks should be done about it. It's a three to six month period of getting all the statistics on a particular issue, meeting a broad and diverse set of perspectives representing a well-rounded view of the challenge and selecting a few individuals for in-depth interviews. The final objective is to capture the nature of the challenge at hand as comprehensively as possible.

		PROBLEM	PEOPLE	PLACE	PROCESS
		Researching studio theme			Matching possible studio topics to the vision and trajectory of the organization
	Months before	Build network around studio theme			
		Identify expertise profile for studio	All studio members and support staff recruited and confirmed		Meetings with internal and external stakeholders to build awareness
	1 Month before	Challenge briefing done	Meeting and vetting potential field visits and guest lecturers		
				Studio location confirmed and final furnishings and equipment being secured	
	Weeks before	All guest presentations and field visits confirmed			
		Electronic copy of challenge briefing sent to studio		Studio assistants work in the studio for 1-2 weeks beforehand so that the space feels lived- in	Studio assistants are working on initial questions that studio members ask about the challenge briefing
	Week before	Paper copy of challenge briefing delivered to studio members			
					All hands meeting with host team to review details for studio week
Studio week	Monday	Introduction to how things are 'supposed to work'			
	Tuesday	Field visits to see the on-the-ground reality			
	Wednesday	Synthesis ramps up			
	Thursday	Ongoing synthesis			
	Friday	Studio presents its strategic architecture of solutions to invited guests			
	Week after			Studio assistants are in studio for 1-2 weeks afterwards while documenting the work	Studio assistants are working on initial questions that studio members ask about the challenge briefing
	Weeks after		Check in with studio team and guests to get feedback. Check in with stakeholders to explore the possibility of continued collaboration around studio outcomes		
	Months after		Collaboration with key stakeholders to develop sketches from studio into viable projects		

Figure 6.3   Overall timeline for a studio structured around the four key dimensions (problem, people, place and process)

Source: In Studio: Recipes for Systemic Change by Boyer, Cook, Steinberg; Sitra 2011. Reproduced with kind permission of Sitra: The Finnish Innovation Fund

The process of developing the brief assists in building a broad and comprehensive network of people and insights that will be helpful later, in preparing the studio week. The studio week is structured upfront, open in the middle for the team to use time as they see best fit and concludes with a presentation to a key group of policymakers and stakeholders. Monday is a series of presentations from key people on how the problem is understood today and what are known solutions. Presenters may range from the minister on the given issue to a top economist to a leading NGO director. Tuesday is a day of field ethnography, seeing what the issue is like in the field: schools, with parents, in nursing homes, within city planning offices. Wednesday and Thursday are open to the studio to use and Friday ends the week with a studio presentation to a panel of stakeholders and policymakers that concludes with a dinner to carry conversations over in a more informal setting.

Studios require significant preparation and follow-up to have an impact. The studio is frontloaded with a structured program and then tapers off to allow for the studio to start deciding what perspectives it needs to gain or further develop and how (Figure 6.4). The week ends with a formal review session where the studio members present their roadmap for strategic improvements and top 10 opportunities for improvement to a panel of stakeholders.

Identifying the right space is critical in supporting the work. The space needs to be conducive to many forms of collaborative work and acts as a home for the design team (Figure 6.5).

The team presents to a panel of stakeholders its roadmap for strategic improvements including its 'top 10' opportunities (Figure 6.6).

The final review with stakeholders ends in a shared meal where the formal presentation discussion can overflow into the informal ambiance of the meal (Figure 6.7). This is where a lot of the 'what if' conversations happen that help seed the ground for transitional thought and action.

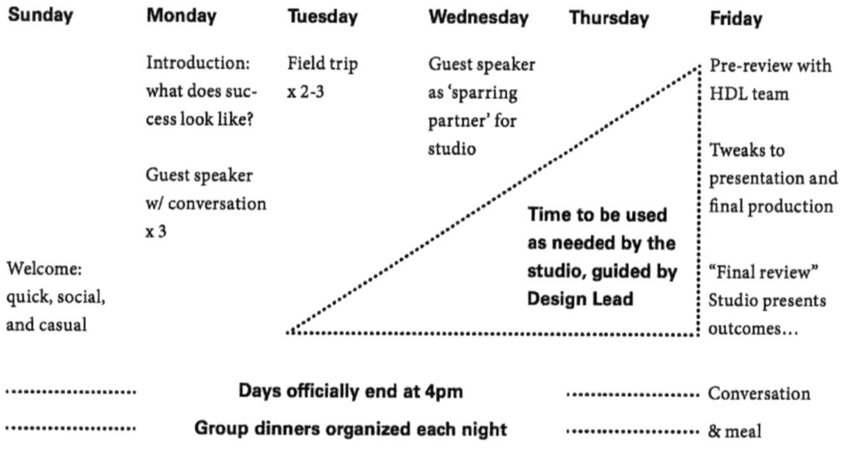

Sunday	Monday	Tuesday	Wednesday	Thursday	Friday
	Introduction: what does success look like?	Field trip x 2-3	Guest speaker as 'sparring partner' for studio		Pre-review with HDL team
	Guest speaker w/ conversation x 3				Tweaks to presentation and final production
Welcome: quick, social, and casual			Time to be used as needed by the studio, guided by Design Lead		"Final review" Studio presents outcomes...

	Days officially end at 4pm		Conversation
	Group dinners organized each night		& meal

Figure 6.4   Structure of the studio week

Source: *In Studio: Recipes for Systemic Change* by Boyer, Cook, Steinberg; Sitra 2011. Reproduced with kind permission of Sitra: The Finnish Innovation Fund

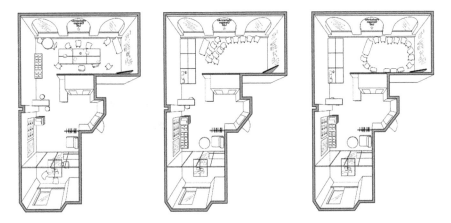

Figure 6.5   Examples of studio space. Left, typical working day for the team; Middle, presentation mode for the final review on Friday; Right, discussion mode for the final review on Friday

Source: *In Studio: Recipes for Systemic Change* by Boyer, Cook, Steinberg; Sitra 2011. Reproduced with kind permission of Sitra: The Finnish Innovation Fund

Figure 6.6   The studio during final review
Source: Reproduced with kind permission of Sitra: The Finnish Innovation Fund

Figure 6.7   Studio meal
Source: Reproduced with kind permission of Sitra: The Finnish Innovation Fund

How Do You Determine What Voices to Include in a Studio?

To gain a comprehensive understanding of an issue you need to systematically gather inputs from a very broad and diverse set of issues. Developing a comprehensive understanding of a complex issue is like parsing together individual drawings, photographs and stories to gain a sense of a city as a whole. In that sense, developing an understating is a process of broadening the angle of view to 360 degrees, to include all that which affects or is affected by the issue at hand. The problem clearly is that you can't look at all the issues because they are by definition endless. A bit like Noah who couldn't save every animal on the planet, you have to select representative perspectives that give you a balanced 360-degree spectrum of the challenge's to the 'animal kingdom'. For this we developed the 'Noah's Ark' principle, ensuring we have the broadest set of perspectives examined through scale, perspective and context. On any given issue we ask ourselves: *Do we have a broad enough representative perspective on the issue?* On the issue of scale that meant looking at a school through the classroom, district and national levels. On the issue of role it meant ensuring we had a teacher, student, parent and future employer perspective. On the issue of geography it meant looking at aging in a rural, urban and suburban context. The Noah's Ark notion is there to challenge us to identify as many categories (new and existing) as possible and ensure we have the broadest range of representative inputs from them. This approach was used in everything we developed: preparing the background work for our studio briefs; selecting our studio participants; selecting where to go for our studio field visits; identifying review stakeholder panelists for the final presentation.

What Happens after a Studio?

The studio was conceived as a way to start a strategic conversation about alternatives with policymakers and stakeholders. It was about identifying the keys to innovate on large-scale issues, and help challenge-owners break away from the existing categories of solutions and logic. As such a studio should be seen as a starter to a longer transformation effort. Stewarding, understood as the art of leading towards impact, a studio (people, resources, stakeholder interest) towards a systemic proposition is critical. This is the first opportunity to have a 'what if' conversation. Once space has been created, it is the job of the strategic designer to steward the opportunity towards impact. This might mean delivering on a single project or run a second studio to build momentum towards a more public and committed roadmap for innovation. Stewarding may also involve identifying and leveraging unexpected opportunities that come during the studio conversation. In our case one of the questions that emerged at the final presentation was: *How can we have more of this capability in our department?* This question led us to develop the Design Exchange Programme, placing designers within public sector departments. This was not a studio recommendation but the studio created a need that we responded to by stewarding interest, resources and knowhow to respond to it.

What Is Design Stewardship and Why Is It Critical?

'Stewardship is the art of aligning decisions with impact when many minds are involved in making a plan and many hands in enacting it.' As such, design stewardship is about the craft of navigating forces outside of one's control, in the case of public sector innovation these include organizational incentives, prevailing investment logic and political mood swings. As a designer innovating from within, the craft of stewardship is captured in the ability to take forces and changing circumstances and re-channel them in ways that keep the original objective clear and focused. Like a navigator using a sextant on a sailboat, the designer has to have the capability to understand a project's current position, prevailing forces and discern how to steward the course of action by pivoting at critical junctures. The ability to create value while having fluidity of path challenges the public sector's dominant culture where progress is linear and predictable. The dominant notion that one must define ideas in their entirety, vet all major risks and declare a path of implementation that is to be rigorously followed before setting sail, so to speak, is antithetical to the innovation mission. But faced with a risk-adverse culture of plan and implement, the design steward needs to find the navigational tools to deliver innovations without disrupting the institutions he or she is serving.

Stewardship is about the design approach needed to coherently shape cultural, political and economic interests through unpredictability towards a desired goal and to ensure impactful delivery. Here are six key points in deconstructing the art of stewardship:

1.   Design to multiple expectations, timelines and clock speeds. When working from within the system you have to address multiple realities and expectations: political expectations of quick results, the public servant expectation of how things should be done and the desire to create something new, that breaks from 'business as usual'. Building two timelines, one that is aligned with the political need for progress, and the other one aligned with the innovation needs for progress can be helpful. Likewise nesting projects within projects can help manage, in a 'Trojan

Horse' way, the need to deliver what the sector wants while providing it with what it needs.

2. Work at the extremes and at the margins. When first starting out on a broader innovation challenge, it may be helpful to look at extreme or marginal issues, a small community. Working at the margins usually means that the space is less cluttered with interest, experts and assumption – it can give you the freedom to discover and experiment. Likewise looking at extreme issues can frequently help 'exaggerate' and thus crystallize the nature of a challenge. By the same token looking at the issue from a mainstream or mean perspective may actually muddle the underlying traits: it's hard to understand grey if you have not experienced white and black. The extreme and the margin can give you more freedom and greater clarity.

3. Build innovation coalitions. The design-innovator will always be in the minority and won't have all the answers. As such you need to deliberately build coalitions of people that can see, understand and help support the growth of opportunities; you need people with the expertise to help infuse the right knowledge into initiatives; you need to have the support of people who can champion a different way of doing well beyond the comfortable confines of a project. The design task goes beyond more familiar team building, to designing the stewardship ecosystem: ensure you have built a coalition of teams, individuals and networks of individuals that can help build, support and scale potential innovations.

4. Prototyping as planning. The notion that one can plan first and implement after is not viable when there is a lack of information or little to no precedent. Many of our public sector challenges are coloured by lacks of both, leaving it struggling within a model that is broken. Design stewardship is about connecting problem definition to solution delivery, through an iterative process. In this model the idea of prototyping is planning, meaning prototyping is the vehicle by which one delivers (by making a first version of a real solution) and plans (by using the prototype to gain insights and in turn improve the understanding of how one should plan). Prototyping also makes alternative tangibles and helps de-risk both their future development and the perceived barriers to adoption.

5. Investment design. The public sector is fuelled by its financial resources. The current logic of the system will remain constant for as long as the basis of financial resourcing and investing remain the same. The schism between end objectives and behaviour can be particularly evident, both in investing and the financing. Governments will fund projects to help meet low carbon aspirations while and at the same time increasing their investments (pension plans and so forth) in the same oil dependent markets that they are attempting to reduce. Bringing design coherence by aligning objectives with investment logic is critical. Project financing is also marred by misalignments by applying standardized resourcing approaches. It is counterproductive to impose the financing model that is applied to a project about improving existing solutions to a project about invention new ones. The financial package and investment logic should be very different because the risks and rewards are potentially very different.

Stewarding the financial and investment picture is critical in creating the right conditions for success.

6.   Design the social dynamics. Don't loose sight of the fact that any innovation and transformation process is about people. And people are social beings. Designing the right social conditions to help lower the barrier for teams and organizations to adopt a more innovative approach is critical. Think of this stewardship task as one of nourishing the comfort and social needs of people so they can be most productive and creative at the innovation task at hand. This can frequently lower the stress within teams, help them focus on what is essential and help suspend disbelief as they venture out into uncharted ideas and opportunities. The process is about designing the experience of innovating to both maximize the impact of the expertise available and help make it more likely that teams will want to repeat the experience. Resourcing can sometimes be difficult as public sector organizations are vulnerable to cost saving fallacies by associating nice spaces, food and experiences with luxury. Here, as in many instances, the stewardship task is to shift the resourcing conversation from a cost to an investment one. Something may actually cost a bit more, but it will yield a lot more. Having a strategic meeting with key stakeholders in a windowless basement because it's cheaper is likely to leave people uninspired, unproductive and unengaged. Investing a bit in the right place will likely help relax people, shift the atmosphere from being a barrier to being an enabler and increase the likelihood of people being inspired, productive and engaged.

99

The Strategic Design Challenge in the Public Sector

Resolving the public sector innovation conundrum hinges on the convergence of two major challenges: the shift from innovative parts to innovative wholes and transitioning the role of the public sector from administering to innovating. The first challenge needs to be focused around developing the science and practice of large-scale innovation; the second around the design of large-scale transformations. Let's examine the questions and implications of these two interconnected issues.

First comes the question of large-scale innovation. We have scarce experience or knowledge on how to innovate on large-scale social issues, especially within the context and realities of today's public sector. Furthermore, we don't have the time to first experiment and then deliver. Rather we need to do both simultaneously. This shift will challenge our current systems of learning and it is likely that building the science and discipline will happen in the field first. This organic growth needs to be resourced and tended to. Attempts to burden our current systems of education with that task will most likely be counterproductive and create critical delays.

Second, we are challenged with the question of transformation. The structure and operations of the public sector are not aligned with the kind of work that this paper has outlined. Many of the key prerequisites, such as strategic design competencies, are missing. On the other hand, the public sector has a very real and current obligation to deliver services. The shift towards new competencies, cultures, incentives and resource allocation models cannot happen at the expense of the current delivery needs and long term stability. As such the core issue is to design coherent transitions whereby current obligations can be fulfilled while simultaneously building necessary future ones. This is fundamentally about disrupting people without disrupting institutions.

The lack of a real discipline and aligned institutions leaves us with some key questions to address quickly. Quickly because the clock speed on the viability of current public sectors has outpaced the natural speed at which societies evolve and adapt. First, do we have enough capability within the design communities to scale up to the magnitude of the innovation mission? I fear not, at least not at the current rate of development. Few if any traditional academic institutions are preparing designers for the task of innovating from within public sector structures. Second, is there real political awareness, vision and commitment to address the challenge of innovating the public sector itself? There is little sign that there is clarity of vision, leadership and real commitment to act. A quick and easy measure would be to look at the percentage of public sector expenditure set aside to innovate the way the public sector goes about its 'business'. In the corporate world a 4 per cent figure would be normal, the public figure, I fear, has the decimal point a few notches to the left. Third and lastly, is design being positioned to impact strategic issues? The success of the corporate world has been accelerated by a migration of design from a pure add-on service to the boardroom. The best companies have design as an executive leadership capability. The same path needs to be built in the public sector. This can only happen if design can prove its value at the service level and career paths are built to help migrate that capability higher into public sector offices.

References

Boyer, Bryan, Cook, Justin W. and Steinberg, Marco (2011). *In Studio: Recipes for Systemic Change*. Helsinki: Sitra.

Boyer, Bryan, Cook, Justin W. and Steinberg, Marco (2013). *Legible Practises: Six Stories About the Craft of Stewardship*. Helsinki: Sitra.

Majid, Anouar (2009). *A Call for Heresy: Why Dissent Is Vital to Islam and America*. Minneapolis: University of Minnesota Press.

Tufte, Edward R. (1983). *The Visual Display of Quantitative Information*. Cheshire, CT: Graphics Press.

Section 2

Policy in Practice

EZIO MANZINI

Design and Policies for Collaborative Services

Facing everyday life problems, people are often capable of inventing new solutions: ways of thinking and doing that permit them to tackle these problems and to work them out, opening new possibilities.[1] Initiatives like these, in which people collaborate to achieve results and, at the same time, create social, economic and environmental benefits, can be found everywhere in the world. These *collaborative organizations* have grown out of problems posed by contemporary everyday life such as: How can I improve the quality of my neighbourhood? How can I find healthy food? Who will help me in my daily necessities now that I am becoming old? What can I do to deal with my allergies? How can I go to work every day, avoiding high car expenses and traffic jam stress?

Collaborative Organizations as New Services

Given these problems and the daily life questions they raise, individuals and associations are pushed to search for solutions using their specific experience and their capacity to collaborate, in a creative way, conceiving and implementing new forms of organization. Such collaborative organizations are capable of answering these difficult questions exactly because they break the old economic and organizational paradigm that made the problems behind them intractable. In fact, what collaborative organizations do, at the everyday life scale, is to start economic and organizational models valorizing the collaborative behaviours driven by both the growing social impact of the intractable problems and by the opportunities opened by the diffusion of technology-based social networks.

Because they are based on the interaction of actors aiming to get a result, and offering solutions to socially sensitive problems, collaborative organizations can also be considered as services.[2] More precisely: a new kind of social services that, involving active and collaborative citizens, generate values for them and, at the same time, for the whole of society. For example, in the case of the elderly population, we can find a number of innovative solutions derived from within the elderly community using their own networks and resources, thereby making them possible agents of the solution, and not only as people bringing problems. Examples of this approach are, for instance, groups of elderly mutual assistance; intergenerational residences, where residents

---

1   To read more about social innovation cases, navigate the website of Young Foundation: http://www. youngfoundation.org; Social Innovation Exchange: http://www.socialinnovationexchange.org/; NESTA: http://www.nesta.org.uk; and DESIS: http://www.desis-network.org.

2   Jegou and Manzini 2008; Manzini 2009; Manzini 2011.

of different ages agree to help each other; initiatives in which elderly people living alone in their (large) family houses offer rooms to students who are willing to help them. The same approach has been applied to several other socially relevant issues as chronic disease, social cohesion, immigrant integration and so on, in which in all cases, the capabilities of the people with needs can be recognized and valorized within an appropriate solution strategy.

If we take these examples as a new generation of social services, *collaborative services*, we can ask ourselves if and how public policies could create conditions to support them and if and how the role of public agencies could evolve to support their existence and promote their diffusion.[3] In fact, if it is true that collaborative services bring positive social results and that, therefore, it would be wise to promote and support them, a new wave of public policies and services should be defined. Where to start?

Being a brand new kind of public intervention, both public policies and public services should break their business-as-usual ways of doing things and start new ones. This shift is not easy and should be seen as a learning process in which they, and all the other involved actors, should come to understand what it means to be 'the Public' in the new context in which collaborative services operate that is, as we have seen, the context of the networked society and its social economy. In other words, policymakers and public agencies have to learn what it means to participate in the broad co-design and co-production processes that characterize this emerging, dynamic, unprecedented context. The first step of this long journey is to better understand 'users' when, as it happens in collaborative services, they become *active citizens*.

Active Citizens and Participation

In collaborative services, the active participation of citizens is not just a nice option (as in other typologies of social services), it is a necessary pre-condition. No matter how much the enabling experts (public agencies, private companies and design experts) do, no collaborative service works if the involved citizens do not actively participate in its production and delivery (there are no community gardens if neighbours do not like gardening, there is no transportation via car pooling, if no one likes driving for/ with others, there is no elderly care group, if participants do not care for other peers, and so on). Therefore, if we want to promote, consolidate and spread collaborative services, presenting them as a new generation of public services, the first and main question to answer is: 'how to trigger and support the citizens' active collaborative and lasting participation to a collaborative service?'

To answer this question let's start from a quite obvious consideration: generating a new collaborative service, creatively adapting and managing an existing service idea or simply actively participating in an ongoing venture often calls for a huge commitment in terms of time and personal dedication. And, of equal importance, they ask for trust: the mutual trust among people who, at least at the beginning, do not know each other and the trust in the quality of the achievable results. It turns out that the required time and dedication on one side, and trust on the other, are

---

3   Many design research projects and programs have informed this chapter. However, one of them has contributed in the most significant way and it is the DESIS P&C Initiative: an international design research promoted by the DESIS Network in 12 DESIS Labs in Europe and the United States (http://www.desis-clusters.org).

the main limiting factors to collaborative services' possibilities of lasting in time and spreading. Consequently, to get these positive results, it is necessary to overcome these limiting factors. That means, to understand them better and, consequently, to improve the definition and functioning of collaborative services.

This awareness can be done by increasing, from the users' point of view, the services' *effectiveness* (the ratio between results they get and required individual and social efforts they require), their *trustability* (the trust they inspire in terms of both the results and the way to get them – including the trust between participants) and their *attractiveness* (the users' motivation to activate their capabilities and their networks).

Users' effectiveness, trustability and attractiveness are the three main pillars on which a strategy of promoting and supporting collaborative services should be built. Therefore, to be conceived and developed this strategy asks for adopting a *user-centred design approach* in which 'users' become a main source of information on what to do, how to do it and, most importantly, on why to do it.

In collaborative services, the user-centred approach presents very special features. In fact, if the precondition is the active participation of citizens, in this case, to be user-centred means to consider 'users' acting as collaborative citizens, recognizing not only their needs, but also their capabilities, their social networks and the cultural and economic conditions that motivate their active, intelligent, lasting participation. In short, in this case, the user-centred design process necessarily becomes a *participatory design and production process*. That is, a design process in which everybody participates in the service definition and daily delivery, and in the enabling strategies specifically conceived to support it.

Co-design and Co-production Processes

Collaborative services are generally presented as grassroots organizations because their existence is based on the active collaboration between the interested citizens (and because, very often, the original service ideas on which they are based have been conceived of and developed in bottom-up innovation processes). But closer observation, from initial ideas towards more mature forms of organization, indicates that their long-term existence and, often, their same start-up depend on a more complex mechanism: the initiative taken by active citizens is often supported by professional agents, such as policymakers, civil servants, social entrepreneurs and designers.

For instance, let's examine the collaborative nursery case: a group of parents using their own ability and house to share the care of their children in the daytime hours. This is a rather simple service idea. Nevertheless, looking at its practical applications, we observe that the majority of them started looking at other groups' experience (and often directly interacting with them) and that several of them had been backed by a public agency (to guarantee their conformity to established standards and to support them when educational or medical problems, that cannot be solved within the nursery itself, arise).

When collaboration includes the horizontal collaboration among peers *and* the vertical one with professional agents, collaborative services appear as the result of a broad and dynamic participatory process.[4] It involves both the whole design process (from conceptualization to implementation) and the following phases of production

---

4   Manzini and Rizzo 2011.

and use (with the daily work of the delivered service adjusting and up-grading). In the following paragraphs I will refer to these complex processes across three levels:

- The first and main level is where a collaborative service is defined and delivered. It is a broad *co-design* and *co-production* activity resulting from the cooperation of all the involved actors.[5]

- In the second level we observe how a set of products, services and communication artefacts is systemized in an *enabling solution* aiming at supporting a collaborative service. It is a co-design process in which all the social, political and economic actors are involved, capable of contributing necessary expertise (we will call this group the *enabling experts*).

- Finally, the third level is the one in which specific *design initiatives* are taken by *design experts*, aiming at funnelling new ideas into the process and, most importantly, at empowering the other participants' design capabilities.

Public Agencies and Design Experts

Working with collaborative services, and being willing to support and orient them, public agencies must learn to become enabling agents, which is a change that undoubtedly requires a deep transformation (both cultural and practical). In particular, this change demands new design capabilities and a renewed relationship with design experts.

In fact, to conceive and develop enabling solutions and to create a more favourable environment, a broad and articulated design activity must be collaboratively performed by the whole group of participants (active citizens and enabling experts). Until now this activity has been very often accomplished intuitively by the involved citizens and by a variety of experts, as managers, social entrepreneurs and public servants. In that model, design experts could or could not play a role. Nevertheless, the greater the complexity, the more specific design skills and knowledge are needed and thus a greater involvement by design experts. To better understand their role and the relationship with the policymakers and public servants, it is necessary to take another step inside the collaborative services design processes, starting from the meaning of the word 'design'. In fact, in ongoing debate, the term 'to design' is used with a double meaning.

DIFFUSE DESIGN
Diffuse design refers to the human ability of solving problems and creating opportunity via the conception and realization of meaningful artefacts: human capability. Therefore it can be found in every human being and, as creativity and curiosity, it can be improved or reduced by the nature of the social and cultural context in which these human being live. Today, for several reasons, the recognition of this kind of design capability, and the request for design thinking is spreading.[6] And, of course, this is happening also in the collaborative services arena. A field in which, by definition, 'everybody designs'.

---

5   Boyle and Harris 2009; Boyle et al. 2010.
6   Brown and Wyatt 2010.

EXPERT DESIGN

Expert design refers to specific knowledge and set of tools. It is a mix of cultural and practical capabilities that, to be acquired, require specific studies and practical experiences. Therefore, expert design is performed by professional designers, design researchers, design schools, design-related media and cultural institutions. This activity, that generated its specific expertise and culture, appeared with the industrial second revolution at the beginning of the past century, with the need for conceiving and developing the products that industry was producing. In one century everything changed and design changed too. Today this expression refers to a culture and an expertise applicable to every problem asking for consideration, while keeping in mind people (in their contexts) and technology (with its limits and possibilities).

Given these updated definitions, it is clear that expert design should be applied to collaborative services. And that the specific role of design experts should be one of bringing into the broader processes of co-design and co-production the necessary design ideas, knowledge and tools. Their role is to deliver new visions and proposals, and to empower the design capabilities of all the collaborative service actors (that is, both the active citizens *and* the other partners who are not design experts).

In terms of their interaction with active citizens and public agencies, design experts should help them to design better. For citizens, designing better means to create the cultural and practical conditions to trigger and support the citizens' capability and will to actively and collaboratively participate, bringing their experiences and their ideas. And for public agencies, improvement means promoting and supporting the broader co-design and co-production processes and defining, with other stakeholders, the enabling solutions that could make them more effective, durable and replicable. These activities, in terms of design expertise, are extensions of existing design disciplines such as *strategic design*, which builds partnerships of participants who can implement and deliver new service ideas, *service design* (as well as *interaction, product and interior design*), to imagine and promote enabling solutions and *communication design*, to generate visions and scenarios and to present the entire proposal, both as an overview and as detailed how-to manuals.[7]

More precisely, design experts should use their creativity, sensitivity and skills to conceive and enhance a variety of *design initiatives* at the different stages of the co-design and co-production process, and do so by adopting different tools and methods, in order to achieve different outcomes. This variety of design initiatives can be clustered into two main groups: to co-create *enabling solutions,* aiming at triggering and supporting specific co-design processes (see box on following page) and to create *favourable environments, aimed at* making co-design and co-creation processes easier (see box on p. 110).

Enabling Solutions, Effectiveness and Trustability

Collaborative services are also necessarily based on the use of some artefacts: products, services, places, communication and organization tools that are, more or less consciously, systemized in order to get the desired results. These enabling artefacts may be quite diverse in both their composition and their processes of systemization.

---

7   In order to do that, a whole set of specific design devices has to be conceived and realized (prototypes, mock-ups, design games, models, sketches) to trigger new actions and sequences of events (Manzini and Rizzo 2011).

DESIGN INITIATIVES FOR ENABLING SOLUTIONS

Exploring. Helping in understanding the needs of people and communities as well as their capabilities (applying ethnographic methods).

Triggering. Feeding the partners' conversation with visions and solution ideas (organizing co-design workshops).

Prototyping. Making new ideas tangible (creating working prototypes).

Enabling. Making solutions more accessible for the citizen co-producers (designing dedicated products, services and communication artefacts).

Replicating. Making solutions replicable in different contexts (designing dedicated products, services and communication artefacts).

Synergizing. Systemizing different solutions at a territorial scale (developing planning-by-projects programs).

Deepening. Improving the cultural dimension of the new proposals (applying design culture and sensitivity to the sustainable qualities of proposals).

For instance, in the simple self-organized day care described above, the enabling artefacts are entirely assembled by the involved parents; selecting and adapting what, step by step, they recognize as necessary (a participant's home, the toys to be collected from each participant and the services provided by their personal telephones and internet). But, for this same day care idea, we can also find cases in which a specifically designed set of products, services and communication artefacts (the *enabling solution*) had been proposed.

Continuing with the example of the day care, an enabling solution could include a guidebook, indicating what to do, when and how; a dedicated website, sharing information and facilitating the day to day organization and support services, managing problems that cannot be solved within the day care itself. In parallel, the enabling solution could include initiatives aiming at building trust (for example, first of all, carrying out assessments of the suitability of the sites to be used and parents to be involved). Finally, this enabling solution could include some communication events aiming at spreading information on the advantages of this collaborative service and reinforcing the self-esteem of is the individuals already involved. On the basis of this example we can say that *enabling solutions* are product-service systems designed (or better, co-designed) as a whole, assembling existing or brand new components to support collaborative services.[8]

To better understand their nature and potential, we can look at the well-known example of the Community Gardens in New York City. In the 1970s a grassroots,

---

8   A formal definition is the following: enabling solutions are product-service systems providing cognitive, technical and organizational instruments so as to enable individuals and/or communities to achieve a result, using their skills and abilities to the best advantage and, at the same time, to regenerate the quality of the living contexts in which they happen to live.

alternative neighbourhood movement started up in New York when city residents decided to squat vacant and abandoned city-owned lots (inherited in lieu of tax payments when arson was a common practice during the 1960s and 1970s) and to transform them into green spaces. In 1978, recognizing the value of outsourcing to community groups the maintenance of gardens, a city program, Green Thumb, was initiated to provide materials, coordination and technical assistance to the community gardeners. In 1995 Green Thumb became part of the jurisdiction of the New York City Parks Department. Today there are 500 such gardens in New York, involving several thousands of citizens in their management and care.[9]

This example shows that, today, the Community Gardens in New York are effectively operating as a collaborative service, supported by an enabling solution offering some technical services, helping in some gardening tasks, supporting with tools, materials and expertise, solving administrative problems and, last but not least, giving some light but effective rules. This is a good example of an enabling solution aimed at making the citizens' efforts more effective and, at the same time, helping them in creating mutual trust among peers and with the same institution. The Green Thumb case expresses neatly what public agencies may, and should, do to promote and support collaboration among citizens and between citizens and public agencies in achieving a commonly recognized value.

Attractiveness and Shared Visions

Although the effectiveness and trustability of users are the two most visible pillars on which a strategy of promoting and supporting collaborative services should be built, the third pillar, *attractiveness,* also deserves attention. The attractiveness of collaborative services comes from the participants' deep recognition of what is, or could be the meaning of the initiative they are actively contributing to, or are willing to actively contribute to.

Of course, the attractiveness we are referring to here is not only based on considerations about the way in which a specific need is fulfilled, nor on the service components appearance, as it could be for a traditional service. The collaborative services' attractiveness is based on a larger vision in the framework of which that specific service becomes meaningful. For instance, in the example of the community garden, citizens become gardeners for several reasons; but at the end of the day, the two most important reasons are because they like gardening and because this activity and its results are part of a shared vision of a sustainable city – its green spaces and its citizens.

In fact, as we have seen, collaborative services aren't driven by the simple question: *How can we fulfil our needs?* but rather by the broader one: *How can we achieve the life we want to live?* Therefore, even though they solve specific problems, they also refer to broader visions on the life participants want to live. Visions that, to become drivers of collaborative initiatives, must be shared (at least) with those who will participate in the related collaborative services (that is, with the active citizens and the other involved actors). Therefore, the most effective and trustworthy proposal will not be successful if the potential participants do not deeply appreciate it and the vision of which it is a part.

---

9   Gittleman et al. 2010.

Therefore, building this shared vision is the crucial component of every strategy aimed at supporting collaborative services, spreading them and, in the end, assuming their way of doing things as the 'normal' way of how public services should work. Can a vision like this be 'designed' in order to consider it part of an enabling solution? The answer is 'not', of course, if we imagine producing it as a material product. The answer is 'yes' if we consider the possibility for design experts to feed with images and proposals a social conversation that, in turn, will generate a shared vision (and the main lines of a strategy to enhance it). Doing that, the social conversation becomes a broad process of scenario building. A process in which, for its same nature, design experts can (and should) play a major role creating meaningful narratives (those narratives that will endow the collaborative service with clear and deep meaning).

Favourable Environments and Experimental Spaces

Collaborative services are living entities the survival of which depends on the quality of their environment.

At the same time, they are brand new entities with (very often) a contradictory relationship with the same contexts in which they have appeared, that can be hostile or favourable to their existence and development.

DESIGN INITIATIVES FOR FAVOURABLE ENVIRONMENTS

Amplifying. Providing visibility for existing best practices (applying different communication tools).

Story telling. Proposing narratives to support best practices and emerging ideas (building scenarios).

Cultural development. Promoting a new deeper culture on sustainable qualities and sustainable ways of living and producing (using design culture and sensitivity to develop new conceptual tools).

Tools and methods development. Promoting tools and methods to facilitate co-design processes (using previous experiences, and previous design tools and methods, to define new ones, more appropriate in the field of social innovation).

To increase diffuse design skills. To teach citizens how to use at best design tools for non-professional designers (organizing design workshops and seminars).

The first and essential character of this favourable environment is its *tolerance.* Since collaborative services are, by definition, different from what, in a given time and place, is considered mainstream, fostering them means accepting something that will probably not fit in with existing norms and regulations. Consequently, an appropriate degree of tolerance is needed to permit them to exist.

Given that need, to permit collaborative services to appear and spread, other environmental features must exist and create the social, political and administrative spaces in which new talent (that is, new skills and abilities) has the possibility to emerge and be cultivated, and in which new ideas (that is, new collaborative services) can be implemented. They are accessible infrastructures, economic support programs, friendly norms and, last but not least, open-minded financial and entrepreneurial interlocutors capable to recognize the potential of new ideas. This last feature is particularly relevant. In fact, when this potential is honoured, interesting economic models appear and drive new waves of product and service innovations.

Policymakers and civil servants should, of course, play a main role in fostering these favourable environments. But the available examples up to now tell us that this task is quite difficult. In fact, even if there may be several public servants who individually are very innovative and willing to contribute to a change that seems more and more necessary, the overall systems are fairly inert (if not completely blocked).

A strategy is emerging to overcome this difficulty. In fact, several international teams, working on social innovation and, in particular, on how it impacts public innovation, are converging on the necessity of creating *experimental spaces* where social innovation and public innovation might meet and reinforce each other. These spaces (which are the same Public Innovation Spaces presented in the chapter 'Public Design in a Global Perspective: Empirical Trends') are conceived as favourable micro-environments where different stakeholders, civil servants included, can meet, interact, discuss different possibilities and develop prototypes to verify them. They could operate as promising idea incubators and launching pads – but not only. They could also become seeds for the creation of the broad favourable environment in which positive connections between bottom-up initiatives and public agency innovations will take place. And, therefore, in which larger numbers of collaborative services would flourish and spread.

References

Bason, C. (2010). *Leading Public Sector Innovation: Co-creating for a Better Society*. Bristol: The Policy Press.

Botero, A., Paterson, A.G. and Saad-Solonen, J. (2012). *Towards Peer Production in Public Services: Cases from Finland*. Helsinki: Aalto University.

Boyle, D. and Harris, R. (2009). The Challenge of Co-production, NEF-NESTA, UK, http://neweconomics.org/publications/challenge-co-production.

Boyle, D., Slay J. and Stephens, L. (2010). Public Services Inside Out. Putting Co-production into Practice, NEF-NESTA, UK, http://www.nesta.org.uk/library/documents/public-services-inside-out.pdf.

Brown, T. and Wyatt, J. (2010). Design Thinking for Social Innovation. *Stanford Social Innovation review*. Winter, 2010.

Cipolla, C and Manzini, E. (2009). *Relational Services in Knowledge, Technology & Policy (Springer)*, v. 22. 45–50.

Cottam, H. and Leadbeater, C. (2004). *Open Welfare: Designs on the Public Good*. London: Design Council.

Ehn, P. and Hillgren, P.A. (2010). Participatory Design and Democratizing Innovation, 10th Biennal Participatory Design Conference Proceedings, Sydney, ACM, New York.

Gittleman, M., Librizzi, L., Stone, E. (2010). Community Gardens Survey Results 2009–2010 (New York, Grown NYC), 7; http://www.grownyc.org/files/GrowNYC_CommunityGardenReport.pdf.

Jegou, F. (2011). Design, Social Innovation and Regional Acupuncture Towards Sustainability in Nordic Design Research Conference Proceedings, May 30–June 1, 2011, Helsinki: Aalto University.

Jegou, F. and Manzini, E. (2008). *Collaborative Services. Social Innovation and Design for Sustainability*. Milan: Polidesign.

Manzini, E. (2009). Service Design in the Age of Networks and Sustainability. In S. Miettinen and M. Koivisto (eds), *Designing Services with Innovative Methods*. Helsinki: University of Arts and Design.

Manzini, E. (2011). Introduction to Design for Services. A New Discipline. In A. Meroni, and D. Sangiorgi, *Design for Services*. Farnham, UK: Gower.

Manzini, E. and Rizzo, F. (2011). Small Projects/Large Changes. Participatory Design as an Open Participated Process. *CoDesign*, Vol. 7, No. 3–4: 199–215.

Meroni, A. (2007). *Creative communities. People Inventing Sustainable Ways of Living*. Milano: Polidesign.

Meroni, A. and Sangiorgi, D. (2011). *Design for Services*. Farnham, UK: Gower.

Mulgan, J. (20060. *Social innovation. What it is, Why it Matters, How it can be Accelerated*. London: Basingstoke Press.

Mulgan, J. and Stears, M. (2012). *The Relational State*. London: Institute for Public Policy Research.

Pestoff, V. (2009). Towards a Paradigm of Democratic Participation: Citizen Participation and Co-Production of Personal Social Services in Sweden. *Annals of Public and Cooperative Economics*, Vol. 80, no 2.

Sennett, R. (2012). *Together: the Rituals, Pleasures and Politics of Cooperation*. New Haven: Yale University Press.

Staszowski, E. (2010). Amplifying Creative Communities in NYC: A Middle-Up-Down Approach to Social innovation. SEE Workshop proceedings, Florence, Italy.

SARAH FORRESTER AND JOHN BODY

Synthesizing Policy and Practice: The Case of Co-designing Better Outcomes for Vulnerable Families

Sandra, a hardworking mother of two from Canberra, was compelled to move into private rental after the breakdown of her marriage. Sandra's ex-husband left her with a large debt that she struggled to repay, which along with the cost of her rent forced Sandra to work three jobs to survive. Along with the financial issues, Sandra and her children experienced depression after the marriage breakdown. Reluctant to seek help, they coped as best as they could. However, their situation quickly became desperate when Sandra suffered a workplace injury that left her incapacitated and reliant on compensation payments and government support.

With Sandra's income now barely covering the cost of rent, they were unable to pay their power bills, and the family slipped further into debt. Through the winter they could not afford to heat their house and Sandra was constantly ill. After paying their rent, the family were scarcely able to afford nutritious food or to put petrol in their car with the remaining income. No longer able to cope, Sandra finally sought help in the form of counselling and received food and clothing donations. Sandra's social worker applied to have the family placed on the priority-housing list as a reduction in rent would greatly ease the family's financial hardship. However, the request was rejected because Sandra's income was $1.50 over the threshold for eligibility. From Sandra's perspective this assessment of her situation was cruelly unfair, yet social welfare systems throughout the world have thresholds and eligibility tests. These tests are intended to ration finite resources yet they can lead to perverse outcomes for people such as Sandra.

Sandra's is one of a number of stories we heard as part of a two-phase co-design project aimed at improving outcomes for families with complex needs accessing multiple services in Canberra.

The project deliberately took a considered co-design approach over a number of phases. Phase one, *Listening to Families*, involved face-to-face, in depth interviews with nine families, through which we sought to better understanding their journeys through the services system. The first phase generated three ideas to improve the experience for families. A lead worker would be chosen by the families to help the families set goals and access the services required. A family information profile would be controlled by the families allowing them to tell their story once and decide who could access it. Community hubs would be places where families could be connected to services faster before major issues arose.

Phase two; *Improving Services with Families*, has seen a prototype of the lead worker service model applied in action and the initial development of the family information profile. Subsequent phases would scale the service model and address and use insights to make systemic policy, legislative and structural change.

Through this chapter we will explore how design approaches succeed in linking policy intent with on-the-ground professional practices in the context of the *Listening to Families* and *Improving Services with Families* projects and how they may affect positive change in the lives of families like Sandra's.

The ACT Government

The Australian Capital Territory is the equivalent of a state within Australia. The population of the ACT is approximately 400,000 people. Like any community, there is a group of families, who, despite significant resource commitment, do not find that the services they receive work for them. This is not a new problem and much research has been done to quantify the costs of such families to the community. In this study we did not calculate the average cost to the community. However it is possible to conclude that with multiple workers from multiple service providers involved with one family the cost associated with that family can be multiples of the average annual wage.

The ACT Government sought to take a new approach to improve services for these families. Working with Canberra design firm, ThinkPlace, the government embarked on a co-design project that did not intend to force a rapid solution but to simply listen to families and hear their stories. The project team comprised a cross section of people supplementing the families themselves with people from government, people from the community sector as well as people with expertise in the co-design process.

The Role of Design in This Project

The project followed a flexible design process. The first step was getting a group of senior leaders representing the organizations involved to come together and form a leadership team. There was strong commitment to be involved. Everyone believed the challenge warranted the effort required.

The process followed the ThinkPlace Design System shown below (Figure 8.1). The key element of the ThinkPlace Design System is that there is a time for divergence and a time for convergence. This concept is well entrenched in the design literature and an early reference can be found in the 1970 work of John Chris Jones *Design Methods* (Jones 1970). In the ACT Government project we had to make time for divergence, gathering information, listening and not deciding on solutions too soon. We also had to decide when convergence would be appropriate.

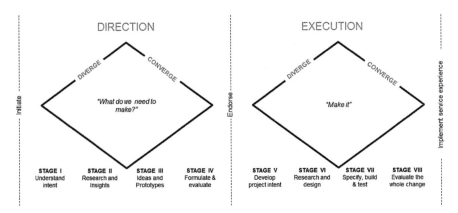

Figure 8.1   The ThinkPlace Design System

Phase One – Listening to Families

The goal of *Listening to Families* was to understand the experience of Canberra families accessing multiple services. We sought to understand their needs, assets and desires and to see their journey through the service system from their perspective. We also sought to better understand the service system and the connections and relationships within it. We sought to understand how the system does or does not fit into the lives of the families and how it does or doesn't meet their needs. To do this we went through stages one to four of the ThinkPlace Design System, including endorsement after the end of stage four.

If a project is to be successful, there are time-consuming activities that are essential to gaining the authority and sponsorship to start, and equally after stage 4 to get the authority and sponsorship to move to the next phase.

A SHARED UNDERSTANDING OF INTENT
Early in the project a leadership group of five people was formed comprising a senior official from the Community Services Directorate within government, two community sector CEOs (Northside Community Services and Woden Community Services) and the Founding Partner of ThinkPlace, the design partner. The leadership group agreed on a shared understanding of the project intent, which guided the project throughout, describing both what was required and the approach to be undertaken. The intent was to listen to families, to hear their stories and, through that listening, to reflect, learn and surface insights.

In addition to the leadership group set up for the project, there were strong connections into existing governance groups within government.

Selecting Families

The families engaged were identified by community sector organizations from which they were receiving support. Because of the existing relationship between the families and the workers who introduced us to them we were in a sense, endorsed as trustworthy and as a result, families were quite open and honest about their experiences during the exploratory interviews. We invited the families to tell us about the life events and circumstances that brought about their interactions with the service system and how the service did or didn't address their needs. We allowed the families to lead the direction of the conversation, which meant that we heard about what was important to them and we were able to identify areas of pain, opportunity and importance from the perspective of the family. Through genuine engagement with families we gained a sound understanding of their experience of the ACT service system.

Synthesis and Analysis as a Collective

At fortnightly intervals throughout the 10-week research phase the government and community sector people along with ThinkPlace designers who had been in the field, came together to reflect on the previous week. The early reflection sessions raised the question 'What is different from what we have always done?' Social workers in the community sector work with families experiencing difficulty every day. They constantly listen and withhold judgement. So what is different? The first few weeks saw everyone involved a little nervous because perhaps nothing was different.

As we arrived at sessions three and four the realization emerged that this was different. Social workers are advocates for their clients, seeking an expedient solution to meet their needs. The *Listening to Families* project was intentionally not seeking expedient solutions to long-term problems. What we sought was to listen and understand, to suspend arriving at premature answers. The problems being tackled are perennial and therefore it would be naïve to think that a rapid fix would point to any sustainable improvements. The co-design approach therefore inserted a deliberate space between sensing information from the families and taking action. This gap was in the form of the fortnightly reflection sessions where the process was one of making sense.

Experience Maps

The family stories were communicated in a way that illustrated what the policymakers needed to understand. The raw interview notes were analyzed and synthesized by the core design team in fortnightly reflection sessions. The family journeys were translated into journey maps that represented key life events/service triggers, service interactions and family perspective of the service interaction, barriers and blockers to positive outcomes or continued service interaction. Family stories told through personas gave a fuller understanding of the family experience. The designers played with many experience map formats before landing on a format that made sense in this specific context. The families did not have typical pathways which followed some logical sequence. The sequence was quite unpredictable. And this had to be shown in the maps if they were to be useful. An example of the map design is shown in Figure 8.2.

Phase One Insights

One of the initial insights to surface was the number of false starts that each family had in finding the right service. The maps clearly showed that in each case there was a long passage of time and a number of unsuccessful attempts before the family received some services that could assist them. In the worst case example the timeframe had been eight years.

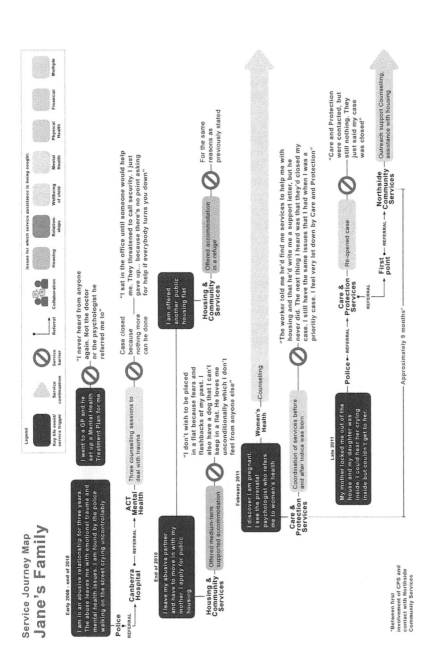

Figure 8.2 Example of an experience map

The maps also showed that families were helped when at least two organizations worked together and cooperated to assist them. This made sense in hindsight because the complexity of the needs of this group of families necessitated a more joint approach to helping them. Many of the families had been managing without extra support until something changed in their situation, forcing them across a line between coping and not coping. These trigger events included family breakup, injury or health issues.

The families all received services from multiple organizations including different levels of government, different agencies within government and usually several agencies within the community sector. Each government and community sector organization had outcomes to achieve for the family – health outcomes, education outcomes, housing outcomes, financial outcomes and others.

The research surfaced the frustration that many families experienced as they told their story repeatedly to all the different organizations they dealt with. Each time they had to tell their story in response to a different set of questions. This highlighted that few if any body knew the family's full story, each having a part.

The project has made considerable progress because of the strong and collaborative leadership of leaders in the ACT Government and the ACT community sector. These leaders have a vision for a new service model and a new relationship between the community, government and the service sector.

GENERATING IDEAS

After a number of weekly design sessions, it emerged that the government agencies were designed to meet the needs of the majority with standardized approaches. For those people with less significant challenges these mainstream services worked. But for those with special circumstances the system did not work well. Most agencies had caseworkers but they were agency specific and they focused only on the needs of the family that were addressed by their service. Without a full picture of the family situation, the families were offered services that they were not yet ready for or that addressed only a small part of their problem. Therefore, the first idea to emerge was that of having a lead worker assigned to each family. The purpose of the leader worker was to gain an understanding of the whole family story and, given the system they were operating in, to authorize the provision of services for the family across the whole system.

The second idea to emerge was to combat the challenge faced by families of having to retell their story over and over again. The idea emerged to have an online profile for the families, where they could tell their story once. This profile would be owned by the family and controlled by the family. The idea was that the family could choose how much of their story they divulged and to whom. Privacy issues were reduced because it is a family-owned and family-controlled profile.

The third idea to emerge was to counter the lag between the family needing services and the family receiving what they need. The concept was for hubs within the community such as through schools and other groups who would be trained to recognize the early warning signs and to help families connect with the services they need.

DOCUMENTATION AND ENDORSEMENT

An important phase one deliverable was the *Listening to Families* report, which was a carefully designed document that allowed people who had not been a part of the research to engage with it. The document comprised the family stories, the maps of their experience, the insights and the ideas. The document was a powerful and effective way to communicate the messages and played a crucial role in getting the support of the senior leadership. The ACT Government project team members navigated the endorsement process through the senior leadership, gaining high level support for the approach and the findings. They also gained agreement to move to a second phase which would involve implementation of the findings. The importance of the endorsement phase cannot be underestimated if all the benefits arising from the co-design activity are to be realized.

Phase Two – Improving Services with Families

In phase two, *Improving Services with Families*, we have continued to follow a co-design approach, but the focus is now on the detailed design, build and implementation of the three big ideas. The project has followed stages 5, 6, 7 and 8 of the ThinkPlace Design System. Through the intent stage (stage 5) we determined that the project must make both improvements for the specific families included in the study and long-term systemic improvements.

THE ROLE OF DESIGN IN PHASE TWO
The role of design in phase two has been to shift the 'power' to the hands of the families and the workers directly involved with them. Families have been given control over the service offer they receive and have been able to design what that looks like – what they focus on, what their goals are, how they will work towards achieving them, how much time they spend with their worker. Families are able to ask for and access more practical assistance, which government-driven services would ordinarily overlook.

An action learning approach was applied, which formalized the prototyping by implementing the service model in practice, reviewing the outcome, then refining and applying again. The reflective stages have once again involved collaboration across government, the community sector and the lead workers themselves. The collaborative effort ensures the complexity of the service system is more fully understood from multiple perspectives.

SELECTING FAMILIES
For phase two there was a desire from the senior leaders in government to select families who had the most complex service scenarios. Three of the families involved in phase one, along with a number who were identified by the government as having the greatest need, agreed to be part of phase two. The phase one families were selected by the community sector. This was fast and the privacy obligations were easy to address. In phase two there was a desire to get to the types of families that would not readily volunteer as they had in phase one. The government wanted to included families who had had interactions with multiple areas such as health, housing, community services, education and the criminal justice system. This approach raised a number of privacy issues that had to be worked through, but it did provide a group of families with very complex needs for the study.

THE LEAD WORKER
The families selected their lead worker from amongst those they are currently involved with and in some cases it was someone they had known for a number of years. As the lead workers commenced, they were provided training in being designers, most specifically in 'not knowing', which meant despite their prior involvement with the family, they would not assume an understanding of the family story, of the issues the family saw as most crucial or how the family would like their lives to be. A key part

of the training of lead workers covered avoiding immediate problem-solving. It was important to observe families hitting barriers in order to understand why and how to overcome them. The lead workers were supported in designing the tools that would be used to engage the families. The tools were varied and innovative, recognizing the varied needs of family members. An example included a tool to capture the family's story that relied on visual queues and conversation to prompt a rich narrative.

Understanding the family story has been a key part of the lead worker role. Lead workers sought to understand what is important to the family as a whole and to each family member, what is their current situation and future aspirations? The lead workers allowed families to tell their stories in their own way and with a focus on what was important to them. There has been a shift from focusing on one family member to focusing on the whole family, as well as a shift from focusing on family problems, to focusing on family goals and assets – something which previous service offerings hard rarely done. This approach is consistent with multisystemic therapy developed in the 1970s by Dr. Scott W. Henggeler, which aims to address risk factors in all the contexts a person (particularly juveniles) finds themselves in.

THE FAMILY INFORMATION PROFILE

While the greatest focus has been on prototyping the lead worker service model, we have begun to develop the family information profile, an online tool that will allow families to enter their information once and share it with the people they want.

The question of how to create a platform that gives the family ownership of their story has posed a number of design challenges. First, the intent of the family information profile had to be clearly articulated. Second, research was required to understand what the families wanted and needed and what they had the capability to use. Questions were raised about how the profile will be used, what would be held there, would it contain core documents and information, logs of interactions or be a real time interactive platform?

PHASE TWO INSIGHTS

The changing relationship between the family, their worker and consequently the service system

Respect is an inherent value in taking a co-design approach and the engagement through this project has been authentic and has sought to redress power inequities.

While it seems to be a blatantly obvious idea, the process of simply listening and understanding the family is something that has previously been neglected. Through this project we have seen the profound effect it has had on the experience for both families and lead workers. Lead workers have reflected a sense of slowing down; of managing the complexity by addressing one area at a time which has made the issues families face much less daunting for them. By highlighting the risks and obstacles and encouraging discussions, the conversation has moved away from being crisis driven. The lead worker conversation has helped families move their thinking from day to day survival to thinking about a new future for themselves. It has allowed more information to surface and made it acceptable for everyone to acknowledge the family's true situation. Including more family members has allowed everyone in the family to be helped more effectively. Getting the family together to identify everyone's desires and goals has been as much of an eye opener for the family themselves as it has been for their lead worker.

Changing the Relationship between the Worker and the Service System

A key aspect of the lead worker role was to change the balance of the authorizing environment. Rather than authority being vested for many small decisions with many different public servants, the lead workers had authority to access information and services. Armed with a much deeper and whole understanding of the family situation, lead workers have been able to assist the families in accessing the services that have made an actual positive difference. An example of this comes from one of the lead workers, Kim. Her client's home needed storage furniture in order to make it safer for her disabled children, to allow her to keep the house much tidier, reduce the risk of losing her government housing and consequently lessen the stress, anxiety and depression brought about by living in constant fear of eviction. The client had identified this as being an important goal for her family and was provided with vouchers to buy furniture. However, the vouchers did not cover delivery of the furniture, which made obtaining it well beyond the financial means of the family. This simple failure to consider the whole situation demonstrates the lack of connectivity between services that would normally be insurmountable for families in this situation. Kim's position as lead worker allowed her to access assistance in transporting the furniture, which meant fulfilment of one goal the family had identified at the beginning of the project. This increase in authority given to the lead worker has brought a stronger sense of optimism that 'We can do that' and demonstrates that simple, practical help can have far reaching effects. It is anticipated that as the project matures there will be increasing systemic change in the service system as it reorganizes, on the basis of lead worker design insights.

Inventing Services as Co-design Solutions

Prototyping has been a key design principle through the project and the small scale of this implementation has posed the constant challenge of understanding how the service model can be scaled up or applied to affect whole of system improvement. An example of this is the opportunity given to lead workers to escalate issues to an executive sponsor. This sponsor is able to make an exception for the family, allowing them to access services they would not normally be eligible for. The escalation process is not in itself a scalable model, because when one family is 'pushed to the front of the queue', inevitably another 'falls off the bottom'. For this reason, through the escalation process we have had to identify what are the large-scale, systemic implications? What does the need for escalation tell us about the eligibility criteria or the process through which families must go to access the service? Why must a family show original, certified documents and go through a 12-month process to be granted a mould-free house in which their son who has severe breathing problems is able to live without constant reliance on a breathing device? Why can't the process to access such essential assistance be faster for every family? The project team faced challenges at times in choosing how much of a blank sheet could be taken out for use with families. As the phase two project has progressed, services have been invented through the co-design process, shifting the engagement in design with the families much earlier in the process than had been done before. This approach has led to design not just of services, but of policy and systemic change.

Where to from Here?

At the time of writing, phase two, *Improving Services with Families*, is coming to a close with emerging prototypes for a future service system informed by changed policy settings. It has provided significant insight into what may or may not work systemically.

It is clear that subsequent work will move into redesigning some of the structural elements in the community sector and the government sector. The next questions to address will be about how government agencies and community sector agencies can work together to assemble their services around the needs of the family, ensuring a tailored service package works for the family.

How did design approaches succeed in linking policy intent with on-the-ground professional practices in the field of vulnerable families in Canberra, Australia? The project intent was to develop new capabilities to design and co-produce services with service users as part of a systemic approach to improving outcomes for families in the ACT. This meant:

- Acknowledging the need to understand the experience and needs of service users when designing services;

- Involving them in the process of designing for the services they require;

- Taking an action learning approach where we start with a small scale prototype, identify the lessons and apply what we've learnt to the next prototype and scale it up;

- It also meant not just designing the service itself but looking at the whole system, the policy, the legislation and the service delivery system.

Through prototyping the service offer on a small scale initially we aimed to understand whether these improvements could be scaled up to affect the whole system and how that might be done. The small scale revealed the failures of the system and the impact of having the barriers broken down. Linking policy intent with on-the-ground practices allowed us:

- To better understand the unique journeys of families in the ACT service system in order to identify what could be done better;

- To link the policy development process and service design in a collaborative effort between policymakers and service users.

The project, while starting small, is likely to provide considerable lessons for how such projects can scale to effect system-wide change.

References

Henggeler, S., Melton, G., Brondino, M., Scherer, D., and Hanley, J. (1997). Multisystemic Therapy with Violent and Chronic Juvenile Offenders and Their Families: The Role of Treatment Fidelity in Successful Dissemination. *Journal of Consulting and Clinical Psychology*, 65(5): 821–33.

Jones, C. (1970). *Design Methods: Seeds of Human Futures*. New York: John Wiley and Sons.

CHRISTOPHER T. BOYKO AND RACHEL COOPER

Using an Urban Design Process to Inform Policy

When hearing the word 'city' one may conjure up a multitude of contrasting and ever-changing images: vibrant streetscapes; food deserts; lively cultural scenes; grittiness and grime; a diverse set of cosmopolitan citizens; dangerous, 'no-go' zones; the place of protest and celebration; traffic congestion; accessible public spaces; noise, air and light pollution and so on. Because of the dynamism of cities, policymakers find it extremely difficult to anticipate and accommodate people's wants and needs. This is especially true for those involved in creating policies for the design of urban spaces and places in the UK today: not only do policymakers struggle with writing their own design and planning policies, they also must integrate design into established urban policies and partnerships around sustainable communities (for example, ODPM 2005a), smart cities (for example, European Commission 2012), eco-cities (for example, City of Vancouver 2008) and low-carbon transport strategies (for example, Department for Transport 2009) in the midst of recessions, budget cuts, influxes of new city dwellers and civil unrest.

Furthermore, cities are not normally planned by just one person or ruling group with one set of principles to guide him or her (see Masdar in Abu Dhabi, Dongtan in China and Konza Technology City in Kenya for exceptions). Urban areas are carved into a myriad of spaces, each with different land owners/developers, and competing interests and ideas about how best to develop that area. While owners/developers must comply with the policies set forth by local authorities and national government – who do not always see eye to eye on things – the end results of such development might stand in opposition to the tight-knit urban fabric envisioned by policymakers. Taken together, then, *how can policy be designed to take account of the shifting nature of cities if we do not understand how, and by whom, cities are designed and operated?*

This chapter's central thesis is that, for cities to work successfully in urban design policy terms, policymakers and other stakeholders need to understand the urban design process and associated decision-making within that process. Thus, the first section of this chapter outlines the need for an urban design process. The second section discusses how using the urban design process can inform policy. A brief case example about creating local spatial density policy using the process completes the chapter.

A Process for Urban Design

Processes provide people with a method, procedure or series of steps that, if followed, should lead to them accomplishing what they set out to do. Many different professions and disciplines, including business/management (Smith and Jackson 2000), non-governmental organizations (English Partnerships 2004; Heritage Lottery Fund 2000) and built environment areas, such as engineering (Macmillan 2002), construction (Cooper et al. 2005; Woodhead 2000), manufacturing (Austin et al. 2001), planning (Bressi 1995; Canadian Institute of Planners 2000; Nelessen 1994; Okubo 2000; Roberts 2006; Wates 1996, 1998), design (Kagioglou et al. 1998) and architecture (RIBA 1999), use processes in an attempt to understand how things are done as well as when they are done and, in some cases who does them and why. These processes may have clear stages, phases, gates, activities and feedback loops that help to bring a clearer understanding to the complexity involved in doing what they do. In contrast, there appears to be a lack of clarity regarding a defined decision-making process for urban design even though some scholars have explored such processes (see Biddulph 1997; Rowland 1995); this may be due to the multitude of stakeholders, decision-makers, tasks and issues contained within city development projects and plans (Boyko et al. 2005; Boyko et al. 2006). In addition, many developers, construction professionals, architects and designers work at the development scale – with local authority development officers often responding to plans at this scale – which means that the process for how the larger urban area is considered may not be critically and holistically contemplated.

Regardless, there is a need for a mapped, decision-making process for urban design. Unless such a process or a model exists, policymakers truly will not know how policies, regulations and guidelines influence and impact – or *should* influence and impact – decision-making at various urban scales, from neighbourhood to city to region and beyond. Intertwined with this notion, which often is discussed in policy and service design circles, policymakers will be unsure of how their policies affect the actual experiences, behaviours and services of stakeholders at individual, local and city scales. Finally, policymakers will not be able to understand how urban design can influence policy without a map. For those cities that are interested in pursuing specific projects or campaigns, or embracing specific ideologies (such as, for example, smart city, sustainable city, low-carbon city, eco-city), a mapped process may be useful to show how, when and by whom various policies have been enacted, or where scientific evidence and knowledge can and should be applied in the process and by whom.

As part of a five-year, £3-million, UK-based research project called *VivaCity2020*, the authors mapped a process for sustainable urban design decision-making. This process was based on a critical review of decision-making processes to understand how processes work in theory as well as case studies of different developments in three UK cities to establish how processes work in practice. Through an analysis of this research, the authors developed a clearer understanding of who makes decisions about urban design, when they should make those decisions, what tools and resources they might use to make those decisions and how sustainability should be an integral part of the decision-making process (see Figure 9.1).

The figure visualizes the process as a series of iterative stages (top orange band) with opportunities for Sustainability Tasks (middle band) and Sustainability Reviews (bottom band). The top band shows five stages, which are mostly consistent with the literature and the processes-in-practice (the number of stages found in processes in the literature varied from three to twelve, with an average between four and five; case study process stages also varied, but there was consistency about what decision-makers needed to do across an urban design project). The middle band contains four Sustainability Tasks that decision-makers should complete as part of undertaking an urban design project. Each sustainability task involves two decision-making teams – a Development Team and a Project Sustainability Group – coming together to decide sustainability priorities at each stage, with both teams agreeing an agenda (just before

Urban design decision-making process

VivaCity has developed an urban design decision-making model to help designers, architects, planners and other professionals make more effective and sustainable design decisions.

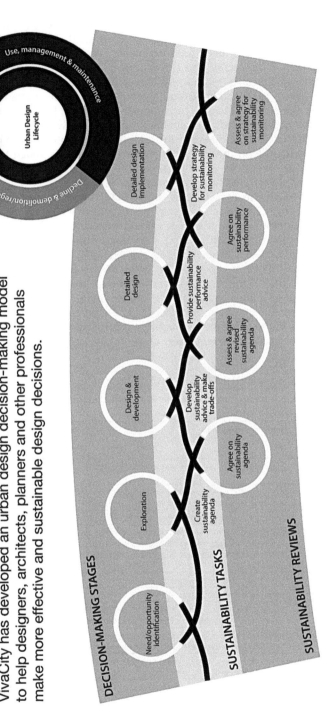

Urban Design Lifecycle
- Use, management & maintenance
- Decline & demolition/regeneration
- Legacy Archive
- Pre-Design

DECISION-MAKING STAGES
- Need/opportunity identification
- Exploration
- Design & development
- Detailed design
- Detailed design implementation

SUSTAINABILITY TASKS
- Create sustainability agenda
- Develop sustainability advice & make trade-offs
- Provide sustainability performance advice
- Develop strategy for sustainability monitoring

SUSTAINABILITY REVIEWS
- Agree on sustainability agenda
- Assess & agree revised sustainability agenda
- Agree on sustainability performance
- Assess & agree on strategy for sustainability monitoring

Figure 9.1 The sustainable urban design decision-making process

Source: Reproduced from R. Cooper, G. Evans, and C. Boyko, *Designing Sustainable Cities*, London: Wiley-Blackwell (2009), with kind permission of the publishers

the Exploration stage), developing advice and making trade-offs (before the Design and Development stage), providing performance advice (before the Detailed Design stage) and developing a strategy for sustainability monitoring (before the Detailed Design Implementation stage). The Development Team incorporates those people who wish to develop an area (for example, developers, architects, financiers/investors) whereas the Project Sustainability Group involves people who can participate during the lifetime of the project (such as, construction companies, local authority planners, residents). The bottom band, Sustainability Reviews, allows both decision-making teams to come to a 'final' agreement on sustainability priorities before moving on to the next stage. Illustrating the Sustainability Reviews as loops, much like the stages, suggests that agreements may not be final and, indeed, discussions may continue until both teams are satisfied with the outcomes.

In addition to the visualized process, a suite of tools and resources were developed during the *VivaCity2020* project that may be used to make urban design decisions. These tools can be employed primarily for gaining knowledge about a particular context rather than for trying or experimenting with ideas. Some of the tools also may be used for highlighting issues to stakeholders (for example, creative arts interpretations of research data) as well as for engaging with stakeholders who normally may not have a say in the decision-making process as a way to create a more democratic, collaborative process (Innes and Booher 1999; Heale 1997, 1998, 2003) (see Halse, Chapter 16, for more democratic engagement in the process). Table 9.1 lists the tools and states where in the process they might be used. Given that there are many more tools available for decision-makers, users of the process have the opportunity to add their own to the list.

Table 9.1   Decision-making tools and resources and when in the process to use them

When in the process to use tools	Decision-making tools
Between Stages 0 and 2	Bibliographic review of mixed-use, organized by theme
	Environmental quality case studiesa: includes innovative, mixed-methods approaches for gathering environmental quality data
	Housing case studies: includes typologies of UK housing from 1820 to the present day
	Liveability postal survey: captures residential satisfaction in an area, divided into four themes: upkeep and management of public spaces and buildings; road traffic and transportation-related issues; abandonment or non-residential use of domestic property and anti-social behaviour
	Night-time economy and crime case studies
	Retail and crime case studies
	Space Syntax analysis: shows relationships between street layout and residential property value as well as the value and formation of urban centres
	Toilet user personas: creation of 'archetypal users' who seek toilet provision in downtowns to help planners decide where to put public conveniences in cities
	Toilet user surveys: used to indicate people's feelings about how provision meets local communities' needs
	Creative arts interpretations of researcher data: working with artists to give alternative insights into sustainability and the urban experience of city users (for example, using data about what local residents like in their neighbourhood and creating visualizations that represent their preferences, and displaying the work in a local art gallery)

Between Stages 2 and 3	Environmental quality case studies (see above)
	Inclusive toilet hierarchy: identifies a hierarchy of away-from-home toilet provision in cities and is used to inform debates about the number and types of accessible toilets in any context
	Intangible Value of Urban Layout (I-VALUL): a presentation that explores residential burglary and street robbery, and the value of personal and property security
	New Urbanist case study: assesses whether the case study area has become a safer, more sustainable place in which to live
	Open Space Strategy: quantitative dataset for 30 housing schemes detailing figure-ground ratios of buildings and open spaces, local street hierarchy and the type, height, transparency and permeability of building facades and secondary boundaries
	Spatial data analysis: used to map economic, social and land-use diversity using GIS. Can be used with Space Syntax to identify street and pedestrian routes, and with on-street surveys to identify pedestrian movement
	Toilet user personas (see above)
	Toilet user surveys (see above)
Between Stages 3 and 4	Toilet design templates: used to help design accessible and inclusive toilets
After and including Stage 4	Urban design process case studies
	Spatial data analysis (see above)

All case studies were completed in London, Manchester or Sheffield in the UK.
Source: R. Cooper and C. Boyko (2010, pp. 265–70)

The above process not only maps out the different stages needed to complete an urban design project, but it also shows who makes decisions (via the two decision-making teams), when they make them and how they make them (via the accompanying list of tools and resources). Such a process can be very useful, particularly to inform urban design policy.

Using the Urban Design Process to Inform Policy

During the last administration, the UK Government established many national-scale policies, regulations and guidance pertaining to urban design and planning (for example, Department for Communities and Local Government 2006, 2007; Department of the Environment 1990; Office of the Deputy Prime Minister 2000, 2004a, 2005a, 2005b, 2005c, 2006a, 2006b; Urban Task Force, 1999, 2005). The current government has maintained some of these policies while consolidating others into the current National Planning Policy Framework (NPPF), aimed to make the planning system less complex, more accessible and drive sustainable growth (Department for Communities and Local Government 2012). This framework provides guidance to local authorities when making plans and planning decisions, *but how are the framework policies interpreted at the local scale?*

Through the NPPF, national-scale policies are applied at the local scale by local authorities via the creation of their own, related policies, partnerships and so forth. For example, every local authority must create a Local Development Framework (LDF), which is a suite of documents pertaining to how the local authority plans to develop their area, how they would like to involve citizens in planning and how they plan to monitor progress (Office of the Deputy Prime Minister 2004b). In theory, the LDF should respond to the general position of the NPPF as well as to specific points made therein. To help decide the priority areas for buildings, infrastructure and facilities as well as local economic and employment priorities, for example, local authorities are encouraged to partner with businesses via Local Enterprise Partnerships (LEPs) (Department for Business, Innovation & Skills 2010). The LEPs play a central role in determining local agendas; to be successful, however, they also need to incorporate global issues, such as climate change and low-carbon transport, into local policies and guidance.

When decision-making bodies and their requirements are aligned, policy creation and successful practical outcomes are possible. However, what happens when national policy, which normally trickles down to local-scale policy or guidance, no longer exists? How do local authorities handle important issues without guidance from above? The urban design decision-making process can help by showing where and how to engage with a variety of stakeholders to create policy that suits the local scale. The next section illustrates an example with the creation of spatial density policy via the urban design process.

Case Example: Creating Density Policy Via the Urban Design Process

Spatial density is important to urban design and planning because it can be used by decision-makers to describe, predict and control land use (Berghauser Pont and Haupt 2007; DETR 1998; Boyko and Cooper 2011). In the UK, the past government developed a policy, known as Planning Policy Statement 3 (PPS3): Housing (Department for Communities and Local Government 2006), in which a national minimum density of 30 dwellings per hectare was established. Planning with this target in mind was encouraged; however, local authorities also were to set densities in line with local housing demand and need, availability of land and current and future infrastructure needs. Since the current Government has been in power in 2010, the minimum density target has been abolished and local authorities are more or less free to establish dwelling densities as they please; they also can work within LEPs and neighbourhoods, via neighbourhood development plans (Department for Communities and Local Government 2011), to develop standards, if any. Under such plans, recognized groups, such as residents' organizations, voluntary groups and community groups, can lead all stages of plan-making and employ a range of tools, both for gaining knowledge and for exploration, for determining local densities and other related issues (for example, land use designations). These plans must sit within the local authority's core strategy as well as national planning policy and EU regulations, and allow neighbourhoods to permit development that they want without needing planning applications to do so. As of August 2014, over 1,000 communities have taken formal steps to produce a neighbourhood plan, over 100 draft plans have been produced for consultation and 28 neighbourhood plans have been passed at community referendums (Department for Communities and Local Government, August 2014).

Abolishing the national minimum density target presents an exciting opportunity for local authorities to use the urban design decision-making process to create policy that is relevant to spatial density as well as relevant to the local context. At present, most local authority policy planners and development control officers make decisions about density based on built form (for example, the number of dwellings per hectare) and population (that is, the number of persons per hectare). However, they often do not consider other, density-related issues when planning neighbourhoods and cities, such as the density of natural form (for example, greenspace), mobile material form (trains, private vehicles) and static form (such as mobile phone masts). Furthermore, decision-makers rarely systematically consider the less tangible conditions that influence, and are influenced by, density (Boyko and Cooper 2011). These conditions include the human dimensions of density, such as perception (such as related to crowding), behaviour and needs, and the context and quality of surrounding areas, including the requirements of those living and working in those areas (see Cohen and Gutman 2007; Day and Day 1973; Raman 2010; Rao 2007; Rapoport 1975). Using the urban design decision-making process gives policymakers an opportunity to ensure that the above issues are considered at different stages.

From the beginning, decision-makers can open up the process and invite people to be part of decision-making, joining the Development Team or the Project Team. Doing so ensures that there will be more people around the table at key decision-making points – which may lead to more tensions but, hopefully, a greater representation of voices – and allows people to join and leave the process at any time. Knowing more about who these people are (for example, their roles in their community and at the local authority scale), what experience and expertise they bring, the myriad of tools and resources to help people make informed decisions and when in the process key decisions need to be made means that a more comprehensive understanding of the dimensions of density can be considered and thus the process of creating local policy around density ultimately can be more resilient to future changes than policies at the national scale.

Conclusions

If cities are going to reach their low-carbon targets by 2050 as well as become more sustainable, 'smart', 'eco' and resilient, we will need to ensure that policy is robust and that they produce positive changes in citizens' behaviour. To do so, policymakers and citizens will need to better understand the process through which cities are designed, as the form of urban environments can impact how we/an area feel(s), how we/an area flow(s) and where we settle. Through the case example of density, we illustrated that knowing who is making decisions about built form, when they are making those decisions and how they are making those decisions can influence the creation of density policy.

Once we have a common platform and understanding of the process, we can tap into knowledge and evidence from experts (for example, scientists, community activists and representatives) to inform planning decisions. We also can adopt digital platforms and visualizations to engage citizens more actively, which may help not just aspects of democracy and open planning, but also the opportunity to model and mediate citizen behaviour. By engaging citizens in all the decision-making stages and using technology to visualize, record and analyze, citizens become part of the process of iterative testing, implementing and reviewing of ideas. Thus, we become a learning society in which places truly are made by the people.

The next step is for policymakers to ensure that policy supports a holistic and innovative urban design decision-making process, undertaken by skilled stakeholders, whilst also engaging appropriate evidence, foresight and citizen engagement to deliver liveable cities of the future.

References

Austin, S., Steele, J., Macmillan, S., Kirby, P. and Spence, R. (2001). Mapping the Conceptual Design Activity of Interdisciplinary Teams. *Design Studies*, 22(3): 211–32.

Berghauser Pont, M. and Haupt, P. (2007). The Relation Between Urban Form and Density. *Viewpoints* 11(1). Retrieved 14 July 2010 from http://www.urbanform.org/journal/viewpoints/viewpoints0107.html.

Biddulph, M. (1997). An Urban Design Process for Large Development Sites. *Town and Country Planning*, 66: 202–4.

Boyko, C.T. and Cooper, R. (2011). Clarifying and Re-conceptualising Density. *Progress in Planning*, 76: 1–61.

Boyko, C.T., Cooper, R. and Davey, C. (2005). Sustainability and the Urban Design Process. *Engineering Sustainability*, 158(ES3): 119–25.

Boyko, C.T., Cooper, R., Davey, C.L. and Wootton, A.B. (2006). Addressing Sustainability Early in the Urban Design Process. *Management of Environmental Quality*, 17(6): 689–706.

Bressi, T. (1995). The real thing? We're Getting There. *Planning*, 61(7), 16–21.

Canadian Institute of Planners. (20000. *The Urban Design Process*. Retrieved 24 June 2004 from http://www.cip-icu.ca/English/aboutplan/ud_proce.htm.

City of Vancouver (2008). *EcoDensity charter*. Vancouver, Canada: City of Vancouver.

Cohen, M. and Gutman, M. (2007). Density: An Overview Essay. *Built Environment*, 33(2): 141–4.

Cooper, R., Aouad, G., Lee, A., Wu, S., Fleming, A. and Kagioglou, M. (2005). *Process Management in Design and Construction*. Oxford: Blackwell.

Cooper, R. and Boyko, C. (2010). How to Design a City in Four Easy Steps: Exploring VivaCity2020's process and Tools for Urban Design Decision Making. *Journal of Urbanism*, 3(3): 253–73.

Day, A.T. and Day, L.H. (1973). Cross-national Comparison of Population Density. *Science*, 181(4104): 1016–23.

Department for Business, Innovation & Skills (2010). *Local Growth: Realising Every Place's Potential*. London: The Stationery Office.

Department for Communities and Local Government (DCLG) (2006). *Planning Policy Statement 3 (PPS3): Housing*. London: Her Majesty's Stationery Office.

Department for Communities and Local Government (2007). *Planning for a sustainable future*. London: Her Majesty's Stationery Office.

Department for Communities and Local Government (2011). *The Localism Act*. London: Her Majesty's Stationery Office.

Department for Communities and Local Government (2012). *National Planning Policy Framework*. London: Her Majesty's Stationery Office.

Department for Communities and Local Government (August 2014). *Notes on Neighbourhood Planning: Edition 10*. London: Her Majesty's Stationery Office.N

Department for Transport (2009). *Low Carbon Transport: A greener Future*. London: Her Majesty's Stationery Office.

Department of Environment (1990). *This Common Inheritance: Britain's Environmental Strategy*. London: The Stationery Office.

Department of the Environment, Transport and the Regions (DETR) (1998). *Planning research programme*: The Use of Density in Urban Planning. London: The Stationery Office.

English Partnerships (2004). *Urban Regeneration Companies: Coming of Age*. London: English Partnerships.

European Commission (2012). *Smart Cities and Communities – European Innovation Partnership.* Brussels, BE: European Commission.

Healey, P. (1997). *Collaborative Planning: Shaping Places in Fragmented Societies.* Vancouver, Canada: UBC Press.

Healey, P. (1998). Building Institutional Capacity Through Collaborative Approaches to Urban Planning. *Environment and Planning A,* 30 (9): 1531–46.

Healey, P. (2003). Collaborative planning in perspective. *Planning Theory,* 2(2): 101–23.

Heritage Lottery Fund. (2000). *Building Projects: Your Role in Achieving Quality and Value.* London: Heritage Lottery Fund.

Innes, J.E. and Booher, D.E. (1999). Consensus Building and Complex Adaptive Systems: A Framework for Evaluating Collaborative Planning. *Journal of the American Planning Association,* 65 (4): 412–23.

Kagioglou, M., Cooper, R., Aouad, G., Hinks, J., Sexton, M. and Sheath, D.M. (1998). *A Generic Guide to the Design and Construction Process Protocol.* Salford: University of Salford.

Local Government Group (2011). *Neighbourhood Planning: A Guide for Ward Councillors.* London: Local Government Group.

Macmillan, S., Steele, J., Kirby, P., Spence, R. and Austin, S. (2002). Mapping the Design Process During the Conceptual Phase of Building Projects. *Engineering, Construction and Architectural Management,* 9(3): 174–80.

Nelessen, A.C. (1994). *Visions for a New American Dream: Process, Principles, and an Ordinance to Plan and Design Small Communities* (2nd edn). Chicago: Planners Press.

Office of the Deputy Prime Minister (ODPM) (2000). *Our Cities and Towns: The Future-Delivering an Urban Renaissance.* London: HMSO.

Office of the Deputy Prime Minister (2004a). Planning Policy Statement 11 (PPS11): *Regional Spatial Strategies.* London: Her Majesty's Stationery Office.

Office of the Deputy Prime Minister (2004b). *Planning and Compulsory Purchase Act.* London: Her Majesty's Stationery Office.

Office of the Deputy Prime Minister (2005a). *Sustainable Communities: People, Places and Prosperity.* London: Her Majesty's Stationery Office.

Office of the Deputy Prime Minister (ODPM) (2005b). *Planning Policy Statement 1 (PPS1): Delivering Sustainable Development.* London: Her Majesty's Stationery Office.

Office of the Deputy Prime Minister (2005c). Planning Policy Statement 6 (PPS6): *Planning for Town Centres.* London: Her Majesty's Stationery Office.

Office of the Deputy Prime Minister (2006a). *Securing the Future: UK Sustainable Development Strategy.* London: Her Majesty's Stationery Office.

Office of the Deputy Prime Minister (2006b). *Barker Review of Land Use Planning.* London: Her Majesty's Stationery Office.

Okubo, D. (2000). *The Community Visioning and Strategic Planning Handbook.* Denver, CO: National Civic League Press. Retrieved 20 July 2005 from http://www.ncl.org/publications/online/VSPHandbook.pdf.

Raman, S. (2010). Designing a Liveable Compact City: Physical Forms of City and Social Life in Urban Neighbourhoods. *Built Environment,* 36(1), 63–80.

Rao, V. (2007). Proximity Distances: The Phenomenology of Density in Mumbai. *Built Environment,* 33(2): 227–48.

Rapoport, A. (1975). Toward a Redefinition of Density. *Environment and Behavior,* 7(2): 133–58.

RIBA (1999). *RIBA Plan of Work.* London: RIBA.

Roberts, M.B. (2006). *Making the Vision Concrete: Implementation of Downtown Revitalization Plans.* Unpublished doctoral thesis, University of California, Irvine.

Rowland, J. (1995). The Urban Design Process. *Urban Design Quarterly*, 56. Retrieved 14 July 2004 from http://www.rudi.net/bookshelf/ej/udq/56/udp.cfm.

Smith, J. and Jackson, N. (2000). Strategic Needs Analysis: Its Role in Brief Development. *Facilities*, 18(13/14): 502–12.

Urban Task Force (1999). *Towards an Urban Renaissance*. London: HMSO.

Urban Task Force (2005). *Towards a Strong Urban Renaissance*. London: HMSO.

Wates, N. (1996). A community process. *Urban Design Quarterly, 58 Supplement*. Retrieved 14 July 2004 from http://www.rudi.net/bookshelf/ej/udq/58conf/cp.cfm.

Wates, N. (1998). Process Planning Session. *Urban Design Quarterly, 67 Special report: Involving Local Communities in Urban Design*. Retrieved 14 July 2004 from http://www.rudi.net/bookshelf/ej/udq/67_report/method_10.cfm.

Woodhead, R.M. (2000). Investigation of the Early Stages of Project Formulation. *Facilities*, 18(13/14): 524–34.

KIT LYKKETOFT

Designing Legitimacy: The Case of a Government Innovation Lab

In my work introducing design processes into government administration I have become increasingly aware of the importance of legitimacy to do so. This realization has lead me to the question of what constitutes legitimacy and if it can be designed and scaled.

If legitimacy is understood as 'a generalized perception or assumption that the actions of an entity are desirable, proper, or appropriate within some socially constructed norms, values, beliefs and definition' (Suchman 1995: 574) then it is key to enacting change. In the case of MindLab, Denmark, an internal cross-ministerial unit was set up in 2007 to promote design thinking and praxis. Because of the relatively long existence of this unit it can be considered a useful case study.

It can be argued that setting up a unit like MindLab is in itself a design approach to change in the public sector. When aiming to introduce alternative praxis, like design, an implicit challenge is the fact that well-established systems are hard to confront and change. The challenge in change agency is not new and has been discussed by theorists of institutional entrepreneurship and institutional work over the last three decades (Battilana and DÁunno 2009). It has, however, rarely been discussed in the setting of the public sector, which comes with different preconditions from private companies.

Looking at the example of MindLab through this lens not only provides a possible explanation as to how agency can exist despite embedding in a larger and more established system, it also supports the increasing awareness of the importance of curiosity and professional empathy when setting out to work with a focus on citizens and design in praxis (Boyer, Cook and Steinberg 2011: 101; Caffin 2011). If design is defined as thinking through doing (Restarting Britain 2 2013: 9), then design legitimacy becomes about both intangible and tangible resources and how they are strategically or intuitively used to create the desired difference in the world. Ultimately it becomes about people, their beliefs and interactions.

Content-wise MindLab has been speaking to and pushing an emerging agenda of public sector innovation and is experiencing an increasing interest both nationally and internationally in how to grow the innovation agenda and in what it has taken to build the kind of capacity that MindLab constitutes. Many administrations are now struggling to find the key to introducing the ideas of more open and yet systematic approaches to policymaking and service delivery. There seems to be an emerging openness to test new forms of governance. MindLab can be seen as a relation network-institution and constitutes one way of arranging an alternative approach that challenges the belief that top-down management is always the best way of solving public sector problems.

MindLab is often requested to share experiences on the components needed to undertake that alternative approach and I therefore decided to investigate how MindLab gained the legitimacy that it holds today. Internal and external stakeholders on different levels and MindLab staff were interviewed for this research. The MindLab experience may offer some lessons learned that could be useful in setting up a similar organization. Additionally questions may also arise on the way forward for MindLab and for the role of design as governance tool.

This study suggests that it is more *how* MindLab has done things, rather than *what* it has done that has helped in establishing legitimacy. Important elements that have emerged are adaptable strategies, shared internal values and empathetic approaches in the work undertaken. Some of these points may be applied in a general sense although the specific setting should always be considered.

Introducing MindLab

MindLab was originally established in 2002 to provide project support for the Ministry of Business. In 2006 it was re-conceived and re-established as a cross-ministerial cooperation project aimed at introduce the Danish government administration to the ideas and praxis of design, innovation and user involvement and to work across silos in devising solutions. Backed and funded by three ministries MindLab was intended to disrupt the existing system in a constructive way and come up with better solutions through experimentation with methods and different options. The concrete method of ethnography was used to learn about citizens' experiences with public services and policies and design methods were applied for prototyping and testing new solutions with end-users. MindLab was created to enhance the cooperation between silos and bring new competencies to the administration.

Drawing inspiration from rising trends in the private sector, where for instance US-based IDEO used similar methods to improve both products and company business plans, this route was to be tried in the public sector (Coughlan, Suri and Canales 2007).

MindLabs mission is as follows: 'MindLab works with its owners to create change which generates the desired value for citizens, businesses and society.' It has three strategic objectives: public sector innovation, strengthening change capacity and visibility/legitimacy.

With a permanent staff of eight to ten, MindLab was engaged to carry out projects with colleagues from the ministries and their agencies and thereby increase capacity. MindLab had the theoretical foundation, funding for the first three years, which has since been renewed twice, and an optimal anchoring in an agreement between three permanent secretaries to give its operation a chance to succeed.[1] However, it needed broad support for success.

---

1   The owner-ministries in 2007 were The Ministry of Economic and Business affairs, The Ministry of Taxation and The Ministry of Employment. In 2013 the owners are The Ministry of Business and Growth, The Ministry of Employment, The Ministry of Education and (from October 2013) Odense municipality, a city of 200,000.

Theoretical Framing

Drawing from the theory of institutional entrepreneurship, MindLab looked at a potential paradox between structure and agency, commonly referred to as the paradox of embedded agency: How can you enact change if you are embedded in the settings you wish to change and your actions are likely to be determined by them? (Garud, Hardy and Maguire 2007: 958; Leca, Battilana and Boxenbaum 2008: 4).

In an attempt to explain how the paradox may be overcome, Lawrence, Suddaby and Leca, recognized that institutions can effect action, but put forward that action and actors can also effect institutions. Looking at the '... the practical actions through which institutions are created, maintained and disrupted' (2009: 7) may be an approach for understanding how change can happen despite embeddedness.

In this perspective the people you put in your organization and how they act become the enablers of legitimacy to do so. This condition raises both questions of what can be done to establish legitimacy both in the creation-phase and in maintaining it over time.

The perspective of *stabilizing* an organization contains an interesting dilemma that MindLab has to bear in mind in moving forward. If an institution sets out to disrupt an existing system and to some extent succeeds and reaches a point of a possible affirmation, how is this done without it then becoming a part of the establishment and losing, if not legitimacy, then perhaps its original identity? And what if from the outset the original purpose included an implicit vision of optimally becoming redundant? Is that not then a contradiction or at least the opposite of success to aim for stabilizing internally?

Change Challenge

Civil servants share the obligation to work towards legitimacy with citizens, as well as to create the desired effectiveness, services and changes in behaviours. Although public sector institutions all over the world struggle to meet expectations, sometimes the solutions offered are produced from the perspective of organizational efficiency rather than citizen need. This may occur to ensure reaching the desired outcome rather than risking error – the risk that comes from trying new ways and that opposes the traditional understanding of how things should be done in the public sector.

Ultimately it is a question of choosing known risks versus unknown risks. Although rarely discussed, it is an inherent paradox that risks certainly also exist in the more traditional model. The reluctance to take risks is mainly for unknown risks, the risks that come with processes not already incorporated in the system.

> That bill, well it didn't hit the spot, but then we just try again. The costs from all these repetitions that we do in the traditional system are not measured. And again, no one measures a lost opportunity. The fact that we could have used our resources better or moved even further with an alternative approach has no price-tag. It can be a lot easier to go for lean-and process-optimizing, because then you know that you have saved ¼ FTE when you are done; instead of taking the chance of perhaps saving 10. It is about risk-taking.
>
> H.V.C., former director of innovation, Ministry of Taxation

This example exposes the paradoxes in the existing system including the lack of incentive to work towards more radical change and the range of choices in the tool-box most commonly used.[2] The ways of doing things need to open up towards the rest of the world. The public sector challenge of needing to create long-term solutions in a rapidly changing world calls for a need for more options in governance. The design approach contributes to aligning the system with today's complexity.

> However dangerous it is, I do believe that there are many places around in the ministries with a closed culture in terms of 'we know our field, we made the laws, we have all the data and we make the analysis and fundamentally it is not that welcome that someone from outside comes in'.
>
> B.S., permanent secretary, member of the MindLab board.[3]

Refining the challenge created by MindLab contained a range of dilemmas. How could design-praxis be introduced without appearing like a condemnation of the hard work being done in more traditional ways? And how could a balance between experimentation and citizen involvement and the culture of zero-mistakes be maintained? How could MindLab operate on all the levels needed and be legitimate within the existing system?

A number of elements can be identified as instrumental in creating and maintaining this needed legitimacy. The following sections discuss how this was done in the case of MindLab.

Organizational Position

The organizing principle of MindLabs has been centred on legitimacy and agency needed for enacting change. Its internal organization anchored by a top-management board provides an overarching strategic view. However it is also essential for a small strategic unit to be manoeuvrable. The potential exists of being overwhelmed by administrative procedures. In the case of MindLab the question of how to leverage resources has had to be attuned to the needs of internal stakeholders on an ongoing basis:

> If all your resources are spent on you writing working-programmes, following up on them and going to meetings with us then it becomes pure bureaucracy.
>
> B.S., permanent secretary, member of the MindLab board

The asset of being on the inside is the possibility of being perceived as colleagues, who simply have alternative skill sets. This position is slightly different from being an expert coming in from the outside. It also opens the potential for creating and sustaining a network over time.

---

2 For more on new tools of Government see Horizons 2012.
3 B.S. left the job as Permanent Secretary and member of the MindLab Board in August 2013.

What is the difference between you and all the others? Why don't I just buy some external consultants? What is it ...? You have this edge. You are free to say no and I get no consultants-hubbub. You know the ministry from the inside and we see you as colleagues. You follow up after a while and ask how the implementation went and if you can assist with anything to support that process further. That gives you credibility and makes it worth coming to MindLab.

S.Ø., middle manager, The National Board of Industrial Injuries

It is, on the other hand a fine balance to be and appear to be only loosely linked with the existing system, to have the freedom of scope and to be independent enough to in fact be that neutral ground on which cooperation can happen while being part of the system. The trust that MindLab is not pushing hidden agendas has to be continuously created via relations and by actions.

Adaptable Strategy in a Learning Organization

While MindLab has a written strategy, its legitimacy is built through its ability to adapt, to learn by doing and to be flexible in implementing the strategy. The strategy has had to adapt countless times over the years. Resources have been leveraged according to changes in stakeholder wishes. Constraints provided by existing structures have been targeted both collectively and individually along the way, often on the basis of intuition in the given situations:

We do what is pragmatic and what functions in the situations that arise.
N.H., project manager, MindLab

MindLab is a learning organization and there is consistent alignment of the employees. Frequent discussions on the next steps to take are often basically summarizing sessions, as the understanding of the strategy is constantly evolving and adapts to the current situation. The strategy is alive and flexible; learning that flows from the 'doing' is transformed into co-produced new actions and becomes co-owned by everyone in MindLab:

... it is something organic, it is something that happens continuously, it is something that happens in-between. Often our sessions are just summing up the always ongoing talks on week-briefings, discussions from the concrete projects in the project-teams, our talks across the desks. Then we sum up every once in a while and cement it; sometimes we also write it down on paper, but I don't think that anyone ever reads those papers we write. It is something immaterial. It is just a common understanding we have between us. It is actually interesting ... I believe that it is a sign of a very healthy culture that people who come to work here for shorter or longer periods of time pretty fast join in on the discussions; it shows that it may be informal but also always present. Everyone gets it instantly; it is not something secret that needs to be read in some strategy-document somewhere.

N.H, project panager, MindLab

Of particular interest are the elements that made it possible for MindLab to be this adaptable. This flexibility is mainly a consequence of the people in the organization, how they work and the leadership being practiced:

> *Leading MindLab is to a high extent to be co-creator of meaning, the articulator of it and to remind us all of that meaning.*
>
> C.B, director, MindLab

Forming the Team

To have credibility in the government administration it is crucial to be good at what you do. Having the right people has been the most important factor for establishing MindLab's legitimacy to act. When setting up MindLab, a thorough external recruiting process was conducted to ensure that the skills and competencies required would be present from the beginning. The focus was on the disciplines needed and the experience using them in complex settings.

> *What I then perceived as the biggest challenge was setting the right team.*
>
> C.B., director, MindLab

A competence model was created that laid out the disciplines needed. The bubbles represent individual skills while the triangle shows what everyone should be capable of (Figure 10.1).

Figure 10.1   Competence model showing the disciplines needed in MindLab

It all comes down to that you need a very high professional level and I believe you succeeded with that ... You are recruiting people with slightly alternative profiles, but also fundamentally really intelligent and skilled people.

B.S., permanent secretary, member of the MindLab board

Recruiting for MindLab is based on the theory that social capital and social skills are characteristics for institutional entrepreneurs (Leca, Battilana and Boxenbaum 2008: 16). Social skills can be seen as the ability not only to use a given position of the organization or the individual, but also to bring 'the right' people together and to be empathetic. From this perspective, a more appropriate model would be adding a circle around the entire model labelled 'social skills' or in the language of MindLab 'professional empathy'.

Shared Beliefs, Consistent Approaches and Empathy

In the same way that both organizational framing and position are a starting point, so is a high level of professionalism within the discipline. In fact it is a prerequisite. While the recruitment announcement was focused on specific competencies, it indeed also attracted people who enjoy change processes and are driven by a higher purpose.

You know ... the ad sounded 'Do you want to revolutionise the public sector?' I wanted to do that.

A.V., designer, MindLab

The headline of the first recruitment ad can be seen as the first public narrative of MindLab. It attracted people who saw themselves within certain norms.

If 'norms' are the collective belief system and 'beliefs' the individuals personal beliefs (Hoffman 1999: 351), the two are not necessarily aligned. However, in the MindLab case it seems important that they are.

Common values are so important, as it is actually where so many of our processes and methods and approaches and relationships flow from.

C.B., director, MindLab

The staff members feel ownership, commitment and are collectively ambitious about making a difference. There is a shared belief that the work done at MindLab matters. The people-focused nature of the methods and the built-in need for cooperation and learning in innovation processes seem to be the guiding stars and impetus for alignment of strategy.

We have a common leading star that we have an aligned understanding of. Everything we do flows from this.

J.S., project manager, MindLab

This alignment seems important to the way MindLab expresses itself and how the work is perceived by others. The perceived authenticity and enthusiasm may be immeasurable but resonates well with stakeholders, supporting legitimacy.

I have noticed that when you communicate your results, when some of the employees for instance present for the board then there is always an enthusiasm and a pride from 'look what we have found out.
B.S., permanent secretary, member of the MindLab board

No one at MindLab has exactly the same educational or professional background. As such the teamwork leverages a powerful sense of 'we'. Being a small team with diverse backgrounds has created a precondition whereby people need to rely on each other. In addition the nature of the design approach calls for cross-disciplinary work. This has led to a praxis of collectively framing the work and for collective learning from not only mistakes made, but also new potential mistakes and successes. This praxis supports consistency and consistency in turn supports legitimacy

I don't believe you can work in MindLab without fundamentally feeling that you want to change things for the better, because you wouldn't all have been consistent in all the different settings you are engaged in. There would be too much divergence in what is being said and done, and I don't believe there is.
C.P., municipal manager for disability services and MA student doing field-work on public sector innovation

The MindLab staff scale their message and methods and consciously aim at creating buy-in through a conscious empathetic approach to stakeholders. Professional empathy is an approach that aims at understanding things from the other person's perspective:

We meet people where they are and adapt the methods and communication to their setting.
J.S., project manager, MindLab

Things play out differently in the daily workings of projects with citizens and civil servants where ethnographic approaches help build a sense of curiosity:

It is a classic anthropological trick to let the other one be the expert: 'I just want to hear what you are saying, I know nothing.' It is a professional trick, but also a human value that only works if it is sincere. Sincere is very important to sustain legitimacy in the connection. Professional empathy is both empathy with the citizens and with the work that is already being done in the ministries.
J.C., research manager, MindLab

Real examples from the lives of everyday citizens are used to help communicate the innovative work of MindLab:

Because you hit [the] target with that very intuitive approach you have. You are also very good at communicating the message that this is the right thing to do. You talk a lot about ethics and moral. You establish some truths. ... I don't believe it is meant as manipulation as I do think that you all believe in it. There is an authenticity. When you are physically in MindLab it is the same. ... You leave a feeling that this is not to trick someone. As if you are free from agendas. I interviewed many people and the trust in you is just big.

C.P., municipal manager for disability services and
MA student doing field-work on public sector innovation

Maintaining legitimacy in all actions appears to be both consciously and intuitively reached through a belief in the value of the approach, the use of professional empathy with stakeholders and learning by doing. Perceived consistency and authenticity flow from this, which in turn support legitimacy.

The Importance of Physical Space

There is a consistency that permeates MindLab's values and approach that is reinforced by the ways in which it uses physical space.

We have to have a very professional and consistent way of communicating. Not only in word-choices and language used, but also on the web-site, pictures that function, the space. It all has to be connected. That is how we connect with people.

A.V., designer, MindLab

Physical space has been however more than a part of communication and branding for MindLab. A safe space is frequently needed when introducing new and potentially challenging agendas. It is, however, important to think through the power of the physical framing as it can also send disturbing signals. A fancy space can imply a superior attitude that removes the intended feel of 'safe'. It is important to create a welcoming atmosphere.

The space comes with both positives and negatives. On the negative side, why is it that innovation can't happen at the rows of desks and chairs on 2nd and 3rd floor (traditional ministerial offices) I mean, that is also a signal: 'we can do it, but you cannot'. There has to be an awareness around that

J.C., research manager, MindLab

A physical space has pros and cons. Creating a neutral zone (preferably that looks a little different than the offices people normally work in to underscore the alternative zone) can be an asset. A physical space can mean allowing people to co-own problems that previously were owned by one silo and discussed by invitation of mandated partners. On the other hand, a physical space can send unintended signals.

When Legitimacy is Challenged: The Dilemmas of Value

There is a dilemma in the fact that it is within the ministries that MindLab has most often been challenged on legitimacy, as it is ultimately also where it is most important. This is where MindLab has learned and is still learning its most important lessons about how to refine its approach.

The quality of the knowledge we provide is not at all determining for if a project becomes a success or not. In this particular project we actually provided some very good points but we were not considered legitimate and we learned a lot from that; never to be more preoccupied with the methods than with the colleagues.

J.S., project manager, MindLab
(about one of the first projects he managed)

The strength of bringing in the user perspective can also be challenging. Sometimes it can be difficult to discuss citizen experiences objectively, which in turn can create tension and potentially undermine the work already being done.

The international interest and recognition that it has generated has been an important part of raising interest and design legitimacy nationally. The fact that MindLab is taken seriously at high levels in other countries seems to provide support for its messages and that cooperation on all levels across borders researching and discussing new ways of working with public sector challenges is strong. On the other hand, there would be no interest from the international network if not for the concrete work that has been done domestically. Part of the legitimacy relies on what can be seen as a mutual feeding system between action at home and attention from the surrounding world.

It is 100 per cent sure that the fact that we can refer to the larger debate and dialogue, the agenda-setting role, not only in the ministries, but in general in Denmark and internationally is supporting for the legitimacy I have in my projects ... What make us completely unique is that we can do both. We can do the agenda-setting work and we can do the projects ... it gives legitimacy to each other.

J.S., project manager, MindLab

Being present on the international scene has to be balanced with adding concrete value at home to maintain legitimacy. If MindLab is not able to explain and add value of the discipline internally in the ministries they will most likely be indifferent or opposed.

On the one hand I think it is very well done that MindLab has become a visible institution, also globally. It markets not only MindLab but also indirectly the Danish central administration and the owner-ministries. But if it becomes at the expense of concrete outcomes it becomes a balance tipping too much to one side.

B.S., permanent secretary, member of the MindLab board

The challenge of measuring and assessing results and creating value is not limited to MindLab but shared throughout the public sector. It can be argued that the optimal way of measuring has yet to be found. Public sector solutions can create value on different bottom lines, such as productivity, service, results and ultimately democracy, but they rarely succeed in them all. In other words value and the meaning of it can play out and be experienced very differently (Figure 10.2).

There is a built-in dilemma when discussing legitimacy of innovative solutions. Defining innovation as 'a new idea that is implemented and creates value' contains a challenge of proof of probable outcome.

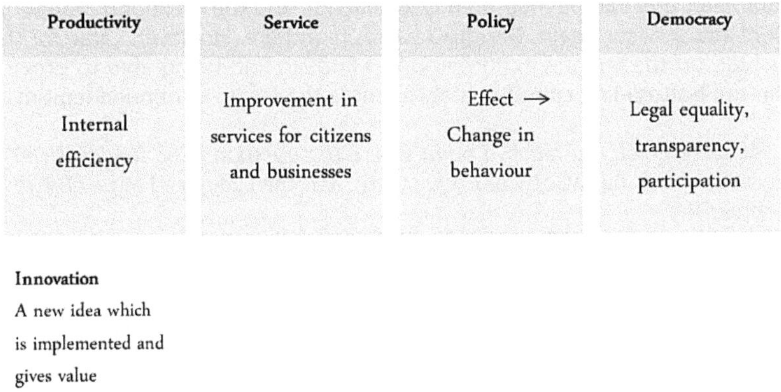

Productivity	Service	Policy	Democracy
Internal efficiency	Improvement in services for citizens and businesses	Effect $\rightarrow$ Change in behaviour	Legal equality, transparency, participation

Innovation
A new idea which
is implemented and
gives value

Figure 10.2   Four bottom lines of success
Source: Model inspired by Bason 2010, Inspired by National Audit Office 2006

It is hard to speak of innovation in a context that demands outcome assurances and proof of added value beforehand, and detailed breakdown of contribution. How can we speak of innovation at all if we cannot also either prove beforehand that it is going to be innovative, or to prove the added value to its full extent or at least which value was added by whom?

> *In my perception MindLab has scored very high on proving that this way of working makes sense and that we can reach better results. Showing the methods and teaching them, showing in praxis how it works and how to involve citizens and gain insights about the users. That has been very good. However I detect a built-in weakness in the construction. Even though MindLab can go further than if you were externals you don't follow the projects all the way through to implementation. If we define innovation as an idea that has been implemented, then what you are doing is not yet innovation. And it is not within your reach to measure it.*
> *H.V.C., former director of innovation, Ministry of Taxation*

Both the kind of value that is being added and the measurability of it present a continual topic of discussion for MindLab. There is no doubt that there is perceived added value on different levels, supporting legitimacy. However, the demand for measurable results arises eventually and there has been an ongoing effort to find the best ways to do that. For instance there is a dilemma in how to measure rising awareness about the innovation agenda to which MindLab may have contributed, but other players as well. The same can be said for increased awareness in institutions within the system:

> *I/we have also this year been very happy to play ball with you in many contexts. It is always inspiring and giving and apropos the much talk about weighing and measuring and after-documentation, I am not sure that it can be done in an 'objective' way in your efforts with us, but you are probably a rather good example that not everything can be weighed and measured. On the other hand no one who has been in contact with you at all doubts your value …*
> *S.Ø., middle manager, National Board of Industrial Injuries*

One parameter that can be measured is satisfaction and the likelihood that people will use MindLab's services again. MindLab scores high here. However, value for the end-users is high on the agenda in and around MindLab and being able to prove added value on the bottom line can ultimately become the key to continued legitimacy.

> At some point you reach a point where the question is no longer _if_ you create value, but what _value you create. And then you need to be able to prove it._
>
> H.V.C., former director of innovation, Ministry of Taxation

There is ongoing work to create a value scale that allows measuring at different points in the process and distinguishing between different kinds of results ranging from 'new knowledge created' to 'implemented innovative solution'. This is an intermediary step, but to a great extent it still relies on providing numbers to the relevant authorities.

Scalability

What happens when legitimacy is established and the work flow and interest mirrors that? What happens when you finally have had success and more institutions want to implement that model across their system? How do you ensure that the solution is scalable and that legitimacy follows a scaled model? Is the concept in fact scalable, are the methods feasible and to what extent can it be translated to new contexts/ countries?

The answers are still theoretical and local contexts may matter. There is an unexplored factor of trust in the system that is high in Denmark compared to other countries when it comes to the use of ethnography with citizens and to experimentation with solutions (Svendsen and Svendsen 2010). Trust in the system may be helpful for the willingness of citizens to engage in, for instance, interviews about their lives and for experimentation with solutions and, ultimately, for legitimacy for both the processes and the solutions. However, it can also be argued that the concept of an operational unit is more dependent on the support of the system that it aims to change.

> By principle you are nothing special. It sounds all wrong, but I am thinking that you by principle are a bunch of very competent people, who have some thought-through and now proven models and concepts you go by. Those two things can be found other places too, luckily. But skilled people and good models do not do the trick alone. MindLab cannot exist in a context where people do not want it. If you want to create a MindLab make sure that the surroundings want it.
>
> S.Ø., head of division, National Board of Industrial Injuries

Ultimately setting up a unit can be seen as admitting to the fact that the system is not yet ready for deploying these skills directly into the sector as a whole. If these competencies were to be found across the sector, then there would be no need for MindLab. As such the goal to build up innovation capacity may be a long-term goal to become redundant as opposed to up-scaled.

> User-driven innovation is somehow something that there will always be a need for. But do you also have a need for someone to help you do it or

*is it something we over time can internalise in the ministries? Maybe it
ought to be?*

B.S., permanent secretary, member of the MindLab board

Becoming redundant in the long run could also call for expanding MindLab
immediately, to speed up the reach of its competencies. Hiring additional staff now
would, on the other hand, create new potential challenges to be addressed. Where
would it, for instance, leave collective learning and the flat organization? More people
could result in a need for more rules and set boundaries around the learning process
and thereby potentially enforce the embeddedness.

Lessons Learned from the MindLab Case

The overall pattern through the research is that is has been *how* MindLab has done
it that has created the legitimacy for the work and the agency for *what* MindLab has
been able to do. Qualities like curiosity, empathy, enthusiasm and authenticity have
turned out to be important for the perceived legitimacy. In a time when measurable
results are the preferred parameter for value this is worth noticing as it potentially
adds a more holistic dimension to the concept of value that arguably should not be
underestimated. Elements like adaptability and sense of meaning support this.

This case has shown that a number of elements have helped in designing the
legitimacy of MindLab and overcome the potential paradox of embedded agency.
Actors can seemingly have an effect on institutions when the organizational framing is
right and the team maintaining it takes on an empathetic approach that is adaptable
and encourages continual learning.

When establishing this kind of organization it is imperative to know *the ideal and
what kind of change you want to make in the world.* This is what drives the employees
and creates the authenticity needed for becoming legitimate. *Anchoring with top-
management* gives the backing for agency on lower levels. However, *forming the right
team* may be the determining factor. Besides being multi-disciplined to be able to
enact the design processes, the skill of *empathy needs to be present.*

A small unit needs to *build relations* and to be *authentic and consistent* in the
meeting of stakeholders wherever they are positioned. The character of the approach
as multi-disciplined calls for *a learning organization,* that again supports *communication
being straight-forward and aligned. Physical space* can, if used right, have a supporting
role in that.

Striking the balance between external and internal activities so they both feed each
other and continuously add value is important and delicate. Being able to *measure and
prove added value* ultimately become determinants for continued legitimacy.

Future Challenges

Now that we know more about the elements of legitimacy in creating MindLab – what
is next? This questions leads to new questions to be considered. What work should be
done to sustain it and what are the best next steps to be taken? Has the learning and
subsequent adjustments made MindLab more integrated into the system? If so, is that
an asset or will it make it less cutting edge or even dilute its potential?

Going forward how does MindLab tackle the dilemma that legitimacy was gained with 'how', while the important question of 'what' is both complex, ever-present and eventually will demand concrete answers; answers not necessarily corresponding with the perceived value of the contribution MindLab gives today? Can MindLab deliver on both and does MindLab have the right competencies in place to do so? These are questions for exploration and attention in the next phase of developing and designing continued legitimacy for MindLab.

On the broader agenda it will be interesting to see if a small-scale example like MindLab can inspire and further the discussion on design and governance. The embedding of design in governance will have to emerge from overcoming the agency to do so.

References

Battilana, J.A. and DÁunno, T. (2009). Institutional Work and the Paradox of Embedded Agency. In T.B. Lawrence, R. Suddaby and B. Leca, *Institutional Work*. Cambridge: Cambridge University Press. 31–58.

Bason, C. (2010). *Leading Public Sector Innovation. Co-creating for a Better Society*. Bristol: The Policy Press.

Boyer, B., Cook, J.W. and Steinberg, M. (2011). *Recipes for Systemic Change*. Helsinki: Sitra.

Caffin, B. (2011). The Empathic State. TEDxAdelaide, http://www.youtube.com/watch?v=UdVdVDvrch8 uploadet 22/11/2011.

Coughlan, P., Suri, J.F. and Canales, K. (2007). Prototypes as (Design) Tools for Behavioural and Organizational Change. A Design-based Approach to Help Organizations Change Work Behaviours. *The Journal of Applied Behavioural Science*, 43(1): 122–34.

Garud, R., Hardy, C. and Maguire, S. (2007). Institutional Entrepreneurship as Embedded Agency; An Introduction to the Special Issue, *Organization Studies*, 28(7): 957–69.

Hoffman, A.J. (1999). Institutional Evolution and Change: Environmentalism and the US Chemical Industry. *Academy of Management Journal*, 42: 351–71.

Horizons (2012). Driving Policy on a Shifting Terrain. Understanding the Changing Policy Environment Amid 21st-Century Complexity. Ottawa: Government of Canada/Horizons of Canada.

Lawrence, T.B, Suddaby, R. and Leca, B. (2009). *Institutional Work. Actors and Agency in Institutional Studies of Organizations*. New York: Cambridge University Press.

Leca, B., Battilana, J. and Boxenbaum, E. (2008). Agency and Institutions: A review of Institutional Entrepreneurship. Working paper.

National Audit Office (2006). Achieving Innovation in Central Government Organisations. NAO.

Restarting Britain 2. London (2013).

Svendsen, G.T., Svendsen, G.L.H. (2010). Social Capital and the Welfare State. In M. Böss (ed.), *The Nation-State in Transformation*. Aarhus, Denmark: Aarhus University Press. 315–34.

Suchman, M.C. (1995). Managing Legitimacy: Strategic and Institutional Approaches. *Academy of Management Review*, 20(3): 571–610.

MARIANA AMATULLO

The Branchekode.dk Project: Designing With Purpose and Across Emergent Organizational Culture

One could easily argue that everything around us is the result of a design decision. In their most essential roles, designers deal with concrete and objective results whose consequences affect us all, shaping the form, function and symbols of our world: from the visualization, ideation and planning of images, products and services, to the strategic conceptualization of systems and environments (Buchanan 1995). When we consider the growth in complexity and uncertainty that characterizes our twenty-first-century society, significant implications for design as a 'reflective' community of practice (Schön 1983), and as a pluralistic field for inquiry adept at tackling formidable problems (Rittel and Weber 1973), emerge.

This is a time when we recognize a sense of urgency for change to happen – perhaps at a broader scope than ever before – and with it, a call for a path creating forms of collaboration and generative modes of intervention. In this sense, the essentially unbounded space of design allows us to embrace alternative futures and shy away from prescribed courses of action (Simon 1969).

When the task at hand is to reimagine our public sector institutions to better meet today's challenges and citizens' needs, MindLab, a Danish cross-ministerial innovation unit that anchors their research and practice in design-centred thinking, as much as in qualitative research and policy development, represents a distinct organizational model that bridges both the public and private sector with the aim of spurring innovation, creativity and collaboration.

During the spring of 2012, I spent time with lead members of the MindLab team and their ministry staff partners, as part of my doctoral research in management and design at the Weatherhead School of Management, Case Western Reserve University.[1] My ongoing research examines some of the key shifts that are occurring for the role of the designer as a change agent (Margolin 2007) when engaged in innovation projects

---

1   I consider myself privileged to have relied on the scholarship and mentorship of colleagues and faculty at the Weatherhead School of Management, Case Western Reserve University throughout this study and my ongoing doctoral research. In particular I would like to thank Dr. Richard J. Boland, Dr. Kalle Lyytinen and Dr. Richard Buchanan, the Chair of my PhD committee, whose clarity of thought provides ongoing inspiration to my own process of inquiry about design's lasting promise in public sector innovation.

that have a participatory, user-centred design framework (Ehn 2008; Manzini 2012), and where the fundamental aspiration is for social change.

The opportunity of having access to multi-stakeholder perspectives from one of MindLab's recent initiatives, the Branchekode.dk project, a Danish government service and digital portal responsible for generating classification categories needed to register a new business, offered me a chance to probe into critical questions about the experience and meaning of undertaking public sector design projects in the high and low conditions of difference, dependence and novelty (Van de Ven 2007) within a multidisciplinary context. The following stream of insights is culled from that original research, and I am greatly indebted to the MindLab team and their partners for generously granting me the necessary access to study the project.[2]

The summary analysis that ensues reveals three critical dimensions that stand out when we consider the promise design holds as a tool for public sector innovation: (1) the role of design as a driver of cross-cutting collaboration and empathic user-centred outcomes; (2) a plurality of views and perceptions about the range of actions that designers are responsible for today within the complex organizational boundaries they traverse; and finally, (3) a profound state of flux, in terms of the roles designers are espousing within this context and the diverse knowledge communities they collaborate with.

In particular, the Branchekode.dk project, and to a larger extent, many of the projects within the portfolio of MindLab, showcase how these modalities of what is often referred to as 'strategic design' in the public sector – design as a means to achieve social innovation outcomes for a class of challenges that are systemic in nature (Boyer et al. 2013) – manifests as work that remains at the edges of an emergent practice.

A Note on Methods and Data Collection

My research for the Branchekode.dk case study benefited from a select number of face-to-face, semi-structured qualitative interviews that I conducted with key stakeholders behind the development of the project; it was also complemented with data gathered from observation, field research notes and from information in extant texts. I adopted a grounded theory approach (Charmaz 2006; Strauss and Corbin 1990), which focuses on eliciting meaning from empirical data, along with case study methodology, which allowed me to explore the world of theory and the experience of practice in order to bridge rich qualitative evidence to mainstream deductive research (Eisenhardt and Graebner 2007; Yin 2009). Throughout the data collection process, a key priority was to remain self-aware, flexible, non-prescriptive, 'open to the new, the different, the true' (Gadamer 1976) and ready to evolve the ongoing interpretation of the data following new insights as they emerged.

Cyclical rounds of coding of the interviews yielded a series of patterns and key concepts that I then reshuffled through language analysis. The latter analytical strategy proved to be essential in allowing me to converge on interesting phenomena at play, while advancing my own understanding of the significance of the project, especially as

2   I am deeply grateful to the MindLab team and their partners for sharing their insights and personal perspectives about the Branchekode project: I would like to extend a special thank you to Christian Bason, Neils Hansen, Runa Sabroe and Helle Venzo.

I was also relying on cross-referencing the Branchekode.dk case study with three other cases of social innovation design that also comprised the original doctoral research.[3]

Branchekode.dk: Making the Complex Less So

In an early report produced by MindLab with the Danish Commerce and Companies Agency, authored before the re-launch of Branchekode.dk and entitled *Clear, user-friendly and simple: New Visions for Digital Government* (2011), the principal objectives behind the Brancheckode.dk brief were outlined as generalizable recommendations for digitization of public service solutions that could prove friendly to citizens as well as cost effective to public authorities. The goals were stated as follows: (1) the purpose of the electronic self-service must be communicated clearly; (2) the system must handle the complexity of the self-service solution, not the user; (3) the self-service solution must be based on the user's reality; and (4) the authorities involved must cooperate in the digital solutions.

As a cross-sectorial unit with the capacity of bridging knowledge and dialogue across various public authorities and ministries, MindLab was uniquely positioned to redesign the industry code site to be responsive of these tenets. Likewise, the expertise and emphasis on deploying design research tools also positioned the MindLab team to translate these strategic goals with a sense of purpose as well as the agility that define effectiveness in our digital age. After all, it is widely accepted that as we become more fluent in accessing knowledge via digital portals and connecting to others via ubiquitous social media, by the same token we are also increasingly expecting to experience technology in ways that make our life and work more relevant.

The *New Visions for Digital Government* report also succinctly describes what the redesign of the Branchekode.dk set out to do:

> The new industry code site transforms the goals to reality. This self-service solution is centred on users and their needs, and features a new self-service solution combined with a super user site for the case-workers who work with industry codes. The new industry code site makes it easier for companies to find the right industry code while also streamlining the authorities' workflow in this area. The business case prepared for the project shows that a new industry code site will provide savings of DKK 24 million over a period from 2011 to 2015, even after the costs of development and operation are deducted. (p. 19)

It is important to understand the larger context for the re-launch of this site: Branchekode is the Danish equivalent to the international statistical system known as 'NACE' codes (Nomenclature des Activités Economiques dans la Communauté Européenne), and represents a mandatory stop for all business owners in Denmark to identify and register their companies with the appropriate industry codes from a pool of more than 700 used by the government to classify businesses for statistics, tax and

---

3 The other three cases are the Design Exchange Program (DEP) an initiative by the Helsinki Design Lab and the Finnish Ministry of Innovation, Sitra; Project Mwana, a mobile health service that uses mobile phones to improve early infant diagnosis of HIV and postnatal follow-up and care in rural settings that is a collaboration among UNICEF, Frog Design and partners within the governments of Zambia and Malawi; and Clean Team, a sanitation business currently being trialed in Kumasi, Ghana, the result of a collaboration among Unilever, Water and Sanitation for the Urban Poor (WSUP) and ideo.org.

administrative purposes. As the reports signals, industry codes are a frequent source of statistical errors, pressure on public sector telephone lines and erroneous company inspections, generating administrative burdens from the perspective of public sector management and potentially considerable frustration for business owners that may end up pursuing confusing searches for their correct category of filing. The Danish Business Authority's (DBA) development group, Team Effective Regulation (TER), therefore initiated a cross-ministerial project on industry codes led by MindLab to demonstrate the value of closing the 'last mile' separating well-considered regulations from effective use by citizens. The office head of the DBA, Sune Knudsen, who initially commissioned the project, had worked at MindLab and was familiar with the group's design research approach and in a position to champion their innovative mode of engagement from the start – this was undoubtedly a distinct factor benefiting this MindLab collaboration, and one which many partners highlighted in their interviews repeatedly (Boyer et al. 2013).

Runa Sabroe, one of the lead project managers for MindLab summarized the big picture rationale and aspiration of the project by stressing what is perhaps the real innovative dimension and importance of the endeavour. Beyond a website that streamlines workflows, integrating information that previously lived in silos and/or was duplicated in the separate offices of public servants (the redesign includes a new feature to connect case officers who work with industry codes across agencies), and beyond a user-friendly design interface that invites interaction to help improve businesses registration processes, the proposed new design stood out as a 'demonstration' project of sorts for what could be accomplished in the public sector with design-driven methods of co-creation and the integration of deep insights collected from users: 'I really hope that this can illustrate that the public sector should think of service and think of the end-user not just because they feel sorry for them or they like them, but because it's actually what it's all about, isn't it?' (Sabroe in interview with the author, 2012).

Ultimately MindLab did not design the final Branchekode.dk service. As it often happens in the strategic role the unit occupies, the team turned their recommendations along with a comprehensively flushed-out prototype to DBA to build it into a functioning service that launched in early 2013. Indicative of the successful alignment between stakeholders that the MindLab team was able to generate as they moved through the design process and prototyping of the new service, is the following statement from one of the ministry staff partners, Special Advisor Helle Venzo at DBA who echoes Runa in the following statement:

> There are huge effects to gain. If we do not do it this way, we risk to loose opportunities because we are too focused on the inside out perspective [...] And by doing that we risk to create monsters that are going to make our citizens frustrated, our companies spending too much time and, as I told you before, we eat from the capital of legitimacy and trust between Danish state and people, which we benefit so much from. (Venzo in interview with the author, 2012)

Challenging the Status Quo: Insights through the Prism of Language

The impetus for including the Branchekode.dk project in my overall process of inquiry about the shifts in the positioning of design in the public sector was driven by a number of attributes that the case presents that are worth reflecting upon. First of all, at its core, the project addresses what Christian Bason refers to as 'the holy grail' of public administration and a key mission within his mandate at MindLab: cross-cutting collaboration, 'when you generate a learning system that will actually enable the system to continuously improve itself' (Bason, in interview with the author, 2013). Understanding the collaborative and complex human dynamics that shaped the progress of the project through the system was of keen interest. Secondly, as Bason observed in his interview, as a rather discreet, but also tangible solution, Branchekode presents a good example about newer ways to foreshadow an alternative future for government, one which is human-centred, participatory and inclusive of citizens, business savvy and outcome-oriented. Finally, and as mentioned earlier, because it was the result of a partnership where there was an intentional decision from the vantage point of the commissioning agency to consciously commission design-led work, it provided a platform to theorize on the designer's role and the process of designing as a contemporary form of rhetoric that incites action through argument (DiSalvo 2012) and engages the emergence of pluralism as 'a recognized feature of human circumstances' (Buchanan 1995).

It is significant to note that despite the undisputable success of the project's outcomes, and the considerable level of synergy between the MindLab team and the multiplicity of stakeholders the team engaged during the design process to jointly arrive at the final solution proposed, the project was also one fraught with complexity. For Bason and his team, an ongoing question was the following: *how do you work within innovation and change not just from an outside-in perspective but also from a dual perspective of outside-in and inside-out?* (Bason, interview with the author, 2012). The question is one the team behind the former Helsinki Design Lab brought up as well in their inclusion of Branchekode as one of six stories about what they refer to as stewardship – a form of leadership that allows 'a constant state of opportunism and willingness to pivot when progress on the current path is diminishing' (Boyer et al. 2013).

As I pondered through the outside-in and inside-out dialectic in my own analysis of the case, the semantic framework I designed for interpretation of the qualitative data in the interviews included a binary frame that organized interviewee perspectives between MindLab designers and project managers, versus viewpoints expressed by the Branchekode.dk ministry staff as principal commissioning 'clients' of the project.

The structure included three categories that attempted to capture the concepts at a more abstract level: (1) a study of the language used to refer to values and goals of the project at hand; (2) a study of the language used to describe activities and methods used in the project; and (3) a study of the language used to characterize the context and situation of the activities of the project. Given my personal interpretative lens and interest in probing where there were commonalities of worldviews between designers and non-designers, I paid particular attention to flagging patterns of common language use between groups for each category, while also noting differences in terms of the constructs that were more, or less, emphasized by each. Table 11.1 presents a synthesis of these recurring patterns across many of the interviews.

Table 11.1   Language analysis: key concepts across interviews

	MindLab	Ministry Staff Partners
1.1	**Values /Process**	**Values/Process**
Commonalities	Entrepreneurialism Collaboration Human/user-centred innovation	Entrepreneurialism Collaboration Human/user-centred innovation
Differences	Co-creation Emotional design Openness Empathy	Reliability of solutions Profitability/productivity Speed Lessen administrative burdens
1.2.	**Activities defined as:**	**Activities defined as:**
Commonalities	Tangible deliverables Visualization/translation	Tangible deliverables Visualization/translation
Differences	Iterative/generative Storytelling/synthesis Experimentation/prototyping Process-driven	Rational/disciplined process Innovation for business model creation Quantitative measures Outcome-driven
1.3.	**Context**	**Context**
Commonalities	Complexity Multiplicity of stakeholders Uncharted territory	Complexity Multiplicity of stakeholders Uncharted territory
Differences	Opportunity and challenge of an undefined brief Cross-cutting collaboration	Metrics for value creation Necessity for business case validation Streamline work flows

Emergence

As a reflexive researcher, the moment of discovery for me in terms of the results of my analysis came by way of the realization of the magnitude of the 'uncharted territory' that design in the space of public sector still occupies. It was pointed out in no uncertain terms, time and again, by interviewees, and also manifested at times in what was not said, but implied. In many ways, my original assumption coming to the study of the Branchekode project had been that for a design-based innovation unit such as MindLab, which is embedded successfully within a consortium of government partners in Denmark's design-fluent society, the willingness to have others value the notion of design as a prepositional discipline that can potentially stimulate, or actually originate change in organizational culture would be a given.

Instead, I encountered what I would qualify as an emergent space, where new meanings, values, practices and new relationships are continually being crafted amidst a dominant culture (Williams 1977). In other words, strategic design seems to be slowly coming into focus in an unmapped frontier of sorts. There are two strands of formulations that are of note. First, a repeated discourse about the 'need to produce evidence' or 'demonstrate value' from this form of design engagement appears as a central preoccupation for all. Second, there seems to be agreement that the process of articulation and validation underway will require ongoing cultural change within organizational practice.

Design as the Point of Departure instead of an End

If we consider organizational culture as a whole as 'the activity of ordering, disordering, and reordering in the search for understanding and for values which guide action' (Buchanan 1995; Buchanan, Doordan and Margolin 2010), the significance of the highly dynamic actions that designers are responsible for as they align decisions with impact and work together and with others to innovate, cannot be over-stated. Their actions can represent the point of departure for greatly significant insights.

In this regard, there might be a key provocation the Branchekode.dk case brings forth: why might we care to delineate more effectively the boundary zones of actionable modes of design engagement and collaboration, such as those present in this case study, which can propel innovation in the public sector? The answer could be, we might venture, because there is hope and significance in better understanding the pathways design offers toward alternative futures for all of us as human beings to lead lives of fulfilment. These are issues of cause and action that matter deeply to organizational practice as it confronts the challenges of the twenty-first century.

References

Boyer, B., Cook, J. and Steinberg, M. (2013). *Helsinki Design Lab: Six Stories about the Craft of Stewardship*. Helsinki, Sitra.

Buchanan, R. (1995). Rhetoric, humanism and design. In R. Buchanan and V. Margolin (eds), *Discovering Design: Explorations in Design Studies*. Chicago: University of Chicago Press.

Buchanan, R., Doordan, D., and Margolin, V., eds (2010). *The Designed World: Images, Objects, Environments*. Oxford; New York: Berg Publishers.

Charmaz, K. (2006). *Constructing Grounded Theory: A Practical Guide Through Qualitative Analysis*. Newbery Park, CA: Sage Publications.

DiSalvo, C. (2012). *Adverserial Design*. London: The MIT Press.

Eisenhardt, K.M., and Graebner, M.E. (2007). Theory Building from Cases: Opportunities and Challenges. *Academy of Management Journal*, 50(1): 25–32.

Gadamer, H.-G. (Linge, D., trans.) (1976). *Philosophical Hermeneutics*. Berkeley: University of California Press.

Manzini, E. (2012). SIE interviews Ezio Manzini. Available from: http://www.socialinnovationeurope.eu/magazine/methods-and-tools/interviews/sie-interviews-ezio-manzini.

Margolin, V. (2007). Design for Development: Towards a History. *Design Studies*, 28(2): 111–15.

Mygind, J. (2011). MindLab and Danish Commerce and Companies Agency. *Clear, User-friendly, Simple: New Visions for Digital Government*. Danish Commerce and Companies Agency and MindLab.

Rittel, H., and Webber, M. (1973). Dilemmas in a General Theory of Planning. *Policy Sciences*, 4: 155–69.

Schön, D. (1983). Designing Rules, Types and Worlds. *Design Studies*, 9(3): 181–90.

Simon, H. (1969). *The Sciences of the Artificial*. Cambridge: MIT Press.

Strauss, A., and Corbin, J. (1990). *Basics of Qualitative Research: Grounded Theory Procedures and Techniques*. Newbery Park, CA: Sage Publications.

Van de Ven, A. (2007). *Engaged Scholarship: A Guide for Organizational and Social Research*. Oxford: Oxford University Press.

Williams, R. (1977). *Dominant, Residual and Emergent. Marxism and literature (Vol. 1)*. Oxford: Oxford University Press.

Yin, R.K. (2009). *Case Study Research: Design and Methods*. Thousand Oaks: Sage Publications.

EDUARDO STASZOWSKI, SCOTT BROWN AND BENJAMIN WINTER

Reflections on Designing for Social Innovation in the Public Sector: A Case Study in New York City

Today, a number of wide-ranging systemic, social, economic and environmental challenges are provoking governments at various levels to rethink their approach to public service delivery. Recognizing these societal and policy trends, and the need for radical social innovation in the public realm, the DESIS Lab at Parsons the New School for Design began in 2011 the multi-year research program, 'Public & Collaborative NYC', to investigate the assertion that design can serve as a catalyst for social innovation in public services in New York City.

In 2012, the DESIS Lab entered a partnership with the Public Policy Lab, a non-profit dedicated to improving public services through design, and the New York City Department of Housing Preservation and Development (HPD) to develop a project entitled 'Designing Services for Housing', which focused on the issue of affordable housing in the city.

This chapter examines the 'Designing Services for Housing' project as a case study for identifying various challenges designers face in working in collaboration with public partners to effect social change in the public realm. Key areas of focus include the acknowledgement of the political position of the designer, the recognition and overcoming of epistemological barriers and the management of risk aversion in the public sector. Building on reflections from this case study, the chapter concludes by highlighting various implications of designing for social innovation in the public sector and offers recommendations for designers, educators, civil servants and policymakers.

Introduction and Overview

Today, a number of wide-ranging systemic, social, economic and environmental challenges are provoking governments at various levels to rethink their approach to public service delivery. Following cuts in public spending and austerity measures to reduce budget deficits, alternatives to big-state welfare initiatives, such as public-private partnerships, the use of new technologies, as well as various strategies for increased public participation are now being considered. In the United States and across the world there is a growing perception of the need for new approaches to providing essential services for individuals and communities to thrive. What these new approaches will look like, how they will take shape and what role design can play in effecting such change is still open for exploration and experimentation. In the United Kingdom – where, in the last few years, there has been a vigorous debate on the relation of design to public service and between social innovation and public policy – a crucial claim has been made by the Design Commission concerning the role of design in the provision of public services.[1] The claim is that 'Design is integral to the DNA of each and every public service', that one cannot improve public services without thinking about design. In their most recent report, the commission emphasizes the value of a design-based approach in promoting the kinds of innovation needed to address the challenges of an increasingly difficult public sector landscape, as well as the genuine need to provide better services to the public who are enduring the effects of continued economic instability.[2] However, while the report strongly advocates the beneficial potential good design can bring to any government operation or service delivery system (or design's role in 'creating cost-effective public services in the twenty-first century'[3]), there is still much work to be done in thinking about what a participatory design-driven approach to public service will look like, particularly in the American social and political context.

The common denominator to any new approach in this field, however, is the requirement of new forms of collaboration across a variety of practical domains. The traditional silos that separate government apparatus from community action can be broken down so new kinds of collaboration can be explored. Such partnerships can be put into place and amplified by means of more participatory, horizontal practices such as co-governance, co-design and co-production – in other words, through new forms of collaboration where people, experts and governments work together to provide better public services. Design can play a transformative role in promoting this kind of change. One of the challenges of a design-driven approach is to accommodate multiple ways of knowing, so that the designer and other experts can employ their distinct forms of knowledge and expertise towards the solving of a particular problem.

Public & Collaborative NYC

Recognizing the need for radical social innovation in the public realm, the DESIS Lab[4] at Parsons the New School for Design began in 2011 the multi-year research program 'Public & Collaborative NYC' to investigate the assertion that design can serve as a catalyst for social innovation in public services in New York City.[5] In the context of such pressing issues, this initiative sought to ask the following questions: What are the roles design can play in building bridges between city government and people

1   The Design Commission is the industry-led research arm to the Associate Parliamentary Design and Innovation Group in the United Kingdom Parliament created to advise government on how design can drive economic and social improvement and to provide a forum for the design community to better engage with policymakers.
2   Design Commission. Restarting Britain 2: Design and Public Services. 2013.
3   Ibid.
4   Parsons DESIS (Design for Social Innovation and Sustainability) Lab (http://www.newschool.edu/desis) is a research laboratory at the New School University in New York City that conducts research into the ways in which design and social innovation can promote more sustainable ways of living.
5   Public & Collaborative NYC (http://nyc.pubcollab.org) is affiliated with the global Public & Collaborative research effort of the DESIS Network (http://www.desis-network.org), an international network of design schools and organizations focused on design for social innovation and sustainability, in which research labs based in different cities are developing parallel projects at the intersection of public services, social innovation and design.

that can bring about new kinds of social innovation in the provision of services for the public good? What are the forms of collaboration or strategies for building strong partnerships between public and private actors as well as local communities and individuals that will promote such innovation?

Designing Services for Housing

In 2012, with the generous support of the Rockefeller Foundation, Parsons DESIS Lab entered a partnership with the Public Policy Lab – a non-profit dedicated to improving public services through design – and the New York City Department of Housing Preservation and Development (HPD) to develop 'Designing Services for Housing' (DSH). DSH was a two-year design effort exploring 'ways to engage community residents in the development of services related to city-supported affordable housing development and preservation in neighborhoods with significant public and private sector investment leveraged by HPD'.[6] HPD is the largest municipal housing preservation and development agency in the United States, and its mission is 'to improve the availability, affordability and quality of housing in New York City' (HPD, 2013). The city's affordable housing service landscape consists of a diverse network of government actors, regulatory bodies, private developers of affordable housing, property managers, community-based organizations, tenant associations and individuals. It is an inherently collaborative field, requiring interaction between a number of different parties, and making it an ideal space to explore the generative possibilities of enhanced forms of collaborative practice between public and private actors. Furthermore, the topic of housing is particularly urgent, as New York City has some of the lowest vacancy rates in the United States coupled with steadily increasing rent costs. Combined with the challenges of an enduring economic crisis, housing has become a crisis of its own in the city.

157

DSH was structured around two interconnected project tracks. The first focused on improving HPD's services and interfaces with current and potential residents of subsidized housing for low- and moderate-income New Yorkers. The second focused on enabling resident social networks and collaborative services[7] in neighbourhoods where HPD programs and initiatives are most active, such as the Melrose Commons Urban Renewal Area in the Melrose neighbourhood of the South Bronx. The project began with a series of public lectures and two courses at Parsons that included co-design sessions with HPD staff, students and Public Policy Lab fellows to create a 'kit of ideas' for the agency. The 'kit' included new service ideas for increasing tenants and landlords' understanding of the city's housing maintenance code and protection of tenants' rights; simplifying application processes for affordable units; improving HPD's information channels and physical spaces and creating networks among neighbours for mutual support.

---

6 Parsons DESIS Lab, Public Policy Lab and NYC Housing Preservation and Development Receive Rockefeller Foundation Cultural Innovative Fund Grant to Design and Prototype City Service Improvements, NYC government. Press release, August 29, 2012, on the NYC government web site, http://www.nyc.gov/html/hpd/html/pr2012/pr-08-29-12.shtml.

7 Collaborative services are a type of services based on collaborations between people. The main interactions of services generally occur between service users and service providers. In collaborative services this line is often blurred: service providers are service users and vice versa.

During summer and fall of 2012, the design fellows convened by the Public Policy Lab[8] continued to work with HPD managers, front-line staff, community-based organizations, affordable-housing developers and potential and current users of HPD's services to identify and refine concepts for further development. Four proposals for enhancing the marketing, lottery and lease-up processes for affordable housing were selected by HPD and transformed into pilot projects to test the efficacy of the proposals. Ideas about how to activate resident social-networks and collaborative services around housing-related issues, however, were considered outside the agency's scope and therefore not developed as pilot proposals but left as recommendations for future exploration. This work has been compiled into a findings document – or 'How-To Guide' – which describes the existing service environment for New Yorkers seeking to access HPD services and/or living in neighbourhoods with significant agency presence. The guide also outlines current opportunities and future possibilities for improving services while providing technical and strategic guidance for implementing the proposed pilots. For the purpose of this chapter, the 'Designing Services for Housing' project serves as a case study to open up the discussion about the role of designers in working with government to effect social innovation in the pubic sector.

Evidence and Reflection

During the DSH project, it was observed that the designers operating in this space encountered a number of epistemological, practical and political challenges. This section describes the nature of the proposals that were put forward by the design team, and examines how such ideas predicated specific challenges identified during the project. It concludes by reiterating the implications of these challenges in order to suggest new possibilities for enhancing this type of interdisciplinary collaboration amongst design practitioners, design educators, civil servants and policymakers.[9]

Acknowledging the Political

> Given the importance of power in defining the problem and identifying stakeholders, it is all too easy to accept the stated goals of the collaboration, which means success is measured from the position of the powerful while equally legitimate outcomes, which favour low-power stakeholders, are excluded. Moreover, while collaboration can be highly productive in solving inter-organisational problems, conflict also has a clear role in challenging existing frameworks and forcing domain change in directions considered by at least some members to be positive. (Hardy and Phillips 1998)

Current societal challenges are generating the need for radical innovation and the redesign of public services. Governments are challenged with finding new ways to

---

8   For this initiative, the Public Policy Lab's fellows included five designers and one staff member at HPD's Division of Strategic Planning, who acted as a liaison between the agency and the other partners.

9   In this chapter the authors reflect on the barriers faced by designers when designing for social innovation in the public sector. These reflections do not include the opinion of public staff participants, who might have felt equally challenged by the design process proposed by the Public & Collaborative team.

provide better services in the context of broader economic crisis. While often resisting austerity measures and tax increases, the public is at the same time demanding better services. In this context, a new 'breed' of (service) designers with expertise in user participation, appear as 'natural' candidates to help governments evolve and enhance services for the public good.

However, designing in the public sector need not be merely exercises in making the State look user-friendly or making interactions with government a better 'experience'. 'User-centred' approaches[10] (that is, 'user as subject') for enhancing service delivery commonly applied in the private sector cannot be automatically transferred to this context without engaging in a discussion about the socio-political implications of this work. A movement towards a 'participatory' approach (in other words 'user as partner') in this case is not only appropriate but also required. Here, citizens are key stakeholders in public problems and should be considered as participants in the construction of their own futures and not only participants in the design process simply as users or consumers.[11]

The challenge for designers operating in this space is how to negotiate their inherent political position as agents of change accountable, not to a client or clients who have engaged them for a specific purpose, but to the diverse needs of the broader public(s). Therefore, the traditional client-consultant relationship in which the designer is an expert beholden to very specific interests is challenged. In this sense, the work of designers in the public realm is not simply a matter of enhancing existing service structures or even maintaining current social practices. It can be thought of in terms of playing a more transformative and political role.

The DSH project is partly an experiment in testing and understanding the limits and opportunities of this new role. For example, DSH explored how designers could be proponents of service co-production in the public sector, or more specifically how the city could look at collaborative social innovations as inspiration for different forms of public partnership and reshaping public services.[12] Thinking of service provision in this manner can constitute a challenge to the existing order in which public agencies operate. Most of the DSH proposals involving co-production and bottom-up social innovation were not immediately or entirely embraced by the agency. Certain aspects of co-production were eventually incorporated into the pilot proposals, but within the limits of existing parameters set by agency partners. For example, proposals in which co-production was directed at reorienting relationships between stakeholders in the affordable housing services landscape (that is, supporting new forms of collaboration between tenants and landlords), did not fall directly within the agency's current mandate or practices. In retrospect, it is clear that the presentation, negotiation and reception of these ideas constituted moments of contestation, wherein design is an explicitly political act. Design becomes a political act precisely because it is a set of

---

10 The term 'user-centered design' was coined by Donald Norman at the University of California San Diego to describe design processes in which the needs of end-users influence the design of a product or service. The term and design approach enjoyed a surge of popularity after the publication of the books *User-Centered System Design: New Perspectives on Human-Computer Interaction* (Norman and Draper, 1986) and *The Design of Everyday Things* (Norman 1988).

11 This chapter refers to the participatory design approach as described in the Scandinavian tradition, in terms of early experiments with employing computers to emancipate workers in their work environment (Ehn 1989).

12 According to David Boyle, a fellow at the New Economics Foundation in London, co-production means delivering public services through an equal and reciprocal relationship between professionals, people using services, their families and their neighbors. Where activities are co-produced in this way, both services and communities become far more effective agents of change.

practices and procedures which directly challenge the established order. It represents a moment of contestation, not only through the promotion of new ideas and policies, but by the very processes in which such ideas are produced.

Overcoming Epistemological Barriers

> Overcoming the distinction between quantitative and qualitative forms of knowledge is politically radical, as well as epistemologically radical. Breaking out of methodological scientific procedures may also mean breaking out of organizational routines that constrain power. (Davies 2011)

The DSH project was conceived as an inherently interdisciplinary endeavour meant to bring together designers (represented by Parsons students and Public Policy Lab fellows), agency leadership (with different backgrounds including strategic planning, marketing and urban development policy) and front-line staff into a collaborative space. Within this space, the different project participants brought to the table different disciplinary viewpoints and approaches to improving New York City's affordable housing-related services.[13] Designers typically operate as experts in experimentation, coming up with a wide array of proposals in a short period of time. Design's mode of operation is heuristic and iterative (where failure during the process is expected and embraced), and it lays a heavy emphasis on 'innovation'. While agency partners certainly maintained a positive view of the value of design – particularly with respect to its potential to identify and fix service inefficiencies, as well to improve the style and usability of 'touch-points' (that is posters and websites) – the role of designer as a catalyst for social innovation and institutional change was not always embraced. Design proposals that sought to discuss and expand policy into areas outside existing mandates were often constrained by legal infrastructure which places strict limitations on the speed and scale in which new policy ideas may be experimented with or implemented.

One such proposal recommended that affordable housing developers and property managers actively facilitate social networks and collaborative services within their buildings in order to help residents recognize each other for mutual support and foster a greater sense of connection and belonging throughout their community. While this concept appeared compatible with HPD's interests in 'strengthening neighbourhoods' and 'stabilizing families' (HPD 2010), the designer's proposed methods for achieving such goals differed significantly from the agency's existing policy mechanisms. Although this proposal was designed to further HPD's goals and social mission, the rationale for such an approach fell outside of existing frameworks for validating strategic decisions and policy proposals. Previous studies on policy innovation reinforce this perception by suggesting that modern bureaucracies 'often struggle to make space for engagement with uncertainty' and operate within a highly

---

13 Public Policy Lab's fellows included designers from different academic and professional backgrounds such as an experienced designer with a focus on participatory design and systems thinking; a service designer specializing in social-sector clients; an expert in public-engagement strategy and an urban planner with a focus on community-based design. Design students in the Integrated Design Program (BFA) and the Transdisciplinary Design Program (MFA) at Parsons were involved in the first phase of the project. Both academic programs emphasize the use of service design and participatory tools and methods to engage multiple stakeholders in addressing pressing social issues.

rationalistic, economized epistemological framework (Davies 2011). The DSH project verified that agencies', governments' and policymakers' 'economistic' approach to problem-solving tends to value new ideas by weighing them against quantitative metrics for an initiative's likelihood of success. The rapid experiments, ad hoc iterations and speculative narratives that designers commonly use to justify their ideas simply do not carry the same weight as rigorous surveying and economic data in the eyes of most public administrators. Both previous research on policy innovation experts and the observations made during the DSH project confirm that the requirements necessary for bureaucratic institutions to incorporate new forms of change often fall outside the capabilities of designers. In meetings where proposals were presented to agency staff that emphasized social innovations outside existing service structures, the designers often lacked the 'epistemological authority' to convey the validity of their ideas to agency partners.

Both designers and policymakers are expected to demonstrate particular forms of expertise; but paradoxically such demonstrations of expertise can actually prevent the very real work required to translate policy intentions into political realities. For instance, a designer could be asked by agency staff to 'do the design' for a set of policy goals; this is not the same as designers working with citizens to envision better societies. If design practices are to be a catalyst for social innovation in the public sector, then it is imperative to further explore the possibility of creating platforms or spaces in which different epistemic communities may work together without reproducing hierarchical power relations where one form of knowledge and practice is valued more highly than another.

Managing Risk Aversion

> The practitioner allows himself to experience surprise, puzzlement, or confusion in a situation which he finds uncertain or unique. He reflects on the phenomenon before him, and on the prior understandings which have been implicit in his behaviour. He carries out an experiment which serves to generate both a new understanding of the phenomenon and a change in the situation. (Schön 1983)

The risks associated with communicating new ideas and proposals must be taken into account when designing for social innovation with public-sector partners. Especially when discussing and promoting more disruptive, or transformative proposals, designers need to be aware of the unique constraints that government agencies face in exploring, entertaining and implementing new ideas. By acting in the public sphere, agency managers and staff are held publicly accountable for their actions and for their use of taxpayers' money. For this reason, strict communications protocols (both internal and external) may inhibit the exchange of ideas and discourage participants of a design project from taking the risks necessary to be truly innovative.

The various ideas, activities and outcomes of the DSH project were subject to different constraints depending on their audience – be it the design team, agency partners or the general public. The more people that proposals and interventions were potentially exposed to the greater the limitations that were imposed upon them. As concepts moved from the design studio to the agency conference room and into the public domain, they were naturally subjected to increasingly rigorous editorial scrutiny and legal restriction.

In the studio, designers often encourage divergent thinking and expansive ideation in order to maximize the exploration and exchange of new ideas. In the conference room, an atmosphere of free and frank discussion may also be cultivated, but ideas must be articulated in ways that do not unduly criticize an agency's existing policies or unfairly overlook its inherent limitations. In public documents and interactions associated with the agency, new ideas must be thoroughly vetted and edited to ensure that they do not create false expectations, unequal opportunities or conflicts of interest among individual constituents or institutional partners.

Since innovation in the public realm is intended for everyone, it cannot be seen to alienate anyone. Unlike the private corporation, which is obligated to act solely in the interest of its shareholders, a public-sector institution is obligated to act equally in the interest of all its constituents. As a result, the work of designers partnering with government agencies is held to a higher standard of public accountability. In this environment designers should expect agencies' legal and communications departments to work closely with design team in developing concepts for the public and authorizing them for public consumption.

The DSH team grappled with the complexities of involving the public in their work well before any of their proposals were ready to be discussed publicly. Design research methods involving public participants or private partners had to be routinely vetted by the agency. The design team's decision to produce and publish a 'How-To Guide' (Figure 12.1), illustrating the project's development and detailing proposals intended for piloting by the agency, presented additional challenges. Publishing concepts before conducting prototyping emphasized editing over experimentation and placed legal and communications procedures before the design process.

Figure 12.1   Layout of the 'How-To Guide' cover.
Source: Design by Claudia Brandenburg/Language Arts

This experience demonstrates how untested ideas risk being evaluated on the basis of how they might be perceived rather than how they actually perform. 'Visioning' and scenario building – design approaches intended to explore new possibilities in order to prompt strategic conversations among stakeholders – risk being interpreted as 'speculative' or 'condescending' for presuming too much about current procedures and future possibilities, and they may be just as likely to offend public managers as inspire them.

Successful innovation in public services must ultimately recognize the challenges of public accountability. Designers and agency staff are wise to think strategically about how and when to involve the public in their work. This requires a delicate balance that can be hard to achieve and manage. The Bloomberg administration, for instance, has been criticized for its so-called pilot programs – essentially a 'do it first; ask questions later' approach. For some, these pilots are innovative ways to skip public-sector red tape, and for others they are a 'tool that undermines democracy by minimizing the public's role in scrutinizing the ideas of government'.[14]

Conclusion

Building on reflections from this case study, this chapter concludes by highlighting various implications on designing for social innovation in the public sector and offering recommendations for designers, educators, civil servants and policymakers.

Implications for Design Practitioners

Although the overall design agenda is growing within governments (with a prevalent focus on the design of 'apps' or digital platforms to increase government transparency), participatory design, service design and designing for social innovation in the public sector are still emerging practices in the United States. As discussed in this chapter, designing for social innovation cannot be merely an exercise of consultation or placing the user at the centre of the design process. Designing in this context is mostly about creating meaningful mechanisms of public participation. As a result, designers must acknowledge the complex political environment in which their work is situated. They would also do well to examine the landscape and existing processes which facilitate public participation in governance. The application of participatory methods and involving final users in the delivery of public services must be carefully examined. The aims of consultation, participation, co-design and co-production can be easily distorted, and the use of these strategies – what Barbara Cruikshank (1999) calls 'technologies of citizenship' – can expose problematic political and power relations. The design community needs to shift the discussion focused on user-centred methods towards a political commitment to participatory and democratic processes.

Designers pursuing social innovation in the public sector must also carefully consider how to position their projects in relation to government agencies, community partners and private individuals, so as to maintain their own autonomy and legitimacy

---

14 David W. Chen and Michael M. Grynbaum, 'Pilot' Label Lets Mayor's Projects Skip City Review, *The New York Times*, June 26, 2011, New York Times on the Web (www.nytimes.com/2011/06/27/nyregion/bloomberg-pilot-programs-avoid-red-tape-and-public-review.html?), accessed Feb. 23, 2013.

without losing the participation, trust and enthusiasm of all stakeholders. As stressed above, in asserting their epistemological authority within hierarchical, bureaucratic policymaking environments, designers will be subjected to increasingly rigorous scrutiny. Therefore, they must adapt their language and tools in ways that are more legible to their public partners and community collaborators. Further comparison and analysis is necessary to determine when and why designers are best served by working within, along side or outside of government agencies.

Implications for Design Educators

The DESIS Network's Public and Collaborative Thematic Cluster initiative is one example of how universities and design schools around the world are trying to create different opportunities for students and faculty to engage with a multiplicity of public and community partners. Exposure to these kinds of project situations is fundamental to the development of future designers' capacity to work collaboratively and engage in cooperative processes.

The DSH project in particular revealed that designers must learn how to better communicate with public-sector managers and at the same time retain their authority to intervene and add value to a field that often resists the kinds of uncertainty and speculative thinking that characterize design practice. In this sense, it is essential to nurture pedagogical spaces that enhance the ability of design students to interact with other fields and disciplines, such as the social sciences, management and public policy.

Although the market for design services in the public sector is growing (with design organizations like the Public Policy Lab and others steadily expanding the field), there is a lack of a strong professional and academic tradition around service design in the United States. Consequently, there is not much of a culture or familiarity with design-led innovation processes within public agencies. As a result, there are few internships or other opportunities for design students to gain experience working in this space. One way to address this issue is for university career service offices to consider establishing relationships with public agencies and to guide design students in pursuing careers in the public sector.

To strengthen the professional authority and credibility of designers working to effect change in the public realm, universities should continue to promote public events, stimulate research initiatives and foster strategic alliances with public agencies in order to build a more robust academic knowledge base in this emerging field.

Implications for Public-Sector Managers and Policymakers

Public-sector managers and policymakers are beholden to practical and political constraints, which can make experimentation with new ideas – even desirable ones – difficult and/or impossible. If public-sector managers and policymakers are interested in experimenting with new ideas, one approach could be to create semi-autonomous spaces for collaboration, or what Christian Bason has referred to as 'authorizing environments' (Bason 2013). Supported by a specific agency, organization or community, these spaces could serve as both exploratory and experimental sites for working towards innovative solutions to public problems (such as, affordable housing, education, healthcare). They could be dedicated to the creation of networks and partnerships; launching projects, events and platforms. Such spaces would bring together a variety of actors, both public and private, with a diverse array of skill sets and expertise around a set of issues. They would provide a degree of freedom from many of the innovative constraints of partner-specific mandates, policy issues and procedural restrictions.

While remaining semi-autonomous and allowing innovators to freely explore new forms and create new knowledge, these spaces could still be supported by the larger institutional bodies whose services, practices and interests stand to benefit from such collaborative work. How the output of these spaces is evaluated and adopted would ultimately be up to the specific agencies, organizations or communities that house them. However, the idea is to proliferate such spaces so that they may (1) work experimentally and freely using design as an instrument for advancing innovation in the public sector/realm; and (2) be collaboratively integrated with all interested parties at every step of the process in order to maximize the potential for innovation and new ideas to emerge.

Governments should consider promoting the creation of 'public innovation places' where professionals from different backgrounds (design, economics, policy and social knowledge) can operate in more horizontal, non-hierarchical ways, and where they can complement each other, as opposed to one form of knowledge dictating how the others will operate.

Acknowledgements

The authors wish to thank the NYC Department of Housing Preservation & Development for providing the extraordinary opportunity for collaboration, and the Public Policy Lab staff and fellows for their tireless dedication to the Designing Services for Housing project. We also gratefully acknowledge the contribution of our colleagues and students at the New School and within the DESIS network. The Designing Services for Housing is a project of Parsons DESIS Lab, the Public Policy Lab and the NYC Department of Housing Preservation & Development made possible through the generous support of a 2012 New York City Cultural Innovation Fund grant awarded by the Rockefeller Foundation. The views expressed here do not necessarily reflect the positions of the Public Policy Lab or the official positions or policies of the NYC Department of Housing Preservation & Development or the City of New York. All errors and omissions are the authors' own.

References

Bason, C. Design-Led Innovation in Government. *Stanford Social Innovation Review*, Spring 2013. http://www.ssireview.org/chapters/entry/design_led_innovation_in_government (accessed March 14, 2013).

Boyle, D., and Harris, M. (2009). *The Challenge of Co-Production: How Equal Partnerships between Professionals and the Public are Crucial to Improving Public Services*. London: NESTA.

Cruikshank, B. (1999). *The Will to Empower: Democratic Citizens and Other Subjects*. Ithaca, NY: Cornell University Press.

Davies, W. (2011). Knowing the Unknowable: The Epistemological Authority of Innovation Policy. *Social Epistemology: A Journal of Knowledge, Culture and Policy,* 25(4).

Design Commission (2013). *Restarting Britain 2: Design and Public Services.* London: Design Commission.

Ehn, P. Work (1989). *Oriented Design of Computer Artifacts.* Hillsdale, NJ: Lawrence Erlbaum Associates.

Hardy, C. and Phillips, N. (1998). Strategies of Engagement: Lessons from the Critical Examination of Collaboration and Conflict in an Interorganizational Domain. *Organization Science,* 9(2).

HPD (2010). *New Housing Marketplace Plan: Creating A More Affordable, Viable, and Sustainable City For All New Yorkers.* New York: HPD.

HPD (2013). Mission Statement. HPD website: http://www.nyc.gov/html/hpd/html/about/mission.shtml.

Kimbell, L. Design and Design Thinking in Public Services. Design Leads Us Where Exactly? November 19, 2012. http://designleadership.blogspot.com.

Norman, D. (1988). *The Design of Everyday Things.* New York: Doubleday.

Norman, D.A. and Draper, S.W., eds (1986). *User-Centered System Design: New Perspectives on Human-Computer Interaction.* Hillsdale, NJ: Lawrence Earlbaum Associates.

Schön, D. (1983). *The Reflective Practitioner: How Professionals Think in Action.* New York: Basic Books.

FRANÇOIS JÉGOU, ROMAIN THÉVENET AND STÉPHANE VINCENT

Friendly Hacking into the Public Sector: (Re)Designing Public Policies Within Regional Governments

How can we initiate a progressive transformation process within and with local public administration? What are the emerging steps of this process? How can we develop a 'friendly-hacking' spirit of design within public administration? As a public-funded but neutral non-profit association playing the role of French public innovation lab since 2008, La 27e Région has always tried to embed design into administrations in an alternative way, different from both traditional external consultancy and from internal support (Durance et al. 2008, Jégou and Vincent 2010). The goal is to emphasize the ability of design to challenge the organization in a systemic way, not just as a one-shot tool.

This chapter presents the lessons learned from the experience of La 27e Région and the network of civil servants, elected representatives, designers, sociologists, social innovators and various players from different disciplines involved in promoting innovation in the public sector and redesign of public policies.

The core hypothesis emerging from these experiences is synthesized in the concept of 'friendly hacking'. The apparent contradiction between the two terms borrows from hacking as a computer crime the idea of challenging the robustness of public policy instruments and services, identifying and acknowledging weak points needing improvement. But the hacking is friendly and not destructive. It is agreed with public authorities to represent an innovation strategy disruptive enough to question public structures often generally criticized in France for their conservatism and complexity, for instance with its 6,000 different kinds of subsidies for companies. As presented in Figure 13.1, showing civil servants from central and rural administrations exchanging theirs job for half a day, and Figure 13.2, showing users and civil servants taking part in a redesign process of administrative letters, hacking in this context refers to the positive culture of hackers as innovative, curious and playful tinkerers in public infrastructure, who are able to achieve promising results by efficiently working with what they have at hand, to build trust among stakeholders inside and outside the institution and kick-start structural change within the innovation culture and practices of public authorities towards more participative, open-source and experimentation-based innovation.

Figure 13.1   Civil servants from central and rural administrations exchanging their jobs for half a day

Source: Romain Thevenet and François Jégou

Figure 13.2   Users and civil servants taking part in a redesign process of administrative letters

Source: Laura Pandelle and François Jégou

Promoting Design as the Government's 'Friendly Hacker'

This chapter reviews the lessons learned in terms of friendly hacking through field experiments. They will be illustrated with examples from La 27e Région's two ongoing programs 'Territoires en Résidences' and 'La Transfo', as well as forward looking exercises and sustainable transition processes conducted with public authorities at regional, national and European levels.

A PROCESS BASED ON SUCCESSIVE PROGRAMS

Territoires en Résidences consisted of immersive-oriented sessions, contracted with regional authorities that wished to experiment for the first time with an alternative way to reframe a specific policy. After a partnership and financial agreement was signed between La 27e Région, the region involved and the places of residence (for example, a neighbourhood, railway station, high school, university, local authority, library and so forth), a cross-disciplinary team hired by La 27e Région worked closely with the local community over the course of five to six months, including three weeks of total immersion with ethnographic, co-design and prototyping activities. The whole process was documented through blogs, videos and notebooks, and the lessons learned not only benefit the local community and the regional governments but also the national network of regional governments (Jégou et al., 2011). After nearly five years, fifteen residencies have been organized in diverse fields: reshaping high schools, rural multimodal transportation, the future of libraries, sustainable procurement, democracy within local governments and others.

La Transfo is a lab implementation program launched in 2011. After testing one, two or even three residencies, some regional councils have expressed the wish to build their own capacity to use such methods. La Transfo consists of prototyping a temporary lab through a two-year program simultaneously engaged in four pilot regions: Bourgogne, Pays de la Loire, Champagne-Ardenne and Provence Alpes Côte d'Azur. In this program, each cross-disciplinary team spends a total of ten weeks embedded in the regional organization. Its role is to empower a group of managers and civil servants with design and ethnographic skills through practical cases, and to co-design the protocol of the lab after the team has gone.

Seven Key Lessons about 'Friendly Hacking'

THE INSIDE-OUT POSTURE

Hacking relies on the meeting of different cultures that stay on the edge of the institution but are immersed enough to engage and team up with civil servants, however sufficiently detached to preserve a critical point of view and relative freedom of action. After the first experiences of the Territoires en Résidence program, some public authorities expressed their intentions to recruit designers in their staff (and some did). Other institutions also subcontracted designers through the traditional consultancy route. In both situations, adopting and sustaining a hacking attitude was difficult owing to, respectively, a lack of autonomy among in-house designers or a lack of involvement in design competencies for temporary placements. The best solution that was found for the public arenas of Résidences and in the following programs of La 27e Région was the immersion model: the hacking team was set up in a school, a library, a neighbourhood and even the Région offices for several weeks, which created an atmosphere of in-depth collaboration, growing trust and being a part of the institution far beyond the classical formats of participative design (Jégou, Vincent, Thévenet, and Petit 2009). Long stretches of immersion also means that the team is involved and able to metabolize the experience from the inside, yet also able to step back and rebuild a critical distance. This inside-out posture is valuable both from being involved as a quasi-new employee and being a free external observer to rethink, at least partially, the focused public institution. Each intervention context requires adjustment to strike the right balance and get in the rhythm between being inside and outside.

THE INDEPENDENT-ACTIVIST ROLE

The independent-activist role requires both independence towards stakeholders (when it comes to getting people with different positions to work together) and activism (as exemplified by adhering to values such as freedom of speech). Since 2008 La 27e Région has worked to build and maintain a position of relative independence working as a third party, promoting open-source practices and sharing of experiences between regions, leveraging co-financing and maintaining its status as a partner and not a subcontractor, building a community of the compassionate 'hacked' and friendly hackers. But this independence is also obtained through a contract and a protocol signed by the principal stakeholders prior to each experiment, by the fact that la 27e Région contributes to the budget of these experiments up to a certain level (around 5%) and by initiatives like the 'Manifesto of the Ingenious Regions' which contributes to creating common ground for all stakeholders.

The public sector, and its shared foundation in such values as equity, freedom and common interest, is open by definition and cannot reject mild and reasonable forms of activism. In many cases when confronted with a mix of internal inertia, bureaucratic silos and external social, economic and environmental challenges, the public sector calls for these forms of soft activism: How can we build a school that is open to inhabitants and shares its resources with them? What do we do with rural train stations with fewer than 50 travellers per day? How can sustainable procurement comply with European public procurement rules and active construction of regional ecological transition? These are all core questions that have emerged from collaborative processes between civil servants and stakeholders requiring disruptive innovation.

The design attitude responds to these challenges by hacking the established public framework (resetting the problem), but while maintaining a constructive and project-oriented attitude (problem-solving). This hacking is driven by a set of positive, constructive public values ensuring a balanced, acceptable and efficient activism.

THE ENABLING COLLABORATION

Beyond being friendly and positive, the hacking is intended as *increasing capacity* through a co-creation process, the use of collaborative tools and also the intention to enable the public structure to adopt these tools and innovate on their own. Résidences have been analyzed as local development projects, whereas their value lays not only in their capability to support progress on the specific field hosting the Résidence, but also in the lessons learned in the field to transform regional policies (Jégou, Vincent and Thévenet 2010). After the first program of Territoires en Résidence, the second program launched by La 27e Région called Transfo shifted the focus from experimenting with the design-driven approach and tools to equip the regional public administration with a temporary innovation lab using these approaches and tools and effectively transforming from the inside the way public policies and implementation processes are made. Within the range of the Résidences and Transfo methods, the participative approach is the default: 'doing with' instead of 'doing for' requiring availability from civil servants to take part and production 'on centre stage' rather than remote from the design team.

This collaborative mode is also reflected in the administrative relationship between the hosting regional administration and La 27e Région's hacking team, establishing a partnership as much as possible, exchanging the power and control of usual commissioning or subcontracting with a collaborative and mutual learning process. Establishing a partnership is generally difficult for public authorities that are accustomed to relying on the outsourcing as seen in the past few decades. Partnering facilitates a shift that enables mutual learning and adoption of new innovation practices.

THE DOING BEFORE THINKING

Hacking is a hands-on activity that gains credibility because it provides proof of success, in our case not by breaking into the public structure, but by positively delivering improvements that work. The usual local public development process tends to be based on in-vitro project engineering followed by large-scale deployment in the field. It often lacks field studies carried out with users and especially of experimentation within the engineering of the solutions. For instance, a particular experiment conducted between La 27e Région, Strategic Design Scenarios and the two French regional education departments of Champagne-Ardennes and Nord Pas-de-Calais permitted the mapping of the process and stakeholders involved over two to three years in the construction of a new high school (Jégou, Vincent and Thoresen 2011). It revealed from political decision to inauguration a quasi-absence of user involvement. Pupils, professors, school technical and administrative staff (with the exception of the headmaster) were not involved in the design process of the new high school and innovative inputs were only visible from the external architecture.

Résidences' approach on the other hand tends to turn the process upside-down, starting with experimenting with the populations involved in the participating institution, focussing on low hanging fruit to build trust between parties, testing ideas and new features in a simple setting that can be further developed if it is convincing or simply withdrawn if not.

THE MULTILEVEL INTERACTION

Hacking is not the work of a single activist but the involvement of a supportive community. Similarly, the transformation of the public sector calls for cooperation between territories, government levels and cross-fertilization within a heterogeneous community of interest. Stakeholder processes are not the default public way of conducting action. And when stakeholders are brought in for consultation or participation in a project process, they tend to reproduce the scheme of representative democracy: non-profit and civil society stands for citizens, professional federation stands for private sectors and so on. Consequently, the people at the table generally sit far away from the people whom they are supposed to represent. This barrier can be partially overcome by taking into consideration stakeholder's legitimacy instead of sticking to the strict official democratic process: certain players may be considered more legitimate by their peers or by the other participants to contribute to a project because of their experience in the field, their broadly recognized authority or their successful practice even if they may or may not be legally representative of the category of stakeholders they belong to.

The approaches taken by Résidences and Transfo include the progressive construction of a heterogeneous community of stakeholders eager to contribute to a certain project and with the legitimacy to do so: the social map around apparently vague topics such as young people in the Champagne-Ardennes region, the future of villages in rural Burgundy or employment perspectives in the PACA Region includes both inhabitants, pupils, workers, families as well as elected representatives, policymakers, experts and scholars. This community of interest includes legitimate stakeholders within the core of the project but also at its periphery taking the big picture into consideration, the broader levels of the system within which the project is located. Such a use of a 'macro-scope' to enlarge the focus and consider a problem in a systemic way combined with the investigation at the micro-level described above and the continuous interplay between macro and micro specific to our approach facilitates the breaking-down of technocratic silos, the involvement of multilevel governance (Committee of the Regions 2009) and inter-territoriality perspectives (Vanier 2008).

THE ENVISIONING PERSPECTIVE

The community of hackers focuses on forms of mutual improvement, works in progress and is by nature oriented toward a collective construction of the future. The hacking we promote in the public sector also encompasses participative and forward-looking activities. Insights at the ground level are generally the purview of expert-based activities to integrate the local context into the big picture of regional, national or global strategic environmental perspectives. Broad views point to grand challenges, threats and limits but often lack local relevance and specificity. Complementary bottom-up, participative, user-based foresight activities are more likely to identify potential opportunities and solutions rooted and emerging from the local context.

Regional foresight processes focus on a diagnosis of steps pointing toward urgent problems leading directly to the discussion of strategic orientations and agreement upon an action plan. A phase of shaping a collective and concrete vision of a desirable future is often missing prior to taking action and initiating projects. In the approaches used by Résidences and Transfo, an early visioning step points out the necessity to step back from the urgency of the present, take the necessary time to build an image of where we want to go and discuss and agree collectively on it. Design capabilities to simulate in a tangible (visualizing, rapid prototyping) and realistic (feasible) way possible alternative futures facilitate the fruition of the vision into a range of ideas, projects, solutions potentially answering the future challenges. Positive hacking provides alternatives and concrete perspectives and stimulates the strategic conversation between stakeholders. In this approach, having foresight is not merely a theoretical exercise but a way to build actionable proposals. This collective construction of the future works also as a knowledge brokering process with a convergence building effect in a heterogeneous/divergent stakeholders context.

HACKING DOCUMENTATION

Hacking is also part of the open-source culture of disclosing processes in order to share experiences and enable diffusion and reproduction. It requires finding ways to publish both the success and the failures so that anybody can learn from them and improve the solutions developed as well as the process used to reach them.

The public arena is in theory close to the open-source culture putting forward values of commons good, transparency and equity of access compared to the private sector with property rights, secrecy agreements and competitiveness barriers. Field investigations in the course of the activities of La 27e Région nearly always revealed a lack of a sharing culture in the public administration. Public facts are public and therefore accessible to everyone. Making experiences available in an easy and accessible way for other similar public institutions in the same area or same level therefore shouldn't be an issue. However, there are firewalls preventing civil servants from accessing basic online dissemination and social networking tools; and top-down control of public communication services to streamline every output into 'politically correct' information add to the filtering of 'so-called' best practices preventing the sharing of real experiences, the learning from failed practices in order to avoid repeating the same mistakes and learning from others experiences.

The design orientation towards narration (story-telling, user journey and so forth) and focus on the process as part of the result (educational dimension, transformation of stakeholders through the project process and so on) provide the basis to initiate a systematic and progressive documentation process. The Résidences gave each participant the opportunity to publish a short easy-to-read and highly illustrated booklet intended to capture and share openly each of these experiences and to enable systematic benefit and dissemination of lessons learned for further friendly and constructive hacking.

Limits and Strengths of 'Friendly Hacking'

- The **risk of neutralizing the 'friendly-hacking'** oxymoron: the virtuous opposition of a 'positive disruption' in the concept of friendly hacking may also lead to a weak and flat 'do-gooder' attitude. Friendly hacking requires both a capability of strong hacking to effectively break into the established and oppressive public infrastructure as well as a strong capability of compensating for the disruption caused by co-designing pertinent and innovative solutions. A design oriented towards problem-solving rather than problem-setting, together with a highly inertial public body, may lead to patching projects rather than in-depth collective rethinking of public infrastructures and policies. The friendly-hacking spirit needs the adoption of a solid protocol, strongly supported by both the administration of the services of public authorities and elected representatives.

- **Hacking as a stand-alone performance** lacking follow-up: design culture is already focused on the performances of the project rather than on its implementation. Beyond this general description, the service design arena focuses even more on the project pointing to the importance of the design process as part of the result as shown above. It sometimes tends to 'overdesign' the design process and thereby loses even more the purpose of the final implementation, generating substantial frustration among stakeholders. To limit this risk, practitioners like Charles Leadbeater (Leadbeater 2011) suggest embedding people in charge of creating disruption in the scaling-up and future business models at the earliest stage of the process.

- **Lack of knowledge and experience of design in the public arena** and public policies: design capabilities are known for benefiting from a certain level of freshness to 'look at old problems with new eyes' but the risk within the public arena is that it seems to be a close and familiar area to designers and that the proper investment (that is at project preparation, at school levels) to acquire the public culture/process is not enough. There is a strong need for a richer exchange between design and administrative/political sciences, as well as a mutual understanding between designers and civil servants/officials.

What Kind of Governance Could Leverage 'Friendly Hacking'?

Design as friendly hacking for public administrations might play a major role in the future

- by promoting an immersive and collaborative approach with civil servants and elected representatives in order to transform the internal public culture of innovation rather than relying on external consulting projects;

- through forward-looking activity emerging from the stakeholders (user-based) and rooted in action (solution-based) to both provide long-term perspectives and kick start the transformation towards these perspectives;

- by inspiring a systemic and open-source culture going back to the very principles of the public sector where promising innovations, virtuous processes and effective tools are part of the commons and made available and shared as such.

Yet goodwill and methods are not enough if a systemic transformation is the target. It takes time and long-term investments supported by diversified and patient stakeholders. One of the main difficulties is that public procurement does not encourage 'friendly hacking' and the public sector is still a narrow market for service design agencies even though the first pioneers began more than 10 years ago.

Beyond the disruptive capacity of design, there is a need for new kinds of agreements and contracts that could provide a better framework for 'friendly-hacking' activities. They could support new interfaces: for instance, independent design labs working for multiple partners, cooperative design companies, new business models based on crowd sourcing or new design programs inspired by action-research. Exploring new power and governance patterns could enable the independence required by design into governments, in an alternative approach to the traditional supplier/client business model.

References

Committee of the Regions. (2009). The Committee of the Regions' White Paper on Multilevel Governance. CdR 89/2009.

Durance, P., Kaplan, D., Puissochet, A. and Vincent, S. (2008). *Technologie et prospective territoriale*. Fyp Ed. Paris, France.

Jégou, F., Thévenet, R., Vincent, S, Rautureau, C. and Seyrig, A. (2011). Les residences de la 27e Région, Manuel d'Utilisation. In *Strategic Design Scenarios* (internal publication).

Jégou, F. and Vincent, S. (2010). *Residencies in Public Institutions Supporting Local Transition to Sustainable Ways of Living in Human Cities, Celebrating Public Space*. Brussels: Stichting Kunstboek Publishers.

Jégou, F., Vincent, S. and Thévenet, R. (2010). Sustainable Transformation Through an Acupuncture of Residences in Nord-Pas-de-Calais periurban areas. *Design and Creation*. Wixi.

Jégou, F., Vincent, S. Thévenet, R. and Petit, S. (2009). *Developing a College as an Open Campus. Design-driven Residences to Foster Innovation in Public Institutions*. Artifact.

Jégou, F. Vincent, S. and Thoresen, V. (2011). *My College Tomorrow: Innovation Labs to Enable Collective Public Action on Education Environments*. Enabling Responsible Living Conference Istanbul, PERL.

Leadbeater, C. and Wong, A. (2011). *Learning from the Extremes*. CISCO Systems, UK.

The Manifesto of the Ingenious Régions launched by La 27e Région in November 2011, http://fr.slideshare.net/27eregion/manifesteregioningenieuse.

Vanier, M. (2008). Le pouvoir des territoires. Essai sur l'interterritorialité. *Anthropos-Economica*. Paris.

Design Tools for Policy

JOHN BODY AND NINA TERREY

Tools for Intent: Strategic Direction by Design

By the time a public policy is implemented it is not uncommon for several hundred people to have been involved in its design, development and delivery. With each different team involved there is the opportunity for the policy intent to be distorted or lost. Frequently what gets delivered into the community is not what the original policymakers intended. On occasions, what is delivered can be diametrically opposed to the original policy intent. Too often in the policy design process there is the implicit assumption that once a new government policy has been decided, then the implementation of this policy will naturally follow (Smith 1973). This division between the people who design the policy and the people who will implement and administrate the policy promulgates the loss of policy intent.

An effective way to improve the way that policy design is delivered into the community is to invest time into articulating and managing an integrated understanding of the policy intent. The intent being a clear expression and description of the intended change in terms of the outcomes being sought, who the change is aimed at benefiting and what is required to ensure this can be met. The approach entails a strategic conversation about the intent that involves leaders involved in the policy as well as those that will be involved in the legislation development and the administrative implementation. The strategic conversation seeks to build a strong argument for the policy that can be conveyed across the many different teams that will play a part in the progression of the policy idea through to reality. It is about breaking down barriers, to generate the dialectic abilities of multi-perspectives, and galvanize a shared understanding of the intended policy. An implicit assumption in taking a strategic conversation approach is that it requires organizations to go beyond their traditional bureaucratic tendencies, and to seek post-modern ways of working which support collaborative approaches. These organizations embrace more innovative approaches, are less risk averse, experiment and innovate resulting in better products and services (du Gay 2011: 21). The post-modern public organization challenges contested domains, and supports non-bureaucratic control regimes (Reed 2011: 250).

The Policy Design and Implementation Landscape

In the Australian Government context there are three distinct domains that must be developed when the government seeks the implementation of a new policy (ANAO 2006). First, the policy is initiated. It is conceived by the government typically driven by political, social, economic and environmental reasons. Policy designers then conceptually design this policy. Second, the legislation is drafted that will give effect to the policy. This involves technical writing of the intended policy. Third, all the elements required for the administration of the policy are designed, built and implemented. Depending on the policy, the implementation can entail IT system development, staff training, business process change, call centre changes, marketing materials, explanatory materials and considerable engagement with people or businesses in the community that may be affected or play a part in the change.

In some cases, the policy, legislation and administration functions may sit within the one government department. However, in many circumstances, many administrative agencies are responsible for the administration of policies and laws set by central agencies.

This landscape is the context in which new policies become reality. In many situations, there is a sequence as policy is developed, then converted to law and then converted to a number of administrative components. In such a sequential development process, the likelihood is high for intent to drift. It drifts through communication breakdowns and through different disciplines putting the stamp of interpretation on their work. In much the same way as the children's game of 'Chinese whispers' results in surprising results, so too can the policy implementation process. Without careful management of the intent, the likelihood that the intent will change through the course of the project is very high. This will inevitably result in the project failing to meet expectations. Significant embarrassment to the government can occur, along with audits and enquiries.

Managing intent is only one of many design considerations for a successful policy implementation (McPhee 2006). It is however a foundational consideration. The intent process works across existing domains, increasing cohesion across disciplines while still allowing specific disciplines to deliver their parts of the overall integrated implementation.

The Importance of Managing Intent

The importance of managing policy intent from conception through to delivery cannot be underestimated. The carriage of the government's intent is critically important to maintain community confidence in the government, and in society. If the policy intent is either poorly formulated, and or poorly executed then the role of government to provide public value is undermined and community confidence, amongst other things declines. The following example from Australia illustrates this point.

In late 2008, the Australian Government initiated a series of new policies that aimed to reduce the rising living costs for families and society. The initiatives proposed included developing a Grocery Choice website. The government's policy intent was to give families information about prices of household goods across all retailers, so that they could choose where to shop. The policy intent was to increase competition into the supermarket sector, hence drive prices down. Australia has two very powerful supermarket operators and the government was concerned that given their size they may become uncompetitive. The focus of the policy became a website, which intended to provide shoppers with information that could help them to decide where to shop. During the implementation process it was decided that with thousands of supermarkets and even more thousands of grocery items it would be better to give an average price of goods in each city. Administratively, this was much easier. But unless the shopper was prepared to travel several hundreds of kilometres to another city the information did nothing to achieve the government's policy intent. In many cases in told shoppers what they already knew, as one shopper stated on a blog:

> *What's truly absurd about this is that if the site works as intended (which it doesn't, apparently), it is still not helpful. It gives broad brushstroke information whereas the (alleged) audience has extensive lived experience on the specifics. Only a career bureaucrat could possibly come up with an inquiry and informational website that merely sets out, at a uselessly high level, what every household shopper, and every market participant, already knew. The only people to whom these results come as anything of a shock are solidly upper-middle class types for whom real household budgeting is a mystery and for whom the weekly grocery shop is not a significant portion of their living costs.[1]*

Somewhere in the translation of the policy idea through to the website design and the supporting processes, the intent drifted to such an extent that the result was unrecognizable. This initiative was axed within a year and followed with a Senate Economics Committee inquiry.[2] This was very embarrassing for the government and for those involved in the development of the idea. It was an expensive exercise that failed to take into account people's needs, and there was no design of the intended experience into the policy intent.

GOVERNMENT SCRAPS GROCERY CHOICE WEBSITE
The Federal Government has scrapped its Grocery Choice website, set up to help shoppers find the lowest grocery prices in supermarkets around the country. Consumer Affairs Minister Craig Emerson made the announcement late today. The website immediately attracted criticism last year. Information was updated only once a month and price comparisons were broad and generic. Mr Emerson had said from the outset that it was not feasible to publish reliable, timely information on grocery prices for consumers, a view held by many critics. 'The fact is that in Australia, there are thousands of supermarkets and even more thousands of grocery items', he said. 'The information requirements would have been enormous and they're just not feasible, in my view.' (26 June 2009)[3]

While this example is from the Australian Government context, every government could provide its examples of similar issues. It is a feature of the complex nature of government policy implementation. A policy design project is often quite abstract. The new policy will be implemented across millions of people in contexts that have huge variation and cannot be fully appreciated. The policy will need to work in high density cities through to remote districts. It will need to work for the technologically savvy and those with no technology. It will need to work for speakers of the majority language and those without those language skills. It will need to work for a variety of family or business contexts. It will need to work for young and old. It will need to work for employed, unemployed, retired and students. And it will need to work for those it is meant to work for and not for those with criminal purposes. When government announces a new policy the issues described above could not have been expected to

---

1   Source: http://www.petermartin.com.au/2008/08/fuelwatch-and-grocerychoice.html. Accessed 26 May 2013.

2   Source: http://www.treasury.gov.au/PublicationsAndMedia/Publications/2011/Senate_Economics_Committee. Accessed 26 May 2013.

3   Source: http://www.abc.net.au/news/2009-06-26/govt-pulls-plug-on-grocery-choice-website/1333540. Accessed 24 May 2013.

be fully thought through. What can be articulated is the context for change and the drivers that make this new policy needed. The desired outcomes from the new policy and the desired change in experience for people can be described. Also at this stage of policy design there is also generally a hypothesis that can be described.

Shift to Recognize Policy Intent

This concept of intent was developed in 2000 within the Australian Taxation Office. This followed a significant review of business taxes in Australia late 1999 (Ralph July, 1999). One of the foundational recommendations from the review was to take an integrated approach to designing policy, and the following quote from that report highlights the need:

> It is essential that policy, legislative and administrative expertise be brought together through the design process, to ensure that:
>
> - administrative implications are at the fore when policies are formulated and consequential legislative provision are drafted;
> - reciprocally, the policy intent is reflected accurately when elaborated in legislation and the systems for its administration (recognizing that legislation is the practical expression of policy); and
> - more generally, "feedback loops" are strengthened between policy formulation, legislative drafting and administration (including systems design).
>
> *(Ralph Review of Business Taxes 1999)*

The extent to which it has gained acceptance as a way of understanding new policy design is evidenced in this extract of a speech by the Commissioner of Taxation in 2005 to the business community about a new policy that had been implemented.

> In July 1999, The Review of Business Taxation, chaired by John Ralph, noted in recommendation 15.1 of his report the general principles for Consolidation.[4] The report said that 'introducing a consolidation regime will involve significant change' and that the 'motivation for embarking on such significant change stems from the high compliance costs and high tax revenue costs (and concomitant complex of anti-avoidance provisions) associated with the current tax treatment of company groups ...'
>
> The Ralph Review set out six principles encapsulating the framework and intent of the proposed Consolidation regime:
>
> 1. That Consolidation is optional, but it is a 'one in, all in' for all members of wholly owned Australian-resident groups;

---

4 The Australian Commonwealth Government introduced consolidation to reduce compliance costs for business, remove impediments to the most efficient business structures and improve the integrity of the tax system. Consolidation allows wholly-owned corporate groups to operate as a single entity for income tax purposes from 1 July 2002. Source: http://www.ato.gov.au/businesses/pathway.aspx?pc=001/003/126. Accessed 26 May 2013.

2. That treatment is to be as a single entity for consolidated groups of wholly owned Australian-resident entities with a single common head entity;

3. That former grouping provisions would be repealed;

4. That losses and franking account balances are generally able to be brought into the consolidated group by the entering entities;

5. That losses and franking balances remain with the group on an entity's exit;

6. That tax values of assets and liabilities be determined by the asset-based model.

The intent of the Consolidation regime can be seen as part of a wider intent to cover Business Tax Reform as whole. The overall objective was a stable, simpler, and more coherent business tax system, which would:

- *optimize economic growth;*
- *promote equity;*
- *promote simplicity and certainty.[5]*

This strong reference to policy intent, many years later reinforces the power of a shared understanding of intent. The following section describes how to develop intent in practice, to increase the likelihood that new policy will implement successfully.

Developing Intent in Practice

The outcome sought by managing intent is the successful implementation of the new policy design. This is achieved by having a clear and well-understood argument for the change that is successfully communicated to all people involved in the design, build and delivery of the change.

Four components go towards managing intent successfully.

1. First, a clear argument for the new policy;

2. Second, identification champions of the intent;

3. Third, build a shared understanding of intent through strategic conversation; and

4. Finally, the clear argument is recorded so that it can be shared and referenced as the policy is implemented.

---

5   Speech by Michael D'Ascenzo to the Taxation Institute of Australia Consolidation Symposium, 19–20 May 2005. Source: http://www.ato.gov.au/content/59313.htm. Accessed 24 May 2013.

To illustrate each of these components we will draw on the 'Listening to Families: Understanding the journey of families through the ACT service system project'.[6]

A Clear Argument for Intent

The argument takes account of the drivers, describes the desired outcome and provides a sketch of the big policy idea. The argument considers the complex system from multiple perspectives, including the perspectives of multiple stakeholders. The argument makes sense by taking a user perspective.

Identify Champions of Intent

Strong advocates needed for the new policy idea are amongst those who are leading aspects of the policy design, the development of the law and the design and build of the administration. The change literature is unanimous that a successful change has a champion, or group of champions. John Kotter (2007) talks of a guiding coalition for the change. A new policy project not only supports this assertion, it strengthens it. Where most of Kotter's examples come from within organizations, government policy projects span multiple industry and government partners that affect the lives potentially of a whole nation. The challenges of implementing changes to government policy mean that there must be a small number of leaders who are the champions of the intent of the change.

> In the Listening to Families project the champions of intent identified early were senior leaders from the local government directorate from Community Services, two CEOs/Directors from not for profit organizations involved in the providing services for families in need and a design expert from Industry.

Build a Shared Understanding of the Intent Through Strategic Conversation

The clear argument that is understood by the intent champions is communicated to the many hundreds of people who are designing, building and implementing the change.

Having a small group of people who champion change is a prerequisite but on its own is insufficient. Another feature of a government policy change is the time it takes to implement and the number of parties that the change must pass through before it is implemented.

---

6   See Chapter 8.

> The Intent Champions and representatives from across government and the community sector, including frontline workers, managers and leaders, met for a one-day strategic conversation workshop. The design industry experts ThinkPlace facilitated the workshop. The current state exploration involved participants taking a role from the system – some were themselves, some were families and some were government. We explored the system as it is now, drew out who we were talking about, and called out the observed issues from multiple perspectives. The tools of design used included mind-mapping the issues, sketching the user experience and modelling the complex service system.

Those parties include the policy developers, legislative drafters, IT system developers, marketers, trainers, communications people, compliance officers, operational teams and help desks. Many government policies also require change from people in industry such as software developers, or relevant industry participants to the change such as those in the finance industry, those in the travel industry or those in the energy industry.

All those with key roles in architecting the change need to have a strong shared understanding of the intent of the change. With something as abstract as a policy change, the change must be shared as an argument for the change. Those who are architecting the various components of the change must understand the rationale for the new policy. They must understand what the government sees as the problems being faced, the outcomes the government seeks to achieve and how the policy idea will make the required difference. If those architecting the change do not understand and appreciate the argument then it is unlikely that the change will succeed.

One way to achieve this is to run a strategic conversation.

A key part of the tool for understanding intent is strategic conversation. It is strategic because the conversation considers the breadth of issues and temporal dimensions that are driving the need for change. It considers which elements are in scope for this new policy and how this new policy fits with other policies and the work of other agencies in this area. A conversation implies an unimpassioned consideration of all the dimensions. It is not a debate where each side holds entrenched positions. Neither is it 'group think'. It is a genuine and authentic desire to understand the problem in all its dimensions and through that conversation to reach some shared places of agreement about the problem, Mengis and Eppler draw an elegant summary:

> *A knowledge-intensive conversation is a synchronous, co-located or mediated interaction between two or more people who have extensive level of expertise of in often different area. (Mengis and Eppler 2005: 4–5)*

The strategic conversation is far reaching but that does not mean it is without form. The description that follows draws from over a decade of experience by the authors in the design of government policy implementation.

The first part of the strategic conversation considers the *current state*. The change drivers are identified. A picture of the people currently involved or that will be affected is developed. And design considerations are listed that may present constraints of opportunities.

The strategic conversation then moves to the *future state* where the ultimate outcome or result is defined. Success is often subjective so the different user and stakeholder perspectives of success are defined. And the evidence that would indicate the successful implementation of the new policy design is given. This articulation of the current state and the desired future sets up the tension that creates the argument for the new policy idea itself. This is the change or the hypothesis that the *new policy suggests will bridge the gap* between the current state and the desired future. The change can be expressed as the strategic shifts required, the citizen experience that is sought and the tangible components that will be made to produce the solution.

An important dimension of the intent tool is to take a *human-centred perspective*, and make explicit the use of design thinking and design methods to illuminate the human-dimension to the policy design. Human-centred design concerns itself with creating purposeful interactions for people by designing products and services that are useful, usable and desirable (Junginger 2006: 4). A participatory approach is implicit in human-centred design and the strategic conversation is key to generating the intent.

Record of the Intent

We strongly advocate for the argument to be expressed on one page (Figure 14.1). This forces the argument to be strong, succinct and able to be communicated.

The document may be similar in part to a project initiation document but the differences are important. The differences are that it is developed as part of a process to gain a shared understanding of intent. It is developed through a strategic conversation, never alone. It also fits a format that is literally millennia old to construct an argument, by constructing a gap between the current state and the desired future state, then bridging the gap with the hypothesis for change. The discipline of condensing the whole argument onto one page is also in our experience essential. Each word is carefully chosen. Each concept on the page is thought through for its relevance and importance. The drivers and outcome are debated by those leading the change. The one page becomes a control document throughout the change process.

> The artefact produced from the strategic conversation workshop captures the key points raised within the framework. The policy argument is held within, and the approach to co-design services with families is a clear part of the change.

Having the intent statement documented is particularly valuable because the duration and breadth of policy design and implementation projects means that key personnel will inevitably move on before the project is complete. Having the intent documented allows any incoming people to be part of a conversation around the intent statement so that they can also gain a shared understanding of what is being done. It may not appear possible that the answers to the intent questions posed above could be written on one page and do justice to the conversation. But with careful thought and deliberation on the points of substance it is the authors' experience that this can be done. And it can be done in a way that is not superficial.

Co-designing an integrated service system for 'Vulnerable Families'

INTENT — *To develop new capabilities to design and co-produce services with current service users as part of a systemic approach to improving outcomes for vulnerable families in the ACT*

Drivers
- Recognition that a group of individuals/families are experiencing complexity in receiving the support they need and want, resulting in poor service outcomes and ineffective use of public resources
- The desire to work as 'one government' – better collaboration between governmental organizations, community-based work and citizens to create a cohesive service system for citizens
- Introducing a collaborative design approach – great interest in co-design approaches, concepts and tools to improve outcomes for citizens and the effectiveness for service delivery

Current reality	*Desired reality*
What is the situation at the moment?	**What is the situation in the long-term future?**
Service System - Service system has evolved in a largely reactive manner without considering the user experience which results in increased service system complexity and duplication - System is experienced and compartmentalised – by provider, funding source and program logic – forming parallel streams of services that are poorly integrated and difficult to navigate - Focussing on fixing symptoms rather than addressing the causes of the actual issues for families resulting in ineffective use of resources and migration to higher cost and or intrusive services and interventions - Examples of existing local initiatives/knowledge that have sought to tailor services in conjunction with citizens	**Service System** - A systemic approach to service delivery across ACT human services which is person centred, outcomes focussed and operates as 'one system' regardless of provider or funding resources - Reframed view from service delivery to a service system dealing with all services, their interfaces and interconnections - Focussing on the overall outcomes for people, rather than their problems, to create better use of resources (productivity) and a better citizen experience - Established culture of innovation and conditions for future success
Vulnerable Families - Families that cannot, or choose not to, access the multiple (breadth) and/or intensive (depth) support they require, including mainstream, targeted and statutory (involuntary) support services - Difficult to define, quantify what characterizes a 'vulnerable family' - Despite involvement with services, some families and individuals still experience poor outcomes. This may involve under or over servicing and can trigger non engagement or prolonged involvement with services	**Vulnerable Families** - Better understanding of vulnerable families and their experience by 'Testing the Narrative' in a clear and descriptive way - Engaging citizens in collaboration around services by better identifying their experiences and desires - Optionally, a breakthrough idea
Culture/Environment - Individual services focused on pre-specified 'delivery' rather than creating desired outcomes for citizens as part of a systemic approach	**Culture/Environment** - Introducing/applying/adapting a collaborative design approach in order to improve future approaches - Co-producing outcomes with citizens and other relevant actors of society

Focussing question
How can we initiate capabilities for an ongoing engagement and learning to give citizens a voice in designing and co-producing services?

How do we get there?
We will form two individual streams of work:

(1) Theory – skill building & reflection
- Train field work team and provide skills, tools and methods they need to understand and design person-centred services weekly skillbuilding sessions
- Reflect about the experiences made while applying the learning in the field weekly learning reflection sessions
- Iteratively, build, update, review and refine the co-design methodology

(2) Practice- applying the learning
1. Prepare for citizen engagement by developing the co-design research protocol
2. Gather information on the current situation by concluding fieldwork with citizens and analyse outcomes of fieldwork in workshops
3. Identify and innovate possible solutions, opportunities and ideas into 'fieldshop' sessions
4. Evaluate and refine possible ideas in workshops and propose solutions for the implementation as part of the final report

Figure 14.1   Example statement of intent – Listening to Families (2012)

What Is the Effort Involved?

The value of the intent process is proportional to the amount of time put into it. Some would see the questions posed above could be answered quickly by one person. We have run intent conversations in two hours, half a day or a full day. The difference is the quality of the understanding. A two-hour conversation is unlikely to highlight any new understandings whereas a full day conversation is likely to uncover some insights not considered before that could be the clue to a different approach for the new policy project.

Apart from the strategic conversation itself, there is effort in the preparation for the conversation, and the careful documentation afterwards. And generally the intent statement goes through two or three iterations before it is fully accepted as the shared understanding of the intent of the new policy project.

Where there is no appetite for the senior leaders to engage in the strategic conversation about the intent, this can be an early warning sign of issues that will be faced as implementation progresses.

How Is It Endorsed?

The intent statement is a formal project document and as such it must be formally endorsed by the group responsible for the governance of the new policy design and implementation.

How Is It Used?

The intent statement should never be far from the minds of all those involved in the design and implementation of the new policy. It should definitely be used as the measuring device for any key deliverable signoffs along the way. Therefore the high level design for the new policy should be assessed against the intent statement. The detailed designs for all the components should also be assessed against the intent as should any prototypes of final solutions.

The intent statement therefore becomes an important part of the design documentation, sitting alongside the project management document set. The design documents and project management documents are used as project governance tools throughout the project.

How Is It Maintained?

The intent is the beacon for the project and in many projects the original intent is what gets delivered. But in some projects the intent does change. The research phase of the project may uncover new insights that mean the intent should be modified to take account of new information. Because of the care taken to develop the intent statement, the intent statement should not be changed without the acknowledgement of those leading the change. Those who developed the shared understanding should be those who arrive and the new understanding.

Therefore, changing the intent statement is not an administrative issue. The same approach that was used to develop the intent statement should also be used to modify the intent. That is, a conversation about the need to change the intent is needed and the change is formally acknowledged.

Conclusion

The management of policy intent is complex and challenging due to the complex nature of policy and the many interactions and people who are involved in the process. This chapter set out to present a tool called the 'Tool for Intent' as a way to stabilize and build a shared understanding of policy intent. This intent is defined early in the process, and acts as a guiding tool throughout the policy design and implementation process.

References

(2006). Implementation of Programme and Policy Initiatives: Making implementation matter, Australian National Audit Office.

(2012). Listening to Families: Understanding the Journey of Families Through the ACT Service System. A. Government. Australia, 9.

du Gay, P. (2011). With Regard to Persons: Problems of Involvement and Attachment in 'Post-Bureaucratic' Public Management. In S. Clegg, M. Harris and H. Hopfl, *Managing Modernity: Beyond Bureaucracy*. Oxford: Oxford University Press. 11–29.

Junginger, S. (2006). Human-Centred Interaction Design: A Study in Collective Creativity. Academy of Management Conference Atlanta.

Kotter, J. (2007). Leading Change: Why Transformation efforts fail. *Harvard Business Review* (January).

McPhee, I. (2006). Successful implementation of Government Programmes and Initiatives. Department of the Prime Minister and Cabinet and the Australia New Zealand School of Government Conference.

Mengis, J. and Eppler, M. (2005). Understanding and Managing Knowledge-Intensive Conversations: An appreciative Reading of the Literature on Conversation in Organizations and an integrative Approach for their management, Institute for Corporate Communications. 1–46.

Ralph, J. (July, 1999). Review of Business Taxation: A Tax System redesigned: Chairman's Introduction. Canberra, Department of Treasury.

Reed, M. (2011). The Post-Bureaucratic Organization and the Control Revolution. Managing Modernity. In S. Clegg, M. Harris and H. Hopfl, *Beyond Bureaucracy*. Oxford: Oxford University Press. 230–56.

Smith, T.B. (1973). The Policy Implementation Process. *Policy Sciences*, 4: 197–209.

ANDREA SIODMOK

Tools for Insight: Design Research for Policymaking

This chapter sets out a range of practical tools and methods that can be used to inform the development of a new policy. It discusses innovative ways to open up policymaking to embrace the insights and experience of the general public, professionals and wider stakeholders in the system. It is based upon practical experience formerly as the Chief Designer of a local authority and Chief Design Officer at the British Design Council and more recently as Head of Policy Lab at the UK Government's Cabinet Office, working with a range of Government departments to apply design techniques in policymaking.

What Is Design Insight?

Developing insight through design refers to the act of turning intuition and observation into a vision, or plan of action. We have all experienced moments of insight, when the solution to a difficult problem presents itself, often unexpectedly. Using design methods offers a way to increase the likelihood of these 'epiphanies' occurring by applying research methods that are grounded in design ethnography and observed behaviours.

Better approaches to gathering insight can not only improve the evidence base for a policy, but it can also help bring momentum to change programs by developing a shared understanding of a problem (or opportunity) and increasing the impetus for action. In today's fast changing, highly interconnected, culturally diverse world our current approaches to the development of policy can benefit significantly from being grounded in real world experience of end users. Additionally, the lack of certainty and the prevalence of ill-defined problems set against the absence of concrete datasets to back up decision-making calls for different, more creative and collaborative approaches.

How Can Design Help Build Insight?

Professional designers offer value to the policymakers as experts in managing innovation and creativity, guiding a range of different people through the practical process of turning new ideas into workable policies.

Design brings an approach and set of tools that can be used to maximize the potential for new ideas to emerge. This process unlocks creativity and delivers innovative solutions.

Insights can occur at any stage of a project, they can be both radical and incremental. Over the course of time they can turn out to be instrumental or incidental to the success of the policy. In order to use them effectively, it is important to harness, foster and manage them – recognizing they may come from many different sources and be of varying quality.

This is very different to traditional forms of consultation that typically present a fixed number of potential solutions for feedback. Design insight in contrast to consultation tends to be:

- Holistic – investigating the broader issues with open ended questions;

- Qualitative – often based on small samples of users;

- 'Softer' – dealing with feelings, perceptions and behaviours;

- Contextually based – dealing with users in their environments;

- Empathic – Touching on experiences rather than reported data.

In the early stages, using design methods can help frame problems, bring people together and discover latent needs of citizens, customers and service users. However design can also help shape, develop and deliver new solutions with the user or customer in mind that are both desirable and workable. It is typically through the synthesis of a range of different insights that breakthrough ideas are formed and that weaker ideas are tested, improved or rejected.

Real World Experience

Real world experience is a major trigger of insight that leads to innovation. It may be that localized ad-hoc solutions or workarounds have been developed through local people's ingenuity that can be integrated into system wide solutions. Or it can be the act of seeing a policy in action that begins to reveal the complex interaction of behaviours, values and relationship to other policies that drives the need for improvement. Most often, it is the simply the act of applying 'conscious observation' of real life situations that reveal how people's lives are shaped by the products, services and environments they interact with. In the absence of direct experience, our perceptions may be shaped by formal and informal influences that range from commissioned research to popular media.

People-centred Policies

Putting people's experience at the heart of service provision has been a major driver of policy changes in recent years across local and national governments. This has often meant rethinking service provision from the individual's point of view rather than purely the system or professional's perspective. Put simply this means moving from professionals solving problems 'for' citizens to professionals working 'with' the public on shared interests. Early collaboration between local people and experts, working with designers can help create the conditions for communities to participate in policy development. This reduces the risk of policy failure when it is scaled by testing out ideas early and getting feedback from users.

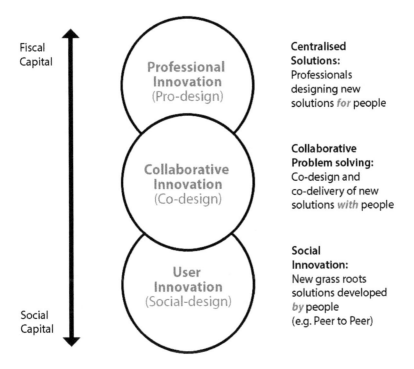

Figure 15.1   Different kinds of innovation in the public and professional realm

Co-design in Policy Development

New forms of collaboration can be a significant source of innovation, efficiency and effectiveness of new policies (Figure 15.1). Co-design refers to the act of collaborating with different stakeholders, professionals and users in the design of a policy or service. Co-design techniques can help address the increasing complexity of public sector problems through the lens of the citizen, encouraging and facilitating new forms of dialogue between the public, private, social and citizen sectors.

It is important to note that in a highly participatory design process, citizens (more often known as 'end users') can work with professionals throughout the process and become part of the 'design team' building and testing concepts and therefore can be better placed to 'own', co-deliver or adopt the solutions. This works on the premise that change is no longer top down, but rather will involve dissolving the boundaries between service providers and end users, thereby allowing knowledge and capabilities to be reconfigured in new ways. These new Hybrid Value Chains (HVC) (Ashoka n.d.) or Social Value Chains (SVC) promise to reform the way that services are designed and delivered, increasing the potential for efficiency and innovation. In the private sector consumer 'sweat equity' has been widely deployed to bring efficiencies, flexibility and reduce the cost to end users of the products and services they buy. In a hybrid value chain users become active co-creators of value, whether it is booking airline tickets or building IKEA flat pack. This could unlock potential for significant service improvement if services were 'co-produced' (Boyle, et al. 2010). The term co-production, first used by Elinor Ostrom, describes the idea that both paid and unpaid labour can deliver public services. However, it also raises fundamental questions of the role of the state in delivering services.

Example: Design in the Development of Local Government Policy and Service

In Cornwall, the local authority Cornwall Council developed a design-led approach to policymaking from 2009 to 2013, initially through a Design Council partnership program called 'Designs of the Time' (Dott) (Figure 15.5) and then led by the council's Chief Executive's department. Designs of the Time (Dott Cornwall) applied a 'living lab' approach (Von Hippel 1986) where 10 projects used design approaches to enable local people to prototype and develop innovative new services.

The ambition was to deliver more for less, improving the quality of services by re-forming and redesigning the way services were conceived and delivered. We set ourselves the challenge of making public services 'ten times better with no extra budget'. Given that Cornwall has 50,000 public sector workers and 500,000 citizens, the goal was to rebalance the economy towards the social sector and citizen sector.

Professional service designers such as Sea Communications, Think Public, Standby and Livework applied a range of bespoke service design methods and tools to social policy problems within a common framework. What was unusual about Dott was that design was used specifically to enable citizens to make a greater contribution to the development of new policies. Each 'project' formed a prototype for policy ideas to be developed and tested.

In 2011, the Chief Executive's department developed a shared approach for innovation using design techniques. This methodology, called Thinking Room, sought to demystify innovation and build a 'common sense' approach that could encourage wider take up of design beyond professional designers to support creative practices in all public sector employees as well as the wider public (Figures 15.2 and 15.3).

The phases combined divergent and convergent thinking, opening up possibilities before narrowing down to a preferred idea. We used the term 'double diamond' to describe this combination of inductive and deductive enquiry at the Design Council (Design Council 2005) (Figure 15.4). Design insights for policy can occur at any stage, however, are most commonly associated with the early stages of projects.

Whilst no two projects followed the same process in detail, the program applied a consistent methodology to underpin project activities. The key value of a methodological approach was in setting expectations and recognizing what cultures and behaviours were helpful in different phases. Spending too long developing insights might hamper delivery, however, conversely, spending too little time opening up possible directions at the early stages could result in the scope of the project being too constrained.

A Methodology for the Development of Policy by Design

Across a range of projects the process typically followed the following stages: diagnostic phase, co-discovery, co-design and co-delivery.

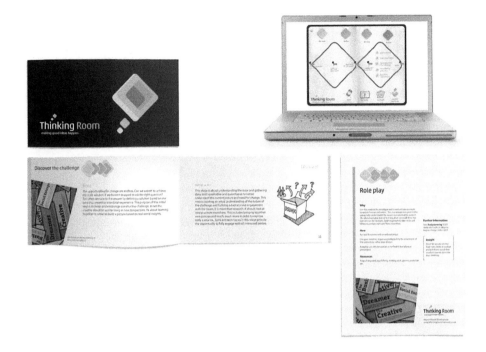

Figure 15.2   Thinking Room toolkit for design in policy development
Source: With kind permission of Cornwall Council

Figure 15.3   Top-down and bottom-up combined in collaborative innovation

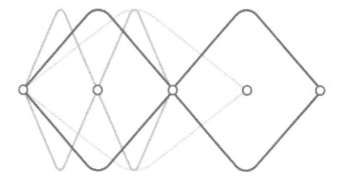

Figure 15.4   Design Council 'double diamond', showing divergent and convergent phases

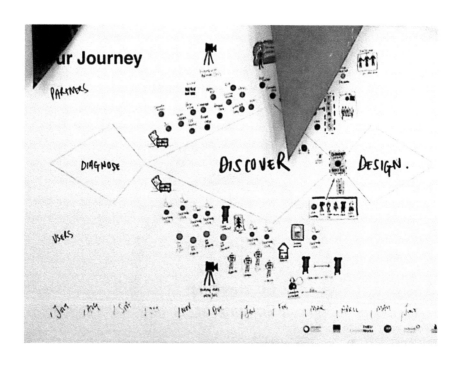

Figure 15.5   'Cornwall Works 50+' Designs of the Time project led by Think Public designers

Diagnostic phase: This phase is about setting up the project, and diagnosing the nature of the problem, including identifying existing policies, research, stakeholders and activities on the ground. It also includes formalizing procurement and bringing together a collaborative team. The key outputs of this stage include a more accurate picture of the existing services, expertise and resources that might be available.

Co-discovery phase: This stage brings critical enquiry and insights. It involves developing a more focussed understanding of the issue that is aligned to the frontline experience and community's needs. Various design tools and methods can be used such as observation, cultural probes, design ethnography, user diaries. The most important insights are often 'latent', the things people do or want that they don't always tell you. Most significantly this phase typically involved re-framing problems bringing into play new actors, resources or information that has the potential to be transformative. This phase can also include gathering and sharing inspirational examples of best practice locally, nationally and internationally. Bringing together experience from different sectors and places can catalyze new ideas and give team's renewed energy to develop their proposed policy ideas.

Co-design phase: Co-designing is where the team and/or community are involved in the idea generation with professional designers and other experts. The design team uses the research with local people in the co-discovery phase to generate new ideas and innovation. Often the design team will build on the key ideas from the co-design stage, creating tangible aspects to them so they can be communicated and prototyped with the community, including prototyping of ideas to get immediate feedback and ideas for improvement (which can be 'low fidelity' mock ups or working prototypes).

Co-delivery: Outputs and outcomes at this stage vary widely; from architectural plans to policy recommendations. Our projects typically created innovative ways that people can engage with the design solution in the medium or longer term.

Design Methods for Insight

Design methods can be used to help establish a compelling qualitative evidence-base to underpin the mandate for change. The process of gathering design insights can inform and influence policy direction by both sharpening our understanding of the problem the policy needs to address (analytical insights) as well as building awareness of the potential solutions on offer (creative insights). Whilst many research techniques can help identify the exiting situation, in addition to this, designerly approaches consciously seek to turn these observations into new ideas and solutions with or for users.

ANALYTICAL INSIGHTS (PROBLEM DEFINITION):

- Build a better understanding of current world, challenging stereotypes and existing assumptions (for example, 1:1 interviews);

- Reframe questions and help unearth where the real problem lies;

- Identify failure points, duplication and inefficiencies in existing service provision (for example, user journey mapping);

- Reveal end users' motives and latent needs in order to create the right incentives for behaviour change (for example, gaining insights through user diaries);

- Connect policymakers to front-line experiences.

CREATIVE INSIGHTS (POLICY IDEAS):

- Bring fresh perspectives from other sectors or fields as well from designers' own experience;

- Identify latent resources (both physical and social) that can be reconfigured or integrated into new solutions;

- Develop active networks of citizens, stakeholders and employees who can bring their experience to service design and delivery (for example, through Hacks and Jams).

What follows are some of the tools, methods and techniques that can be used to build insights.

1. **Co-design**
   Co-design and participatory design means including users in the design team rather than gathering user feedback through observation and testing. The approach can be invaluable to bring user's perspectives and creativity to new solutions (Figure 15.6). When people are involved through all stages they typically gain a greater sense of ownership and empowerment.

2. **Community reporters**
   Community reporters can be effective in accessing a trusted community network and engaging 'hard to reach' individuals. Peer to peer community reporters bring new insights for policymakers into different people's lives. By training a community champion in listening and interviewing skills, and equipping them with audio equipment or cameras they can get beyond the barriers that may exist where communities distrust or find it difficult to share ideas with the state.

3. **Cultural probes**
   This is a research technique for probing attitudes and aspirations across different cultural groups, developed by Bill Gaver and Tony Dunne at the Royal College of Art (Gaver et al. 1999). Digital cameras are an effective way to get users to record incidents, or environments to use in later discussions and workshops.

4. **Design ethnography**
   Design ethnography uses observational techniques in real contexts. It is a form of primary research, where the designer watches people carrying out tasks in their own environments and asks open-ended questions

Figure 15.6   Sea Communications co-design using cake to enable local children to build their vision of a community centre
Source: With kind permission of Sea Communications

about their actions, thoughts and feelings. This method can be valuable to understand the reality of what people do rather than what they say they do, and to gain insights to inform the development of ideas.

5.   **Discovery workshops**
Discovery workshops can be used to bring a range of users and stakeholders together to better understand the problem and 'sharpen' the brief or question. Workshops may include presentation of initial research findings or themes which have emerged from service mapping, user-journey mapping and initial interviews. The process can also include other methods such as co-design.

6.   **Hacks, service Jams and charettes**
Similar to discovery workshops, Gov jams, service jams and hacks bring a range of stakeholders or 'hacktivists' together to 'tackle' a problem, imagine a new service or develop a policy idea. Service Jams are spreading across the world and run a particular methodology. In the built environment there is some similarity to the ethos of the 'charette'. A charette is a collaborative technique where people come together in small teams to intensively work up solutions.[1]

---

1   The term 'charette' evolved from a pre-1900 exercise at the Ecole des Beaux Arts in France. Architectural students were given a design problem to solve within an allotted time. When that time was up, the students would rush their drawings from the studio to the Ecole in a cart called a charette (http://dli. library.cmu.edu/charette/what-charette).

7. **Journey mapping**
   Journey mapping is often used to understand existing service delivery to identify failure points and opportunities for improvement. The journey map may show that the service works well and can be improved or that there is a need for fundamental transformation. The journeys can be visualized for 'discovery workshops' to bring the problem or challenge to life for a wide range of users and stakeholders.

8. **One-to-one interviews**
   This method is useful to develop personas and get in-depth information from individual users. One-to-one interviews can help build insights in sensitive issues, where people might exaggerate in group situations, for getting information from interviewees where individuality is particularly important. Interviews can be open, semi-structured or tightly structured and can take from 30 minutes up to 2 hours.

9. **User diaries**
   User diaries are a low-cost 'fly on the wall' observation technique for getting in-depth insights into how people live their lives, the challenges they face and the opportunities for improvement. Diaries are completed by user groups, usually to a format and covering topics specified by the researcher. User diaries can provide the context for interviews and observations. The diary can be kept over a week or sometimes longer. Photo diaries can also be used in conjunction with a written diary or as a stand-alone tool.

Design methods have been shaped and evolved to respond to changing problems and new technologies, and they will continue to evolve. The Helen Hamlyn Centre, at the Royal College of Art, has collated a number of methods for building insight working with citizens and end users.[2] However, in design for policy it should be recognized that there is no rulebook or prescription to apply, as the Joseph Rowntree Foundation observed: 'Radical public service innovation involves a process of social discovery, not a template to copy' (Hambleton and Howard 2012).

References

Ashoka. https://www.ashoka.org/hvc.

Boyle, D. et al. (2010). *Right Here, Right Now: Taking Co-production into the Mainstream*. London: Nesta.

Carnegie Mellon University Libraries: What is a Charette? http://dli.library.cmu.edu/charette/what-charette.

Design Council (2005). http://www.designcouncil.org.uk/designprocess.

Gaver, W., Dunne, A. and Pacenti, E. (1999). Cultural Probes, Interactions. *Design*, 6(1).

Hambleton, R. and Howard, J. (2012). *Public Sector Innovation and Local Leadership in the UK and the Netherlands*. York: Joseph Rowntree Foundation.

Von Hippel, E. (1986). Lead Users: A Source of Novel Product Concepts. *Management Science*, 32.

---

2 http://designingwithpeople.rca.ac.uk/.

JOACHIM HALSE

Tools for Ideation: Evocative Visualization and Playful Modelling as Drivers of the Policy Process

With this chapter I wish to contribute to the understanding of how two core design competencies, namely visualization and modelling, may become valuable tools for ideation and engagement in the public policy process. (Note: the concept of 'the policy process' is not narrowly defined here as formal ministerial work, but taken broadly to entail processes of social regulation and financing on the municipal and national government level, as well as more general public debate about how to collectively create desirable and viable futures for present and coming generations.)

Visualization and modelling are fundamental aspects of the professional language of designers for making physical, and making visual, proposals for future possibilities that may not otherwise be available for experience and critique in corporeal forms. The designer's capacities for creating images and physical forms that communicate concepts seem to hold also a great potential if imported to processes of policy development. But let us first distinguish two principally different reasons for employing these capacities: They can be aiming to convince, or they can be aiming to explore. It is this latter case that we are interested in, in the pursuit of tools for ideation and engagement.

To capture particular generative qualities of visualization and modelling that are important for meeting the challenges of the policy process, I will talk about visual tools for early engagement, then discuss the concept of 'evocative sketching' as a particularly inviting and exploratory genre. When confronted with complex and abstract issues in policy work, design tools can work to make these issues experientially available through images and physical models. Finally, I will show how a game-oriented frame for ideation may allow a range of diverse stakeholders to engage with images and tangible representations to explore and redefine a complex issue, and what possible futures it may entail from different viewpoints. The case example is on the issue of waste, which requires collaboration from stakeholders with vastly different interest ranges, from the national environmental protection level and municipal waste planners, to technical specialists and garbage collectors, to housing associations and individual citizens.

Compelling Visual and Physical Representations to Convince

There is a strong tradition in design for using images and scale models for 'getting your message through'. Designers of all specializations routinely develop beautiful renderings of imagined artefacts crafted specifically to convince peers, clients and non-designers about the purported qualities of a proposed design. Through these images and models designers try to support and nurture a desire in others to bring into being something that otherwise exists only in the abstract. In product design this process may entail focusing on harmonic curves of a 3D model as well as accounting visually for the complexities of inner circuits or mechanical workings, such that it becomes plausible that the proposed artefact in its entirety will be desirable and actually work as expected. When used to convince, visual representations and physical models are generally characterized by a finished look and feel that induce a sense that all important details and decisions have been carefully attended to.

The work of Edward Tufte has become a major reference in the particular genre of developing a visual language to present complex data and information in ways that are clear, efficient and credible. In 'Visual Explanations: Images and Quantities, Evidence and Narrative' (1997), Tufte explains the principles of the display of dynamic information, that is information that changes over time. Tufte focuses on ways to visualize process and dynamics, causes and effects, explanation and narrative, in order to support decision-making. The book's visual examples range from the genealogy of rock music and corresponding market shares to the causes of the 1854 cholera outbreak in London. Information graphics have greatly demonstrated their potential for 'getting your message through' and are increasingly used in both public media and marketing material.

Visualization and Modelling for Learning and Exploring Alternatives

However, visual images and physical models are also used in more unresolved and open-ended design situations to explore new possibilities that have yet to be understood. Driven by a glimpse of inspiration, an intuitive hunch, or simply by limited knowledge, in the early development phases designers strive to discover the full range of implications of a new idea; How could it work? What would it look like in concrete detail? Who could benefit from it? Or more fundamentally, what is 'it' in the first place (for recent descriptions of prototyping in the early exploratory phase of design and innovation see Brown 2009; Clark 2012)? In other words, visualization and modelling are also employed by individual designers and design teams to support their own line of inquiry into the implications of a premature design direction in richer visual-material detail. This type of exploration is at the opposite end of the spectrum from the goal of convincing, or getting one's message through. It is rather about trying out what the message ought to be in the first place.

In designers' everyday sketchbooks and team based project rooms we find this more exploratory mode of visualization and modelling practice. Designers use these competencies to develop and challenge their own preconceptions of the design situation. Preliminary models and sketches enable designers to carry out what Donald Schön called 'frame experiments': 'When he finds himself stuck in a problematic situation which he cannot readily convert to a manageable problem, he may construct a new way of setting the problem – a new frame which, in what I shall call a "frame experiment" he tries to impose on the situation' (Schön 1983: 63).

Building early models and composing images of half-known future opportunities may reveal to oneself what was not possible to predict by sheer cognitive effort. As Tim Brown states about complex problem-solving: 'a series of early experiments is often the best way to decide among competing directions. The faster we make our ideas tangible, the sooner we will be able to evaluate them, refine them, and zero in on the best solution' (Brown 2009: 89).

When visual imagery and tangible models are used to explore the possibilities and limitations of a premature design decision, they are often characterized by a playful attitude of just trying it out, and a roughness indicating that the specific features could be changed relatively easily.

From Design to Public Sector Innovation

Visualization of dynamic information has been particularly important for the field of service design, where the flow of time is crucial for understanding the interdependence of many actors and resources in sequences of events. The idea of visualizing a user's different touch points with a service provider in a service blueprint is well established (Shostack 1982). To get closer to the perspective of an individual's time-based service experience and integrate it with systemic consideration of the necessary infrastructure and back stage logistic 'experience modelling' and 'customer journey maps' have been established as powerful design tools through numerous examples (Polaine, Løvlie and Reason 2013).

When developing concrete public services with a focus on the experience of citizens it has proven highly valuable to visualize and model the suggested experience journey, either through visual mapping or through modelling proposed workflows with its various physical touch points. In the United Kingdom, NESTA's Public Services Lab has pushed the boundaries for service design and developed and documented a long list of successful implementations of citizen-oriented public services (Penny, Stay and Stephens 2012).

Building on the success of bringing design thinking and doing to public services, there seems to also reside a great potential in bringing – and inventing – design tools to public policy development (Bason 2013). With public policy development, however, it has proven more difficult to implement design tools for ideation for a number of reasons, of which I briefly mention a few:

- The scale of the problem situation is large, often nation-wide;

- The level of complexity, abstraction and generalization is high;

- The predominant cultures of public governance do not immediately embrace the inclusive, or even participatory aspects of co-creation and playful experimentation that are often built into the design tools and techniques for service design and social innovation;

- The hierarchical organization of the governmental bodies that develop bureaucratic measures for regulating societal life as well as the linear logic and technical rationality of the policy development process is not at ease with the playful attitude of learning from mistakes, characteristic of exploratory design.

We need design-oriented methods that directly address the fundamentally thorny questions of how an issue is democratically presented in the first place, and how conflicting interests and aspirations can be allowed to play out in dialogical ways, respectful of mutual differences. Or as researchers from the national public innovation agencies Mindlab (DK) and Nesta (UK) put it, and which is relayed in the earlier chapter in this volume:

> In order to respond effectively to a changing context of complexity and uncertainty, governments and other public service organisations need to consider innovating the processes and practices of public policy itself. (Christiansen and Bunt 2012: 3)

How may policy development processes engage more voices in the early phases of defining an issue?

Examples of Visualization Tools for Engagement

At the heart of policy work resides a political struggle to define what the important issue is from different viewpoints, and how to understand it. Major issues of contemporary societies like imbalances of industrialization, social stratification, expanding welfare costs and depletion of natural resources, intersect conventional borders between science and politics, culture and technology, morals and economy. Represented in public media, but institutionalized in policy development, these issues must be explored in a mode of shared uncertainty: situations where actors agree on their disagreement.

Visualizing Disagreements

To investigate such controversial situations of socio-technical debate Bruno Latour and others have developed a set of techniques known as controversy mapping (Venturini 2010; 2012). Controversy mapping is both about observing how controversies play out, and representing their complexities in a legible visual form. In particular this is done through various digital visualizations aggregating information on public debates (see http://www.mappingcontroversies.net).

The techniques of controversy mapping cover a range of analytical parameters such as the scale of the disputed issue, its dynamic development over time, the diagrammatic relationship of actor-networks, multi-branched trees of disagreement on different levels and, ultimately, how the controversial issues imply conflicting visions of the world.

The produced visual maps of controversies enjoy an indisputable success in education and research, but from an action-oriented perspective they somehow remain external to the controversies they map (Figure 16.1). They remain peculiarly distanced as analytical devices, rather than devices for engagement or for generating alternative ways of seeing the issue, and the possible future directions this may imply.

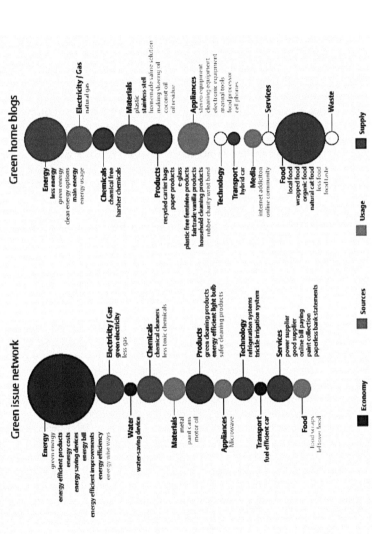

Figure 16.1   Example of discursive differences between official bodies of knowledge and public debate distributed on blogs regarding environmental issues and green living

Source: Noortje Marres (http://www.mappingcontroversies.net/Home/PlatformSustainableHomes)

Design for Public Engagement

Design researcher Carl DiSalvo has suggested that design has a special capacity for contributing to developing the relationship between controversial social issues and public action. He turns Latour and Weibel's (Latour and Weibel 2005) question of 'how things are made public' on its head and asks instead: how are publics made with things (DiSalvo 2009)? DiSalvo argues that there is an important role for design to play in the forming of publics. Not by giving form to the publics as such, but by giving visual and physical form to issues that deserve broader democratic discussion and contemplation before decisions are made. To play this role, DiSalvo suggests that designers must make use of their skills in articulating new possibilities before these are fully realized. Carefully designed objects may allow us to express conflicting perspectives about how our social world should be structured and experienced (DiSalvo 2012).

In public campaigns society's complex situations are routinely put on display with the goal of enhancing people's awareness and possibly their ability to act. However, the prospective mode, to inquire through proposals, is a distinctive feature of design. Design proposals are important for bringing otherwise vague or distant possibilities into the range of visibility; they are important in order for both professional experts and non-experts alike to be able to grasp the change implied and its particular world view.

Taken together, design committed to democratic processes of world-making can make controversial issues experientially available for a broad range of stakeholders, from experts and politicians to laymen, and thereby spark new configurations of publics into being (see Figure 16.3).

Visualization and Modelling as Tools for Ideation

The attention to involve many diverse voices in the early phases of policy development requires new skills of the designer, something along the lines proposed by DiSalvo. Compelling visualizations focused on clear and efficient means for 'getting the message through', are not the most relevant tool to import. What we are after is more like visual sketches and preliminary models that enable further questioning of the issue at hand. Foverskov and Dam, themselves trained in industrial design and architecture respectively, point out that such open-ended sketches are typically for '... the designer's own exploration of tentative options. They serve the purpose of getting familiar with emerging ideas but in a way that is not meant to let anyone in but the designer herself' (Foverskov and Dam 2010:45). They coin the term 'evocative sketch' to capture a central quality of early design proposals that are open-ended, but at the same time entail a communicative and engaging invitation to diverse audiences. While Foverskov and Dam's example material are hand-drawn sketches, the more conceptual argument they develop about the evocative style, is relevant for a broader range of sketching techniques across different media (Figure 16.2).

Foverskov and Dam have begun developing a visual language of evocative sketching techniques, which seek to balance a number of opposing qualities. It is important that evocative sketches are not too definitive, yet they have to be suggestive enough of something concrete to get people started imagining. The motives have to be recognizable as concrete features or situations, yet estranged enough that they convey a sense of one or more alternative options. Stylistically the evocative sketch balances the fine line between too unattractive roughness and too persuasive beauty.

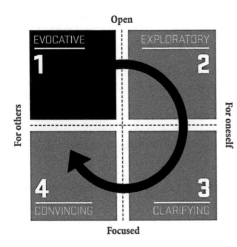

Open

EVOCATIVE **1**   EXPLORATORY **2**

For others   **For oneself**

4 CONVINCING   **3** CLARIFYING

Focused

Diagram B
In co-design the visualization becomes a means to convey the design suggestions of both designers and non-designers. This opens up the opportunity for a new kind of sketching that is both open and directed towards others – the evocative sketch. Aiming to evoke shared stories and to create a common space of opportunities, the evocative sketch probes for possible directions for the design. From the perspective of the professional designer, such sketching precedes conventional drawing formats.

Figure 16.2   Relating the evocative sketch to three more conventional modes of visualizing
Source: Diagram reproduced from M. Foverskov and K. Dam (2010: 46). Reproduced with kind permission of Joachim Halse

They have the capacity to make a complex issue available for discussion in a way that invites multiple perspectives on the issue, and above all they evoke the participant's imagination of how things could be different in a variety of directions (49).

Make it Playful: A Game Frame for Ideation in Policy Development

Evocative sketches do not do anything by themselves, but with the right procedural guidance and receptive materials to capture imaginative explorations of alternatives, they may play a prominent role as drivers in the policy process. Design games may provide a frame for just that. Design games constitute a particular genre for formatting open-ended dialogues about existing issues and possible futures. Originating in exploratory design research, design games enable diverse players to gather around a collaborative activity, guided by simple and explicit rules, assigned roles and supported by pre-defined game materials. The game materials typically point to either or both existing practices and future possibilities. The games are played within a confined and shared temporal and spatial setting, removed from the everyday context of the players. The purpose of the game is to establish and explore novel configurations of the game materials and the present and future practices to which these materials point. At the end of the game, the players will have produced representations of one or more possible new design options (Brandt, Messeter and Binder 2008).

One of the challenges for enabling broader circles of participation in the policy process is to find a common language. The specialized professional languages of each of the stakeholders may be used to describe problems and specify solutions. But the specification in the language of a public administrator, an engineer or a social worker may not make much sense to those outside these professions. Stories and scenarios on the contrary have qualities that make them accessible and understandable even to listeners with very different backgrounds.

There is no 'one size fits all' recipe for design games, so instead I will present a set of general guidelines for creating design games, and provide a particular example of a game exemplifying the guidelines.

- *Avoid overly coherent accounts.* Individual game materials must be fragmented enough to allow re-configurations of the issue.

- *Make it tangible.* The players make design moves by creating new configurations of game materials on a game board. The physical configuration becomes something for other players to react upon in a tactile negotiation process.

- *Take turns.* Ensure that the privilege of talking and making design moves is evenly distributed among the players.

- *Encourage experimentation.* Game playing works by temporarily suspending some (but not all) of the ordinary constraints locking up a problematic situation.

- *Relax and have fun.* Design games are not competitive, but guided as a common journey of discovery and creation towards collective achievement.

Reframing Waste (Figure 16.3) is an example of a design game that facilitates participation and dialogue about waste handling and waste management (Halse and Rasmussen 2012). The game materials in Reframing Waste are based on a research project on recycling and waste management (Halse, Brandt, Clark and Binder 2010). Parts of the game materials point to future possibilities. In a playful way Reframing Waste opens up for co-analysis of existing practices, and in the end of the game the players produce representations of one or more future visions (Figure 16.4).

Figure 16.3   Design students playing 'Reframing Waste'. This was part of a design research course at KADK. The players are forced to negotiate and prioritize the importance of their suggested new configurations.

Source: Reproduced with kind permission of Matylda Rasmussen

Figure 16.4   Game pieces in action. Game pieces afford 'frame experiments' that encourage
questions like 'what happens if we look at it this way ...?'
Source: Reproduced with kind permission of Matylda Rasmussen

During the research and development project on waste, various versions of the
design game were developed and tested through different settings, and played by
participants from the national environmental protection level and municipal waste
planners, over technical specialists and garbage collectors, to housing associations,
small business owners, NGOs and individual citizens.

One of the issues that was explored and momentarily redefined was based
on the fact that in Denmark waste from small professional businesses and private
households must currently be kept separate, and belong to two different sets of waste
handling regulations. In conjunction with small shop owners and individual citizens,
the municipality of Herlev raised the speculative question of what would happen if
private inhabitants and customers near local shopping centres could combine their
efforts and share recycling facilities? The evocative visualizations and models provided
and generated by the design game opened new opportunities for public-private
partnerships and new roles for small businesses with environmental concerns. But more
importantly, methodologically speaking, the design game demonstrated an ability to
create an experimental moment where the regulatory implications of policymaking
are brought into direct dialogue with the most concrete everyday practices. And the
process goes both ways of course, so that if the players generate a sense that they
want to nurture a particular waste handling practice on the ground, then they are led
to discuss what would be adequate regulations to achieve this.

Design games are by no means suggested as a substitute for current policy
development practices, but they may be adopted and adapted into policy development
for their potential to integrate abstract conceptualizations with very concrete life
experiences for a diverse set of participants.

Conclusion

Despite the success of bringing design to public services, it remains a challenge to bring playful tools for ideation into the public policy process. In order to realize some of the potential for the public policy process that seems to lie in designerly ways of creating new opportunities, it is not enough to look for tools for ideation. We need to make room for more playful, iterative and inclusive processes of creation in public policy.

The persuasive skills of visual communication design can be fruitfully coupled with the democratically committed attention to unsettled controversies and respectful disagreement described by Bruno Latour, Michel Callon and others (Callon, Lascoumes and Barthe 2011).

I have used DiSalvo's work (2009; 2012) to argue that design has a capacity for configuring materials, spaces, objects and atmospheres in ways that invite experts and non-experts alike into experiential encounters with complex issues.

Design games are a new tool for the public policy tool box that employs evocative sketching, visualization and physical modelling for profoundly democratic processes of proposing and considering alternative future regulations. Thereby we have a chance to collectively stop and think through the possible implications of a proposed policy initiative and ask ourselves from our different, and sometimes opposing vantage points, how would life look different around any proposed new regulation, be it a new highway projection, migration control, taxation system or food services for the elderly.

The bureaucratic cultures of public governance may still be a barrier for carrying out design games in policy development. The visual and tangible formats in conjunction with playful encouragements to momentarily disregard well-known constraints sometimes appear childish or unprofessional to people more comfortable with white papers and authoritative summaries. But if the game material and rule set are well crafted it becomes less difficult to create a momentary suspension of disbelief. It does, after all, not require more than one to three hours for the players to experience first hand what a design game can do to enable a new kind of policy dialogue.

References

Bason, C. (2013). Design-Led Innovation in Government. *Stanford Social Innovation Review*. 15–17.

Brandt, E., Messeter, J. and Binder, T. (2008). Formatting Design Dialogues: Games and Participation. *CoDesign*, 4(1): 51–64.

Brown, T. (2009). Building to think or the power of prototyping. *Change by Design*. New York: Harper Collins Publishers. 87–108.

Callon, M., Lascoumes, P. and Barthe, Y. (2011). *Acting in an Uncertain World: An Essay on Technical Democracy*. Cambridge, MA: MIT Press.

Christiansen, J. and Bunt, L. (2012). Innovation in Policy: Allowing for Creativity, Social Complexity and Uncertainty in Public Governance, 38, Nesta & MindLab.

Clark, J. (2012). Pretotyping@Work: Invent Like A Startup, Invest Like A Grownup, PretotypeLabs.com.

DiSalvo, C. (2009). Design and the Construction of Publics. *Design Issues,* 25(1): 48–63.

DiSalvo, C. (2012). *Adversarial Design*. Cambridge, MA: MIT Press.

Foverskov, M. and Dam, K. (2010). The Evocative Sketch. *Rehearsing the Future*. J. Halse, E. Brandt, B. Clark and T. Binder, eds. Copenhagen: The Danish Design School Press. 44–9.

Halse, J., Brandt, E. Clark, B. and Binder, T., eds. (2010). *Rehearsing the Future.* Copenhagen: The Danish Design School Press.

Halse, J. and Rasmussen, M. (2012). Reframing Waste – a Design Game. Copenhagen: The Royal Danish Academy of Fine Arts.

Latour, B. and Weibel, P. (2005). *Making Things Public: Atmospheres of Democracy.* Cambridge, MA: MIT Press, ZKM/Center for Art and Media in Karlsruhe.

Penny, J., Stay, J. and Stephens, L. (2012). People Powered Health Co-Production Catalogue, 89, NESTA.

Polaine, A., Løvlie, L. and Reason, B. (2013). *Service Design: From Insight to Implementation.* New York: Louis Rosenfeld.

Schön, D.A. (1983). *The Reflective Practitioner: How Professionals Think in Action.* New York: Basic Books.

Shostack, L. (1982). How to Design a Service. *European Journal of Marketing,* 161: 49–63.

Tufte, E. (1997). *Visual Explanations: Images and Quantities, Evidence and Narrative.* Cheshire, CT: Graphics Press.

Venturini, T. (2010). Diving in Magma: How to Explore Controversies With Actor-network Theory. *Public Understanding of Science,* 19(3): 258–73.

Venturini, T. (2012). Building on Faults: How to Represent Controversies With Digital Methods. *Public Understanding of Science,* 2(7): 796–812.

SIMONA MASCHI AND JENNIE WINHALL

Tools for Implementation

Under the Blair and Brown governments, design tools were applied to support the implementation of UK public policy: both to communicate new direction and a new relationship between government and citizen, and to bring the experience of using public services up to par with private sector services. This was most tangibly seen in the design of the spaces and ways in which public services were delivered. The future of education was illustrated through Building Schools for the Future. The barriers between client and advisor were broken down in the design of the new Job Centre Plus spaces. Self Assessment Online and the DWP's TellUsOnce project streamlined the user experience of bureaucratic systems.

'The key to reform is redesigning the system round the user – the patient, the pupil, the passenger, the victim of crime', said Tony Blair in 2001. And so placing the user at the centre of public services became a priority. It led to increased choice of provision and personalization of services. It should have meant that services were re-conceived from the perspective of the end user rather than the architecture of the system. In reality it often meant bringing the user into the world of professionals and wrapping the same menu of services around them in a different way. The role for design was in achieving better value for public money in the way existing models were delivered.

These advances were in service of a public policy agenda which was not tackling the new systemic challenges facing British society – the ageing population, an epidemic of chronic disease, climate change. More recently the financial crisis has brought the need for whole systems to be redesigned into sharp focus. The emphasis now is on finding radically different ways of delivering more for less, making use of new technology and engaging people themselves in playing an active role. This has coincided with consumer trends more widely where interest has shifted towards more collaborative forms of consumption. Both the public and private sectors have begun to embrace service models based on meaningful relationships rather than the efficiency of transactions.

In this context design has a different role to play. Policy changes such as outcomes-based payments, investment in the third sector as alternative providers, tax breaks for start-ups, new commissioning responsibilities and new forms of social financing have opened up the space for new kinds of social innovation. Some of these innovations are design-led and have used design thinking to re-conceive services and systems; most are not. Each of them however uses design to manifest characteristics or values that make these innovations distinctive.

In this chapter we look at a number of those characteristics and how they have been designed and implemented into new services and systems. We illustrate these with a range of examples and more detailed case studies from our own personal experiences as designers and educators.

Design for Behaviour Change

All design activity aims to bring about desired situations, and each of the sections that follow uses design to enable people to interact in new ways. However the 'new' challenges mentioned above – climate change, chronic disease – present a specific opportunity for design. Solutions to these require mass changes to individual behaviours but cannot be brought about through the more rational policy tools of compulsion or economic incentives. Rather they require us to design services, interventions and relationships that tap into irrational motivations, and engage people in actively making changes in their everyday lives.

We see this design for behaviour change happening in three ways:

PROMOTION

Governments use design tools to educate citizens and promote desired behaviours. These range from sophisticated social marketing campaigns, to simple ways of presenting information to influence the choices citizens make, such as food labelling. These act to reinforce social norms.

SHAPING BEHAVIOUR

Design has long been employed to shape individual behaviours through our experience of spaces, interfaces and processes. Think of Jeremy Bentham's Panopticon prison project, more than two centuries ago, which used spatial design to remove individual autonomy, and the design of modern supermarket experiences which use visual layout, music and even smells to increase the average basket load. Designers use visual cues and affordances to influence how we move through spaces and processes which can be crucial both for designing out error in critical processes (such as air traffic control) and for increasing positive outcomes (such as designing hospital environments to increase recovery rates).

There has been renewed interest in this area among policy thinkers since Richard Thaler and Cass Sustein published Nudge – their research into the potential of 'behavioural economics'. They demonstrate that gains on a large scale can be achieved by making small changes to the default settings in systems to influence decision-making. The Behavioural Insights team at the UK Cabinet Office has increased the repayment rate amongst taxpayers by 15% through tweaking the messaging of tax collection letters. The power of combining the increasing evidence base of behavioural economics with the design of physical experiences and tangible interfaces presents real potential when applied to areas of mutual benefit.

ENGAGEMENT

The third approach relates to services designed to engage people in changing more ingrained patterns of behaviour, such as sticking to an exercise regime, conserving energy or managing their diabetes. These move beyond unconscious influencing and use design to create services that draw users to them and retain their participation.

Lift.do is one of the most successful 'quantified self' apps, which supports people to build lasting habits around goals they choose. It uses carefully designed visual feedback on progress reinforced by peers in the Lift community, and was developed through constant design iterations that gradually increased its effectiveness.

PreventNow is a service for people deemed to be at high risk of developing type 2 diabetes. It combines individual online video coaching with visual progress tools and support from a community of peers.

CarbonCulture is a community platform that supports workplaces to lower their energy consumption. It uses digital tools to engage employees and measure collective progress.

Some of the design principles employed by these services include:

- *Making progress visible* – many systems use positive feedback to reinforce a sense of progress. Smart electricity meters such as Wattson, and the Copenhagen bicycle counter are good examples.

- *Making it aspirational to take part* – many platforms such as Runkeeper use ways of increasing participants' social status in the online community to maintain motivation.

- *Meaningful measures* – allowing people to set their own benchmarks for progress (rather than those the professionals assume are important) is a powerful motivator.

- *Peer pressure* – buddy systems, collective rewards and social pledging are all ways of making use of social pressure not to let your 'team' down.

- *Shared interfaces* – shared data between people and professionals increases engagement. Gaming, rewards and incentives are also used but these have limited impact – the more successful services build people's intrinsic motivation to stick to changes and reinforce their new identity by building new social networks around them.

215

Anti-Fragile Design: Systems That Gain Strength from Participation

Nicholas Taleb writes about the need for financial systems that get stronger in volatile conditions. With shrinking public resources, one response to public service delivery is to ration services: cut eligibility for social care; limit access to professional support. A different response designs services to be strengthened by increased participation, rather than burdened by demand. It considers people not as bundles of needs to be served but as potential assets in the system. What happens if we create services that are open to all? Employability services for both employed and unemployed? Wellness services for people with and without long term conditions? We remove stigma, build capabilities and increase the resources available. These services have the potential to become more resilient as the capabilities and shared knowledge of participants grow.

BigWhiteWall is an online mental health service which combines a forum where members experiencing depression or anxiety can post images that reflect their feelings and participate in an open online discussion mediated by guides trained as counsellors and psychologists. As the membership grows it relieves pressure on acute services and builds the collective knowledge of coping strategies among members.

Circle is a membership service for older people that provides practical help and social connections through a network of members and neighbourhood helpers. Rather than assessing people according to their levels of need, it is open to everyone, meaning it can cross subsidize through more premium offers, making the basic platform more accessible to lower income members. It allows the families of older people – who want them to have practical help and a good social life – to contribute financially at a distance, makes it possible for members to contribute their own skills to help others and makes it possible for neighbours to help out on their street. It creates a resilient network around older people, and at the same time increases the pot of resources by combining state, private and voluntary resources.

Ushahidi runs an online platform initially developed to map incidents of violence and peace efforts throughout Kenya after the post-election fallout at the beginning of 2008 and now widely used to support rapid response efforts in crises, such as the Haiti earthquake and the war in the Democratic Republic of Congo. Its goal is to create a simple way of aggregating information from the public, who submit reports via the web and mobile phones, and make it visual, so that citizens, NGOs and public bodies can collaborate in planning responses.

Whilst these services are often based on mutual contribution, systems which can become reliable alternatives to state provision will not develop organically out of a stronger volunteering culture. They depend on enabling platforms, which need careful design to ensure that people who contribute have a rewarding experience.

Designing a New Narrative

Narrative is an important ingredient in human development. The stories we tell about ourselves shape our outlook and measurably impact how well we do. Major consumer brands understand this, and endeavour to ensure that every part of their service experience contributes to the story they want their customers to be a part of. Apple's Genius Bar is as important a component of its narrative as the iPhone's user interface.

Where public services fail – where there is a breakdown in the relationship between people and the state, or where the intended goal of the service is not achieved – it is often because the service experience is telling the wrong story. People are actors in these narratives and just as their expectations are shaped by the service experience, so are their responses.

At their worst, youth services tell young people the story that they are risks to be contained – to be protected from underage pregnancy, prevented from engaging in antisocial behaviour on the streets. At their best, they position young people as valuable assets to the community. Prisons and probation services tread a line between conflicting narratives of punishment and banishment or rehabilitation and reintegration.

New policies often have their root in new narratives. It is becoming increasingly important that rather than delivering services to people, public services engage them in new activities, actions, behaviours and relationships. Creating a new narrative, and redesigning every aspect of the experience to manifest that narrative – from the physical environment to the scripts used by telephone agents – can be a very powerful way of achieving better outcomes.

Redesigning the Balance of Power

If we want to reduce dependency on public services then enabling people to take responsibility for their own lives is critical. However many services become disabling,

CASE STUDY
Backr.net

An analysis of people's experience of the UK employment system showed that the 'narrative' they absorb once part of it is one of stigma, shame, low expectations and a lack of momentum. This has a negative effect on their own ability to tell a positive story about themselves to prospective employers or to make the kinds of connections that bring them opportunities, reinforcing a downward spiral. Reversing this narrative to be one where people are able to differentiate themselves, to feel productive and useful, increase their momentum and feel equal members of society, gave rise to a new set of designed interactions that significantly improved outcomes.

Backr is a new type of network-based service, open to both employed and unemployed people that supports members to increase their employability through new connections to others in their field of interest, productive activity and peer-to-peer coaching. It both engages people differently and outperforms current employment programs. As people feel an increased sense of momentum, identity and status they are able to tell a new story about themselves and progress.

rather than enabling, owing to power imbalances between institutions, professionals and people.

Web 2.0 showed us that it was possible to design platforms that fundamentally changed our relationship with institutions, and many of these principles have been successfully applied to public sector innovation.

Developers and entrepreneurs are building platforms that allow people to connect to one another in ways that disrupt the monopolies held by public and commercial institutions. Zopa has made peer-to-peer lending possible and now presents genuine competition to traditional banking services. Start-up company OpenUtility allows people to choose who generates their electricity supply, connecting them to alternative sources and small producers. The suite of webtools developed by MySociety (FixMyStreet, HearFromYourMP, TheyWorkForYou) are all aimed at making public institutions more accountable to citizens.

Healthcare is often the site of innovation to redress the power balance between professionals and patients. PatientsKnowBest makes patients the central holders of their medical records, where they give access to health professionals. The Design Council's Agenda Cards is a simple tool to be used in diabetes consultations – a set of cards that allows patients to set the agenda rather than follow the pre-determined check-list format.

PatientOpinion crowdsources individual experiences of NHS services so that in aggregate they can be used to influence decision-making and the allocation of centrally held resources. CureTogether makes people the experts in health solutions that work for them by sharing data on how many people have found which cures work for which health issues.

CASE STUDY
LIFE

Families in chronic crisis in the UK (those suffering abuse, antisocial behaviour, truancy and facing eviction, child protection orders, exclusion and convictions) – often have up to 16 different government agencies interacting with them, costing upwards of £250,000 per family per year. Each of these agencies has its own agenda, none of which is the family's agenda. Families experience blame, hopelessness, shame and defensiveness: they fear that if they ask for help they will have their children taken away. Agencies who have known the family over generations do not expect them to change and experience their own feelings of hopelessness. This situation represents a deep breakdown in the relationship between public service professionals and the families they are there to support. Professionals spend 80% of their time monitoring, assessing and recording activity rather than spending it in relationship with families. The 17% of time they do spend with families is spent gathering information to feed the 80%. Almost all professional effort goes into containment rather than development.

Swindon Borough Council and social innovation catalyst Participle.net set out to reverse this. A team of designers, policy thinkers, development specialists and family members designed an initiative called LIFE that supports families in crisis to design the lives they want. In its first year LIFE made significant savings and improvements to participating families' outcomes. Families choose who they want to work with them as their LIFE team members. They set the agenda for the changes they want to make and lead their own process of change. Team members are trained to build real relationships with families with compassion, and no agenda. This has dramatic effect as families' defences fall away, they reveal what they really want in their lives and begin to move towards that. It works because the program is designed to deliberately rebalance the power – families lead their own change and build reciprocal relationships with team members, who share their own journeys of change. This is reinforced by the design of systems – team members spend 80% of their time in relationship with family members. They record their progress together on an online tool that is openly shared between families and team members. The results have been significant improvements in families' capabilities, confidence and relationships.

Relational Service Design

In the 2000s public services became more personalized, but they also increasingly treated people as atomized individuals, in isolation of their social context. The focus was on improving the quality and efficiency of service transactions. However through advances in social research we now know the extent to which relationships have impact – from the link between loneliness and dementia in older people, to poor bridging capital and unemployment in many social housing estates.

CASE STUDY
Circle

Circle is a membership organization for people over the age of 50 who live in several UK locations. It is a network of members who enjoy social and learning activities together and neighbourhood helpers who provide practical help with a range of skills such as DIY, gardening, teaching technology use. Members are often helpers too, using their skills to contribute to the membership. Helpers can choose how much time they give, whether they are paid for their time, who they want to help and how long they spend with them. The aim is not efficiency but relationships – helpers are encouraged to stay for cups of tea. The families of older people living at distance can contribute by purchasing services – such as gardening or someone to teach their grandmother to use Skype.

There is no assessment process to join Circle, and outcomes are measured both as cost savings to the Local Authority (a Circle is financially self sustaining) and as increases in members' capabilities – for example the number of relationships formed and sustained.

Over time Circle has become a viable twenty-first-century alternative to traditional adult social care. Based on relationships it is a platform upon which local authorities can transfer further responsibilities. For example, Circle provides a home-coming service for people returning home from hospital which involves both practical tasks such as moving their bed downstairs and stocking the fridge, but also social aspects such as calling round to encourage people to take their first steps outside the home and get back into their social scene. Each part of the service journey is designed with the intention of increasing the feeling that Circle is 'for me', encouraging mutual contribution and removing barriers to taking part – especially when people may have become socially isolated after major life changes, such as a period of caring, illness, bereavement or retirement.

This knowledge throws the underlying structure of our public services into sharp relief. Despite the fact that 80% of work is found through word of mouth, our employment services group unemployed people together in activities with other unemployed people. Although we know that to do well, young people need positive relationships with their communities and adults other than their parents, we primarily invest in youth-only services. At the time of writing it was revealed that in some UK councils more than 75% of care visits to older and disabled people are carried out in less than 15 minutes. The growing burden caused by an ageing population means we need to build new types of caring systems – what Charles Leadbeater calls 'intimacy at scale'.

The question is how to create services based on relationships and empathy rather than transactions and efficiency. Peer systems like Alcoholics Anonymous and the National Childbirth Trust are successful formats that have been widely replicated across issues. The Keralan Neighbourhood Network for Palliative Care is a highly flexible social system based on voluntary participation. It only calls in doctors and nurses as they are needed, and covers almost all of Kerala. Rather than the 'heavy' infrastructure characteristic of institutional delivery, new technology is making it possible to design platforms that organize relationships – drawing on the natural motivations behind them – in new ways:

- Casserole Club is an alternative to Meals on Wheels that connects people who are cooking with people with whom they can share an extra plate.

- GoodGym pairs runners with isolated older people. The older person becomes their coach and keeps them motivated to keep running, whilst the runners bring them a newspaper and have a chat.

- Tyze is a secure communication platform that connects the people around someone receiving care. It creates a meaningful and active role for friends, family and neighbours, allowing them to become a critical part of the care equation. Each of these marks a move away from commercial service efficiency towards scalable relationship-based services that increase social value.

Trust

Trust is a key aspect in the design of services in the private or private sector. Trust is built when a party – either the provider or the user of the service – keeps its promises: that is, it does what it says it will do. Thus, trust can work both ways: the public organization trusts the citizens and the citizens trust the public service/organization. In the first case, a lack of trust results in control/checking/monitoring systems to make sure that the citizens are not misusing/abusing the system. If a citizen doesn't trust a public service, a response may be to move to a private sector option where possible or to resist the service where not. In the recent years, in some places, trust has been 'rediscovered' as a starting point and resource for shaping the way a public service works. This is happening for a few reasons, including the opening up of data as well as a more direct engagement of citizens thanks to the digitization of public services administration and coordination. When trust is there, the overall system can use trust to: reduce operational cost, increase brand loyalty, and enable a more participatory, engaged, and symbiotic relationship between state and citizen.

Open

The delivery of public services has often been kept and treated as a less than approachable area, possibly because of its scale and structure. In other words, public services have often been perceived as rather complex and expert environments which require a lot of information from the citizens, but that at the same time release very little information about their own structure and internal workings. Communication with the public has often been from 'one big player' to many citizens. With the opening up of data, participation and transparency are becoming key values in the design and delivery of services.

CASE STUDIES

CPH Metro. The Metro system in Copenhagen is designed and based on the expectation that people will pay for their ride tickets. The experience of being a passenger indicates trust and shared ownership in the system, rather than a feeling of being checked based on an assumption that people can't be trusted to pay. As a passenger there is no feeling of being checked by the system, in fact the opposite: the experience of travelling with the Metro suggests that buying a ticket is the default and expected behaviour, it's the norm.

Open Libraries. In Taiwan, Singapore and Denmark there have been some positive cases of open libraries. An open library is defined as a library branch where part of the opening hours are un-staffed. In Denmark, a staffless library covers the full package of library services – loans and delivery of printed and digital materials, including journals and newspapers, internet access and the availability of the library physical premises as meeting places for people. Apart from implementing ICT solutions to make the self-navigation possible throughout the library, the libraries have looked into generating a welcoming and safe atmosphere in the actual physical space of the library to facilitate the engagement and building of the local community through the library. In the context of this chapter, we want to underline how the value of trust can inspire and justify new service delivery models to match the expectations and needs of local community. On the evaluation side, the staffless library has served to increase the number of loans and attract new groups of people who cannot attend the libraries during regular opening hours.

Family on the Wings (Student project by CIID Education). Family on the Wings is a community service connecting a child travelling alone with a family on the same route in order to create a personal, playful and safe travelling experience. The service facilitates a network of trust by connecting families and their children with other families from their local environment. By connecting these children with a 'host' family, they will travel with the same people, who speak their own language, throughout the entire journey. Therefore, the service also targets the parents of the children travelling alone and the families who will accompany the child on the journey. The service facilitates meetings between families via an online community, where the users can create family profiles and get in touch with each other by shared reference points.

The service improves the travelling experience for both children and the host family by creating a playful, personal and smooth journey from check in at the airport to the arrival at the destination. The value lies in the personal and trustful relationship that the families build using the full-service system, from initiating the first contact with another family in the online community to sending a child travelling with this family, to sharing this travelling experience for other users to read and benefit from in the community.

The service works both on a macro and a micro level, providing the overall framework for families to find each other and meet, as well as handling the practicalities of planning the journey. The value is created by the users, who connect and share their experiences through the community site. Moreover, tangible and intangible benefits are provided for the guest child and the host family throughout the journey in the form of access to the fast track security check, a map of all playgrounds in the airport, a camera and toys for the kids, coffee for the parents and a ride in an airport car to their gate. All touch points are offered to ease the experience of travelling with children. Furthermore the host family has the chance to earn bonus miles when accompanying a child.

CASE STUDY
Teach & Learn

Teach & Learn is a service developed and prototyped by CIID for Blågården library, and not yet implemented. The service provides the tools to facilitate peer-to-peer exchange for sharing and receiving social and cultural knowledge. Teach & Learn is a service created to socially and culturally support the friends and families that live in the Blågården area in Nørrebro, Copenhagen. The service is located in Copenhagen's most ethnically diverse and most controversial neighbourhood – notorious for gang related crime and issues of assimilation and settlement. The entire Blågården community centres itself on Blågårds Plads, where the Blågården Bibliotek, serves as a common neutral space for all community members young and old.

The design process began as an exploration into how the Blågården Bibliotek could find new ways of knowledge sharing as well as encourage safety and trust in the neighbourhood. After weeks interviewing, observing and interacting with people in and around Blågården, the project team recognized a strong need in the community to share and receive knowledge from each other. Teach & Learn was founded on the basis of this strong need and desire to share social and cultural knowledge within the community. It was important for the service to look inwards to the community to strengthen understanding and elevate knowledge between people who were willing to contribute – ultimately to lead to a more unified identity. This was done through positive promotion of good community values such as tolerance and trust, embedded in their cultural exchange.

The service operates on a very simple cyclical peer-to-peer model: know – share – learn. What you know you can share, and from what one person shares, another will learn. And from learning they then have the knowledge to pass on ultimately to someone else. This positive and continuous cycle of peer-to-peer exchange sets the foundation for people to form different relationships, but to also have responsibility to the community around them. Overall Teach & Learn was designed to not only foster trust between the different groups in the community, but also to create a common ground of communication and value attribution to the people and Blågården.

Conclusion

New challenges in the public sector open opportunities to use design to conceive some very different ways of organizing relationships between people and citizens. Design for behaviour change and for systems that get stronger with greater participation can relieve pressure on overburdened public systems. New narratives can be expressed through the way service touch-points are designed, and redesigning interactions between people and professionals can rebalance power. Designing services based on trust and relationships rather than transactions can unlock untapped resources and make public services more sustainable in the long term. Openness enables public administrations to capitalize on assets such as data in new ways. These characteristics are beginning to define a new generation of public services in which design can play a valuable strategic and practical role. Change is what gives design its opportunity, and we look forward to what the next decade brings.

References

alcoholics-anonymous.org.uk

alifewewant.com

Bentham, Jeremy. *The Works of Jeremy Bentham*, vol. 4 (Panopticon, Constitution, Colonies, Codification) [1843].

BigWhiteWall.com

carbonculture.net

casseroleclub.com

charlesleadbeater.net

circlecentral.com

curetogether.com

designcouncil.info/RED/health/#B3

diykyoto.com

goodgym.org

mysociety.org

nct.org.uk

openutility.com

patientopinion.org.uk

patientsknowbest.com

PreventNow.com

Prime Minister's Speech on Public Sector Reform, British Library, October 16, 2001.

runkeeper.com

Taleb, Nassim Nicholas. 2014. *Antifragile: Things that Gain from Disorder.* New York: Random House.

Thaler, Richard H., Sunstein, Cass R. 2009. *Nudge: Improving Decisions About Health, Wealth and Happiness.* New York: Penguin Books.

tyze.com

ushahidi.com

zopa.com

CHRISTIAN BASON

The Frontiers of Design for Policy

If analysts and operators are to increase their ability to achieve desired policy outcomes, they will have to develop ways of thinking analytically about a larger chunk of the problem. It is not that we have too many good analytic solutions to problems. It is, rather, that we have more good solutions than we have appropriate actions

Graham Allison (1971: 267)

Assessing the state of policymaking more than 40 years after the quote above, the challenge of creating policies that truly consider 'a larger chunk of the problem' and 'identify more appropriate actions' is still at the fore. So what will it take to make the transition towards an approach to policymaking that enables a much more intimate and iterative relationship between policy-as-analysis and policy-as-action?

I introduced this volume by suggesting that design is offering a reinvention of the policy process which emphasizes real world impact and change over 'rationality' as an end in itself. Across the dimensions of defining problem space, developing ideas and concepts for policy, I proposed that design holds a unique contribution to the world of policymaking. What are, then, the patterns of design for policy that emerge across the various contributions to this book? Are there particular ideas, insights and potentials which could point to a truly new policy practice? To what degree might this practice be salient over time, geography, political systems and levels of government? And at the same time, what are the critical issues, dilemmas and challenges we must face if those promises are to be realized, not only in practice in single cases, but at scale? What types of recommendations could be put forward to the design community, and to those commissioning design, if design for policy is to unleash its full potential in the coming years?

In this concluding chapter, I consider the promise of design for policy from the vantage point of an alternative model for policymaking. Framed by two fundamentally different sequences of design processes, I examine the claims set forth in this book: First, and briefly: what characterizes the current mode of policymaking, and what is wrong with it? Second, what does design 'do' differently when applied in a policy or public service setting? Without being able to possibly do justice to all the perspectives represented in this volume, I highlight some of the key observations made by individual contributors, both in terms of diagnosis and in terms of the value of design for policy.

Third, what are the discussions we must now have, among practitioners as well as in the academic community, if we wish to bring design to the next frontier in policymaking? What are the recommendations flowing from these discussions?

The 'Rational Man' Policy Model and Its Enemies

The starting point of this volume was that of 'policy' as a political process in which numerous actors are involved, all of which are proposing how people 'should relate to each other, conduct themselves, and be governed' (Shore, Wright and Però 2011, 1). Moving beyond such a basic definition, however, two very different and seemingly opposing understandings emerge of the role of policymaking and policy analysis: Is the aim to 'achieve objective rationality in the consideration of important issues' (Irwin 2003, 19), or is it to achieve an intended societal impact among people, businesses and other actors in society? Although this choice may seem obvious, it is by no means so that the current mode of government operation is fully focused on societal impact.

Drawing on Herbert Simon's conceptualizations of design and vision of management decision, Richard Boland argues that design as applied to management action can be viewed as three major activities: intelligence, design and choice (Simon 1997; Boland 2004). *Intelligence* is the activity which calls the attention of managers to the need for intervening in order to change the state of affairs. Boland suggests that it is 'the process of sensing and predicting conditions that requires action or signal that change is required' (ibid: 108). *Design* is the formulation of 'possible courses of action that can respond to the current situation in a way that makes the possible course better able to serve desired human ends and achieve our goals'. *Choice* is the process of selecting the design alternative that is most efficient and effective in reaching these goals. In examining the interplay between intelligence, design and choice (of which there are six possible sequences), Boland proposes that there are important implications in the way that managers choose to 'punctuate' them. In particular, he highlights two such sequences, and thus punctuations, as almost complete opposites: *intelligence-design-choice* versus *design-intelligence-choice*.

Intelligence-design-choice, or 'rational man' economic theory, is the punctuation proposed by Herbert Simon himself, and later adjusted by way of his Nobel-winning theory of bounded rationality (Simon 1997). This is, broadly speaking, the policymaking model we have inherited, and which we believe to this day. In this view, rational man is intentionally goal seeking and applies intelligence and forethought in order to guide organizational action. Bounded by cognitive limits, we may not be able to select the best possible course of action; instead we 'satisfice', choosing readily available 'good enough' solutions. This picture goes both for the nature of the policymaker, and those intended to be impacted by policy, such as citizens or businesses. By starting the policy sequence with the activity of intelligence, however, insufficient attention is drawn to the question of problem representation: Managers quickly establish alternative actions to be decided on, and move to decision-making. To Boland, the implication is that 'this way of punctuation of management action leads to a finer and finer attention to problem representations that grow increasingly irrelevant to the human condition' (2004: 110). He explicitly mentions public policy domains such as welfare, education and transportation as areas that are particularly prone to this challenge.

The contributors to this volume rather uniformly share this analysis that our current model of policymaking is flawed, not least due to its overly reactive approach to 'problem-solving', and its simplified assumptions about human behaviour inside and outside government systems. As Sabine Junginger highlights in her chapter, 'We might say that "the" problem shapes our policymaking and our lives because we only begin to shape policies that shape our lives in response to this problem'.

Four Challenges and an Opportunity

Across the contributions the following four characteristics of our current policy approaches emerge as particularly problematic, raising the need for design for policy: the changing nature of public problems, siloed knowledge domains, stability over change and the opening of government.

THE CHANGING NATURE OF PUBLIC PROBLEMS

There is a powerful argument that the very nature of the problems the public sector is facing is changing, and that the current mode of policymaking is out of touch with them. In my introduction I discussed this as the growing complexity of our outside world. Says Banny Banerjee:

> Super-wicked problems have most notably the additional attributes of massive scale, urgency and complex interactions between many subsystems that are themselves wicked problems.

Similarly Andrea Siodmok proposes in her contribution that the public sector is facing more ill-defined problems than it used to. Such 'mega-challenges' require a need to 'think big by acting small' in applying a more holistic, qualitative, 'softer', contextual and experience-based approach to policy. Marco Steinberg points out that the complexity at hand is caught between human behaviour, cultural traits, ideals, values, physical principles and perceived facts. The task, says Steinberg, is to find the right simplifiers for issues spanning many domains. From a policy practitioner's standpoint, this raises several questions, where one of the most pressing ones may concern the issue of diagnosis: *How do we come to know what kind of problem space we are facing – ranging from 'tame' to 'wicked' or perhaps 'super wicked'? Given the problem dynamics, the policy environment and the tools available, what kinds of process and solutions should we look for? And how do we learn to represent problems in ways that better enable us to work on them, together?*

SILOED KNOWLEDGE DOMAINS

This is another key legacy of our public institutions, and a challenge in need of urgent attention. Our inner world of government and governance is – also – becoming increasingly complex. Professional disciplines such as economics, law and health work in silos with thick walls that impede communication, thus creating a culture of increasing hyper-specialization. Each discipline or agency looks at the world through their perceptual lens and operates within the rules of the silo, creating significant biases. This is particularly problematic given that the types of scaled challenges discussed above are interlaced, with interdependencies that do not confine themselves to disciplinary silos. The central planning culture and political aversion to real experimentation work against modalities of innovation that are focused on fundamentally rethinking solutions and systems. Are there ways of overcoming the tendency to a reliance on mono-disciplinarity in government? Laura Bunt and Jesper Christiansen raise the issue of the role of authority in this context. How would an authority role look if it focused 'less on sanctioning knowledge and information and more on how to facilitate and enable the generation of knowledge and effective action'?

Current government systems have largely been built to ensure predictability, objectivity and stability – and mass delivery – over adaptation, emergence, flexibility, dynamism and more individualized approaches. However, it is not a question of abandoning existing models and institutions without having anything to put in place instead. Sabine Junginger recognizes outright that there is still space for design as a 'classic' problem-solving activity in government. In Marco Steinberg's perspective, the challenge is that:

> ... a shift towards new competencies, cultures, incentives and resource allocation models cannot happen at the expense of the current delivery needs and long term stability. As such the core issue is to design coherent transitions whereby current obligations can be fulfilled while simultaneously building necessary future ones.

A problematic part of our current legacy is that we largely do not possess the strategies, tools and processes allowing us to make such coherent transitions.

The three challenges above may dominate much of our current conversation about design in government; however there is also a movement which is currently gaining strength globally and may offer a new set of possibilities and opportunities to leverage design at international, national and local level that is described next.

THE OPENING OF GOVERNMENT

A flipside of the changing external dynamic and our bureaucratic legacy is that there are in fact a range of new and different instruments available to policymakers today, in part due to developments in technology, finance and economy. Tom Bentley argues, with the Australian case, that we are witnessing new qualities in the political environment such as openness, focus on the long-term and cross-cutting and deliberative perspectives. Similarly, we see that the notion of open government – to a large part digitally enabled – is gaining prominence globally. In our chapter, Bason and Schneider discussed how the rise of concrete applications of design in the public sector is often closely associated with the open government movement; this holds both opportunities and pitfalls, in the sense that over-focusing on technology may drive out the human-centred emphasis of design. However we also saw how some countries, such as the UK and in part the US, are beginning to connect the dots and introducing design as a key to more experimental, open and collaborative policymaking. Ezio Manzini shifts our attention to the role of design in local policies and the rise of organizations which enable more open and collaborative design. What this all means is that more public institutions are engaged in lines of inquiry which are more susceptible to new approaches to policymaking, and may provide the openings needed for design approaches to take root.

Design for Policy: The Sensemaking Public Manager

What will it take to enable the systematic integration of design in the practice of policymaking?

As design introduces a radically different 'punctuation' to the policy process, the term re-invention may very well be warranted. *Design-intelligence-choice*, or the 'sensemaking manager', is articulated by Richard Boland as the 'antidote' to the rational man model presented above. Here, design is shifted to the forefront of the sequence of management (or policy) action. Design becomes the shaping of things while engaging with others in the flow of action and the production of outcomes:

> Interaction with others generates equivocal enactment that is then subject to a sensemaking process. During sensemaking, intelligence is applied to order those elements of the raw action in ways that make the situation meaningful, aesthetically pleasing, and morally acceptable. This intelligence is followed by a choice of which meanings and sensemaking structures to carry forward into future enactments. (Boland 2004)

In this model, goals are understood retrospectively and the enactments of design become the driving force of organizing. As such, this is a phenomenological appreciation of human action, and one that not only emphasizes sensemaking but essentially collaborative learning in the ongoing endeavour to meaningfully impact the world. This kind of promise of design for policy is inherent to many of this book's contributions. Many express explicitly or implicitly that design is a possible solution to the ubiquitous challenge to provide more and better public services for less money in an increasingly turbulent and complex policy environment. At a more fundamental level – and very much in line with Boland's suggestion above – design offers the opportunity for a different interplay between defining problem space and eliciting impactful, visionary solutions in settings of increasing complexity.

In particular, the following potentialities of design for policy as described in the next sections stand out.

FROM RESISTING TO EMBRACING COMPLEXITY

Design for policy implies a higher degree of humility to the external and internal complexities facing policymakers. Christiansen and Bunt suggest that unlike traditional approaches to policymaking, design has the ability to incorporate the complexity and uncertainty of an ever-changing context. Junginger proposes that a design-based approach can help policymakers become aware of other problems (and thereby other solutions) than they are usually familiar with. Design enables an integrated view of policymaking and policy implementation, which are both important parts of public design activities. Joachim Halse shows that design capacities can be used for convincing and for exploring; design is a way to present complex issues in an easily understandable way, that is through the visualization of data. Making problems experientially available for the involved stakeholders enables a real discussion of challenges and opportunities.

FROM PROBLEM-SOLVING TO ENVISIONING NEW FUTURES

Design is about being able to envision a desirable future and developing a way for this future to become a reality. As Junginger argues, 'designing becomes a means of inquiry and invention, of envisioning and of developing new possibilities for useful, usable and desirable policies'. Francois Jégou, Romaine Thévenet and Stephane Vincent highlight the use of design to challenge the organization in a systemic way; design is 'friendly hacking' to identify and improve weak points. Beyond merely mapping and fixing problems, for Jégou and colleagues design can become a facilitator in the collective construction of the future'. Manzini views this as a unique possibility for design experts to feed with images and proposals a social conversation that, in turn, will generate a shared vision. In doing so, the social conversation becomes a broad process of scenario building.

FROM SYSTEM FOCUS TO CITIZEN-CENTRICITY

Kit Lykketoft asserts that in the public sector, decisions are often made primarily with regard to organizational efficiency at the expense of the needs of citizens, because the system in general is reluctant to risk making errors; and known risks tend to be preferred over unknown risks. Design, by systematically involving end-users, may however offer a shift away from the pursuit of easily measurable results to a more holistic approach and a sense of meaning. Due to the emphasis on functionality, experience and aesthetics, design approaches tend to be highly human-centred. In a public sector setting, this means viewing citizens as uniquely positioned to judge whether a design solution is valuable or not, and uniquely positioned to contribute to the design process. For instance, Manzini calls our attention to the potential of design in involving citizens in collaboratively finding solutions to societal problems at the local level. With design support, users can become the main source of information and action. Similarly, Maschi and Winhall show that using design is a way to enable people to interact in new ways, create more sustainable relationships and facilitate behavioural change. The policy potential is of viewing people 'not as bundles of needs to be served but as potential assets in the system'.

FROM UNILATERAL ACTION TO SHAPING NEW ALLIANCES

As mentioned in my introduction, the range of policy options available to decision-makers is changing. This calls for a more involving, integrative and, one might say, 'designerly' way of making policy – what Boland calls sensemaking through collaborative learning. In Tom Bentley's assessment, the disciplines of policymaking must be

> ... geared towards influencing interdependent systems without abandoning specific responsibilities for particular sets of outcomes. In doing so, policymakers will have to forge alliances with broader coalitions of actors, generating a wider range of organizational platforms and sources of knowledge, than they ever have before.

Banerjee similarly argues that modern society's increasingly distinct and siloed domains of organization and knowledge call for both horizontal and vertical co-creation and co-design. Collaborative approaches to design can ensure more ownership and motivation among those involved in addressing exponentially growing challenges. These are challenges which need to be met with more rapid answers and actions than what is usually allowed by public sector processes of research and decision-making.

FROM FACILITATION TO STEWARDSHIP

Collaborative design may at the surface seem to draw largely on 'neutral' process facilitation. However, design for policy requires something more. Steinberg addresses the issue of stewardship by describing it as the design approach needed to coherently shape cultural, political, economic interests through unpredictability towards a desired goal and to ensure impactful delivery. Stewardship is, in other words, as an ethic that embodies the responsible management and guidance with a particular end in mind. John Body and Nina Terrey suggest an approach which entails a strategic conversation about policy intent that involves leaders involved in the policy as well as those who will be involved in the legislation development and the administrative implementation. They describe the approach as 'having a clear and well-understood argument for change that is successfully communicated to all people involved in the design, build and delivery of the change'. In this vein, the notion of 'stewardship' differs sharply from 'facilitation' by acknowledging that designers give direction, purpose and value to the problem-solving process. Designers are never neutral. This raises the challenge of designers to be transparent about their values as they offer their contribution to the policy process.

FROM POLICY-AS-STRATEGY TO POLICY-AS-IMPACT

The perhaps most radical idea, which has been addressed in a wide range of forms throughout this volume, is the notion of design as a driver of policy impact. This is not the least enabled by the strong human (citizen) focus, but also by the integration of policy with tangible artefacts which can give physical expression to otherwise abstract ideas and concepts. Rachel Cooper and Christopher Boyko conclude: 'By engaging citizens in all the decision-making stages and using technology to visualize, record and analyze, citizens become part of the process of iterative testing, implementing and reviewing of ideas.' What happens is the merging of people and policies. As Junginger argues, 'the moment we link policy implementation and policymaking with the products and services that people actually experience, the human experience moves into the foreground'. By its very nature, design becomes concerned with implementation because it is concerned with the human experience and with the interactions which shape it. As amongst others, Simona Maschi and Jennie Winhall demonstrate there is already an immense range of concrete, new governance models which exemplify how design solutions can be transformed into practical implementation. While some of these new and more human, collaborative and relational models may still be local and small-scale, the promise is there: Design for policy can lead to vastly different and potentially more powerful ways of achieving intended policy outcomes.

Positioning Design on the Policy Stage

Which sequence of 'punctuation' in policymaking will prevail? Will it be the 'economic man' process, well-established in policymaking, of *intelligence-design-choice*? Or will the alternative *design-intelligence-choice* model gain momentum, allowing policymakers to shift their stance and their practice along the lines described here?

Table 18.1   Towards design for policy

Current policy model (Intelligence-design-choice)	Design for policy (Design-intelligence-choice)
Resisting complexity	Embracing complexity
Problem-oriented; reactive	Vision-oriented; proactive
System focus	Citizen focus
Unilateral action	Shaping new alliances
Facilitation	Stewardship
Strategy emphasis	Impact emphasis

As with any model, this one risks oversimplifying the issues at stake, and the relations and dynamics between them. However, it does demonstrate some of the key directions design is proposing as an emerging discipline within the profession of making policy. A number of the contributors highlight the notion of a dominant culture in public sector organizations and the disruptive nature of design within that culture.

Mariana Amatullo, for instance, points out in her case study of Branchekode.dk that even though design skills were anchored in an internal government unit, it was still a very new experience to policymakers to work with design: 'Strategic design seems to be slowly coming into focus in an unmapped frontier of sorts.' Amatullo emphasizes how new meanings, values, practices and relationships are continually being crafted amidst the dominant culture. One might, as Siodmok suggests, say that the search is on for an appropriate, shared design language for policy.

Across the insights shared here, what would it take to enable the next steps in taking up design practice in our policymaking environments? How might design more effectively be positioned on the policy stage?

Recommendations to Strengthen Design for Policy

Several attempts have been made in recent years to ask how design might become a more integrated component of government activity. The European Commission has issued the reports *Design for Growth and Prosperity* (2012) and *Powering European Public Sector Innovation* (2013), both of which directly suggest strengthened roles for design in the public sector.[1] And the UK government in particular, but also a number of other European governments, have proposed ways in which design could add value in a public sector context.

Looking specifically to how design for policy might be strengthened, and to the insights offered by the contributions in this volume, here are some suggestions.

AUTHORIZATION: MAKING DESIGN FOR POLICY LEGITIMATE

One of the absolutely central questions is how to reach a point where design is considered as legitimate a way of conducting the business of government as other social technologies. How does design become a trusted, reliable practice in government? Christiansen and Bunt argue that it is important to identify how to authorize public innovation initiatives within the existing frames of public legitimacy. Such high-level 'authorization' might in turn better enable more organic processes of change. Creating legitimacy is ultimately a question of, in equal part, upper management engagement with design and demonstration of the concrete cases and value creation that design approaches can bring to policymaking. This requires, over time, an accumulation of concrete experiences with design in policymaking environments, and the spread of insight about what it means across multiple levels of government, educational institutions and organizations such as think tanks and consultancies working closely with government. First and foremost, design practitioners in a public sector setting have a responsibility to document and share these cases honestly, not withholding the disappointments, challenges and failures but providing accurate accounts of how design concretely unfolds in policy.

LABS: ORGANIZING DESIGN ENVIRONMENTS

A key question is how design resources, skills and processes might be incorporated into the public sector itself? The global rise of design, innovation and change labs represent one part of the answer, whereby design practice may become a core part of the sector and not perceived merely as a temporary means to achieve a certain goal

---

1   The editor was involved in both these exercises as a member of the European Design Leadership Board, an expert committee and as Chair of the expert group on public sector innovation.

There is no doubt, however, that labs represent a paradox: They are created as part of a system but are there to challenge it. For instance, Lykketoft points out that creating an innovation lab within an existing organization implies that the organization as a whole is not yet capable of the wanted transformation. In that sense, the role of labs is to create motivation and commitment to design for policy; for instance by bringing down the transaction cost of shifting to design-led approaches. Staszowski, Winter and Brown emphasize that design tends to disrupt the established order in the political system. So why invite it all the way in?

The answer, of course, is that in the short to medium term there is no alternative. If we wish to see design become part of the fabric of public organizations, and if we wish to enable more effective policymaking, it must be applied from within the system, in a systematic, visible manner. Labs must be considered for what they are: dynamic organizational structures which reflect the need for more adaptive, outcome- and human-centred policies, and which, on the one hand, can be assertive as they seek to demonstrate alternative methods, but which also need to be protected and nurtured, as the foreign entities that they are. Ultimately, the challenge of labs is to be granted access to policy processes that really matter, and to demonstrate that they have earned the right to that access. As Manzini envisages the new movement of 'innovation places', they could become seeds for the creation of the broad favourable environment in which positive loops between bottom-up initiatives and public agency innovations will take place. There is no doubt that further experiments and studies are needed of when and why impactful policy is best served by designers by working within, alongside or outside of government agencies. Most likely, the answer will vary depending on a wide range of contextual factors. Fortunately, the rise of design-inspired labs for government innovation should provide an increasingly fertile ground for learning.

SKILLS: NEW COMPETENCIES FOR POLICYMAKERS AND DESIGNERS ALIKE

As suggested in Chapter 2 by Bason and Schneider, perhaps Policy Designer really should be a new job title. Just as more and more MBA programs are now including design, we are seeing the rise of graduate and undergraduate programs in public management and governance which include design for public services and policies. There is also a growth in executive education and the desire to spread design skills much more broadly, as envisaged for instance by a European Commission (2013) proposal to train thousands of public managers in design competencies.

The responsibility for creating the future human skills needed to embed design in policy lies however not only with management institutions and schools of public administration: It lies equally with design schools, which have ostensibly been slow to recognize how their own field is splintering – or innovating – and the ways in which designers are now invited into the public sector domain. Many have yet to make the moves in curriculum and assessment forms which would allow designers seeking a more meaningful role in societal change to hone their skills and become motivated and suited for a public sector environment. Apart from the obvious need to gain a basic understanding of the inner workings of public institutions, designers may need to grow a bit less impatient: The rate of change in government is not the same as inside a cutting edge design studio.

There will continue to be a need to bring in design skills from the outside, either via commissioning external design agencies, or via recruiting designers to work alongside their policymaking peers. Public managers would be well served to receive training and advice as to how best to benefit from procuring design expertise; and designers could be advised to simply do it: apply for a job in government.

Design, as it has been demonstrated in this volume, emphasizes the human experience in context. This means that design approaches tend to surface other kinds of value than the economic and legislative indicators that many public managers are accustomed to. User experience, thriving, trust, well-being, resilience and learning are often among the kinds of value discovered through design processes. This places designers in a difficult landscape, where they may need to communicate approaches which are not easily measurable by current and traditional standards. As Staszowski and colleagues suggest, there is thereby a risk that untested ideas are being 'evaluated on the basis of how they might be perceived rather than how they actually perform'. Designers have a responsibility not only to ensure the prototyping of new ideas in order to demonstrate value or build convincing business cases, they also need to be good at communicating what that value is.

Bringing design into policy will thus require new conversations about how we understand public value, and how human outcomes can be measured and considered as meaningful as our current financial and economic metrics.

RESEARCH: LEARNING ABOUT DESIGN FOR POLICY

For some years now the research community in fields such as design, information science and management studies have explored the application of design outside traditional domains such as graphics, digital and product design. However, it is only in the most recent years that design has crossed the radar of public management scholars focusing on innovation and new forms of public governance. That is likely to change in the coming years, but not without support from research institutions, funding agencies and from the government organizations that need to grant access to internal design processes. There is an exciting range of research agendas which could be pursued, many of which are highlighted across this volume. What would probably be a most fruitful first step is simply to start gathering cases and evidence of what happens specifically when design is applied in a public sector setting. A second step would be to analyze the outcomes of design for policy, on the basis of contextual factors: problem and opportunity types, the organization of the contribution of design (via labs, commissioning and so on), policy domains, levels of government, national administrative cultures and so forth. A third step would be to explore value-creation and the long-term impact of design processes, working to identify the attributions of design to policy .

Beyond Practice: Design and Politics

An issue which is rarely addressed is the issue of the domain of politics – political ideas, ideologies and political parties – and how this relates to design for policy. As I raised initially, and as also addressed by Staszowski and colleagues, design in policy may very well lead to sensitive political questions. Insight into human experiences and behaviours can have implications for political perceptions of right and wrong, good or bad; conducting policy processes with certain new forms of stakeholder engagement is potentially disruptive to long-standing power relationships; and by prototyping policy ideas the space for political decision-making might be narrowed down simply because the ultimate solutions become more evidenced and obvious.

Should our political leaders receive training in design for policy? Should there be a new conversation between top executives in government and their political masters? What would need to be the key themes in that conversation?

As design for policy comes to the foreground of policy practice, we must undertake a revisiting of the ways in which we understand democracy, participation and political deliberation. For many societies, both developed and emerging, this should be a welcome opportunity for stock-taking and for invention.

References

Allison, Graham (1971). *Essence of Decision: Explaining the Cuban Missile Crisis*. Boston: Little, Brown & Company.

Boland, Richard (2004). *Design in the Punctuation of Management Action. Managing as Designing*. Stanford: Stanford Business Books.

European Commission (2012). *Design for Growth and Prosperity: Recommendations of the European Design Leadership Board*. http://ec.europa.eu/enterprise/policies/innovation/files/design/design-for-growth-and-prosperity-report_en.pdf.

European Commission (2013). *Powering European Public Sector Innovation: Towards a New Architecture*. http://ec.europa.eu/research/innovation-union/pdf/psi_eg.pdf.

Irwin, Lewis G. (2003). *The Policy Analyst's Handbook: Rational Problem Solving in a Political World*. Armonk: M.E. Sharpe.

Mulgan, Geoff. (2009). *The Art of Public Strategy*. Oxford: Oxford University Press.

Shore, C., Wright, S. and Però, D. (2011). *Policy Worlds. Anthropology and the Analysis of Contemporary Power*. New York: Berghahn Books.

Simon, Herbert (1997). *Administrative Behaviour*. New York: Free Press.

INDEX